REPORTING FOR DUTY

REPORTING FOR DUTY

—— My Urgency for Justice and Peace ——

Andrew Mills

RESOURCE *Publications* • Eugene, Oregon

REPORTING FOR DUTY
My Urgency for Justice and Peace

Copyright © 2023 Andrew Mills. All rights reserved. Except for brief quotations in critical publications or reviews, no part of this book may be reproduced in any manner without prior written permission from the publisher. Write: Permissions, Wipf and Stock Publishers, 199 W. 8th Ave., Suite 3, Eugene, OR 97401.

Resource Publications
An Imprint of Wipf and Stock Publishers
199 W. 8th Ave., Suite 3
Eugene, OR 97401

www.wipfandstock.com

PAPERBACK ISBN: 978-1-6667-5799-6
HARDCOVER ISBN: 978-1-6667-5800-9
EBOOK ISBN: 978-1-6667-5801-6

01/06/23

To Helen, Skyler, Jeremy, Damaris
Rey Ann, Margaret, Jeff,
Hannah, Taylor, Doug,
Tony, Krystina, Jerres,
Rosalina, Winnie, Andrea,
Oksana, Christina, Alex,
Holly, Kurt,
Will, Kyle, Connor,
Chris, Gwen,
Garrett, Savannah, Wyatt,
Hendrik, Lorene, and Arden

With special remembrance of my dear
departed granddaughter, Abril, who was taken
away from us at such a young age.

Contents

Permissions | ix
Prologue | xi

Slavery and Civil Rights | 1
    The Wisdom of Cornelia Van Blake | 3
    Overview of the 1965 March From Selma to Montgomery | 9
    The March | 11
    We Davisites Prepare to Join the March | 15
    On the Road to Montgomery | 20
    In Montgomery | 21
    Back Home | 26
    Long-Term Impact of the March | 29
    Martin's Vision of Peace in Vietnam and Mine | 34

Nicaragua Connection | 39
    Introduction to Nicaragua | 41
    Witness for Peace | 47
    Kidnapped by Contras | 53
    New Jersey Peace Mission | 78
    Witness for Peace After 1990 | 83
    Nicaragua After the Sandinistas' Electoral Defeat in 1990 | 87
        Who to Believe? | 90
        Summary of the Major Happenings During the Protests of April to September 2018 | 92
        The Story of MRS | 99
        Opposition in the U.S. to a "Socialist" Nicaragua | 104
        Spokespeople for U.S. Policy Against Nicaragua | 106
        What Did the FSLN Government Achieve Since 2006? | 112
        To Sum Up | 115

In My Older Years | 119
   El Salvador and Guatemala | 121
   Witness for Peace Mid-Atlantic | 127
   Letters to the Editor | 136

Epilogue | 143

Appendix A: Voices of Ex-Slaves | 145
Appendix B: My Letters and Op-Eds to Newspapers | 187
Bibliography | 209

Permissions

THE MAP OF NICARAGUA in the Nicaragua Connection section of the book is based on Google Maps of Central America and, hence, is freely available provided the attribution is included and the conditions stated by Google Maps are adhered to.

All of the photographs displayed in the book are owned by the author, with three exceptions: (1) the photograph of the group of us on the way back to Davis, California; (2) the photograph of some of the marchers on the highway; and (3) the photograph of some of the marchers in Montgomery.

I have permission to include in the book the photograph of our group from Northern California at a rest stop in Arizona on our way back from Montgomery, Alabama, on March 27, 1965 (in the chapter titled "In Montgomery" in the Slavery and Civil Rights section). The permission to include this photograph has been granted to me by Richard Holdstock, who purchased the photo from its owner Gerald Friedberg. Permission to use the two photos of the march itself taken by Gerald Friedberg (included in the chapter "In Montgomery") was granted by the co-directors of the Hattie Weber Museum of Davis History.

I was told via email by the librarian of the Center for Oral History Research, Charles E. Young Research Library, at the University of California at Los Angeles (UCLA) that I was free to use the quotations of the artist Cecil Fergerson. These quotes from the Cecil Fergerson appear in the chapter titled "The Wisdom of Cornelia Van Blake" in the Slavery and Civil Rights section. The librarian wrote me: "Regarding the quotes, under Fair Use, you do not need to seek permission to quote, just credit the quotes in the publication: Center for Oral History Research, Charles E. Young Research Library, UCLA."

Permission was granted by the editor of the Davis Enterprise for me to quote a portion of what Rev. Dwayne Proett said about the march in the September 6, 2019, issue of the paper. The quotation appears in the "Back Home" chapter of the Slavery and Civil Rights section of the book.

PERMISSIONS

James Jordan, the National Co-Coordinator of Alliance for Global Justice, has given me permission to quote from one article in the Nicaragua Notes publication of "Live from Nicaragua: Uprising or Coup." This quotation appears in the subchapter "What did the FSLN government achieve since 2006" in the chapter "Nicaragua after the Sandinistas electoral defeat in 1990" in the Nicaragua Connection section.

James Jordan, the National Co-Coordinator of Alliance for Global Justice, has also given me permission to quote extensively from a blog by Chuck Kaufman in *Nicaragua Notes* and from an article in the Nicaragua Notes publication of "Live from Nicaragua: Uprising or Coup" on the MRS party in Nicaragua. These quotations appear in the subchapter "The story of MRS" in the chapter "Nicaragua after the Sandinistas electoral defeat in 1990" in the Nicaragua Connection section.

Tom Ricker, Program Coordinator at the Quixote Center, gave me permission to quote from an article by him that appeared on the Quixote Center's website. This appears in the subchapter "To Sum Up" in the chapter "Nicaragua after the Sandinistas electoral defeat in 1990" of the Nicaragua Connection section. Tom said: "You have permission to quote from the blog.... Be sure to credit the quote itself to John Perry, who made this comment in the context of my interview with him."

Prologue

WHEN ONE OF MY sons, Skyler, finished reading my first book *Home in India*,[1] he said he had some questions for me. He wondered why I had said little or nothing about the weather in India nor the look of the countryside in the book. Then he asked when I might be writing another book. I told him that I just didn't have another book in me. But as the weeks went by, I began to feel I wanted to write something about my adventures in activism during other parts of my life. Like when I participated in part of the civil-rights march from Selma to Montgomery, Alabama in 1965 and when I was in a group that was kidnapped by the Contras in Costa Rica in 1985.

This book, written in my 92nd year, is a memoir in the sense that it describes many of the things I have done in my life to promote justice and peace in terms of America's foreign and domestic policies. But it is more than a memoir, as it also includes background for, and analysis of, the peace and justice issues involved.

I have spent many years attending schools and colleges. So many that when I started to describe all those years of study to my wife Helen when we first met, all she could say was: "Did you *ever* work?"! Aside from being a perpetual student and my two terms as a rural missionary in India (1956–61 and 1967–71), my career has been in groundwater hydrology; I worked for several engineering consulting firms in succession. I investigated the groundwater flow and the migration of potential contaminants in groundwater at many sites in eastern United States. Also, from November 1980 through February 1982, I was stationed in Egypt by my then employer, Dames & Moore. I served as the water-resources specialist on a team assigned by the Egyptian Ministry of Development to study, and report on, the Sinai Peninsula's development potential.

---

1. Published by Wipf & Stock in May 2021. It described my thoughts and life when I was a rural missionary in South India under the United Church Board for World Ministries (UCBWM) 1956–1961 and 1967–1971.

I am a convinced Quaker[2] and so justice and peace issues come more easily to me. But I am more frenetic than most Quakers in the way I have felt the urgency to act on these issues. My life has been one adventure after another as I have undertaken actions for justice and peace. My children think my devotion to activism has consumed me. I feel I always tried to strike a balance between my activism, my real job, and my family.

I believe that God loves those who are poor and vulnerable. And he's made me want to protect them. I fear for them, whether in this country or foreign lands, in terms of my own country's power to help or hurt them. In so many places, the Bible mentions the poor with loving concern. I believe God hates people when they belittle or take advantage of people because they are poor or of another color or religion. I know he hates people when they plan wars or torture others.

This belief has led me to participate in several justice and peace movements. This has involved lobbying for just and peaceful policies and legislation, taking part in delegations to areas of conflict in the world, arranging speaking programs and retreats, organizing at the regional level, and taking part in peace rallies and marches. The peace rallies and marches I've been part of involved protests against the Vietnam war, against the war in Iraq (before it started), against the CIA at their headquarters, against the Clinton administration for its unbearable economic demands on Haiti, and against the School of Americas in Georgia.[3]

It's been an honor to be as deeply involved as I have been in matters of justice and peace and to work with wonderful people in these efforts. I believe that the Lord of the earth, the God of Jesus, blesses those who work for peace, fairness, and justice for all people. I believe in him, and he has empowered me to do whatever I have tried to do for all his people.

Events that influenced me greatly and are guideposts for my life were the trials in Nuremberg, Germany in 1946 of Nazi war criminals. I was 15 and 16 years old then. The trials made a big impression on me. One of the lessons we all learned from the trials was that more German citizens (German Christians) should have resisted the Nazi reign and spoken out against the Holocaust publicly as soon as it started.

---

2. A *convinced* Quaker is someone who converted to Quakerism as a teen or adult and is therefore not a birth-right Quaker. I became a Quaker in 1973.

3. The School of Americas, now known as Western Hemisphere Institute for Security Cooperation (WHINSEC) located in Fort Benning in Columbus, Georgia, has trained Latin American military officers who have subsequently led right-wing death squads which have tortured and killed peasant movement leaders, as well as the well-known Bishop Oscar Romero in El Salvador in 1980.

PROLOGUE

xiii

If this was what average Germans should have done in the 1930s and 40s, it behooves me for the rest of my life to call out and speak about practices my own country has followed that has hurt or belittled minorities in my country or that has led to the death or displacement of people in foreign lands by wars my country has imposed on them. I think of, for example, the failure of Congress in 2021 to pass voting rights bills: the John Lewis Voting Rights bill and For the People bill.

Peace work doesn't stop with conferences for peace or praying for peace. It is facing the hard truths about what makes for conflicts and acting on those truths in the most effective ways possible. Since 1947 the U.S. has carried out, or assisted with, more than 38 coups against countries all over the world whose governments our State Department didn't like. Most of these coups involved actions by the CIA, and most were successful in that the desired regime change happened, quite apart from what the citizens of those countries may have wanted. Undemocratic interventions such as these by my government have usually resulted in, or were accompanied by, all-out shooting wars.

Our national leaders who take us into wars or involve us in proxy wars such as the Contra war against Nicaragua don't want us to remember what war is and what it does. They just keep saying we have to fight wars to keep our "freedom." So we feel guilty if we don't support the latest war they come up with. The legacy of war is not just a matter of counting and honoring the dead soldiers. A larger group of veterans comes home wounded, in body and mind, often ruined in mind and body. The suicide rate among veterans is 1.5 times that of the non-veteran population.

I love my country deeply, so I want it to live up to its promise of brotherhood, truth, and fairness and to commit to being a peaceful neighbor amongst the community of nations. As the song "America the Beautiful" says: "God shed His grace on thee, and crown thy good with brotherhood" and "God mend thine every flaw."

How can I then stay silent when Contra fighters, paid by my federal taxes, were tearing eyeballs out of ordinary Nicaraguans and committing other atrocities against them whose government the Contras didn't like? How can I remain silent when U.S. army and CIA personnel were committing torture against Iraqi detainees in 2003 in the Abu Ghraib prison in Iraq?

I have divided the book into three sections: Slavery and Civil Rights, Nicaragua Connection, and actions I undertook In My Older Years. Under Slavery and Civil Rights, the central theme is the march from Selma to Montgomery in 1965, including a narrative about how 35 of us from northern California, chartered a bus, drove there, and joined the march. I give the background to the march and discuss the short- and long-term results. I also include a discussion on the impact of slavery on Black families now. Appendix A includes selected remembrances by ex-slaves as recorded by Works Progress Administration (WPA) interviewers in the 1930s. Also, in this section, I briefly discuss Martin Luther King's opposition to the war in Vietnam and his assassination.

In the section entitled Nicaragua Connection I discuss U.S. policy and actions with respect to Nicaragua and my connections to the country. The section is a bit long in my attempt to untangle the official U.S. untruths about the Sandinista government. I confirm Nicaraguans' right to choose a path different from what my own country, the United States, has imposed since 1909 on this small country of 6.7 million people. What I describe in detail about Nicaragua is just one example of how U.S. policies toward Latin American nations have consistently displayed a ruthless insistence of our dominance over them and a total disregard for the wishes of the citizens of these countries. If any government south of the border chooses to adopt left-leaning social programs,[4] our State Department tends to go on the attack and label the country as "socialist" or a "corrupt dictatorship."

Under the section "In My Older Years," there are chapters on my brief experiences in El Salvador and Guatemala, my role in starting and helping to lead the Mid-Atlantic region of Witness for Peace from 1994 to 2013, and finally, my writing numerous op-eds and letters to the editor on justice and peace issues. Appendix B includes a sample of the letters and op-eds that I've had published.

Those of us who seek to create just and peaceful outcomes have invariably found that semi-truths and outright falsehoods are used to stall or prevent the achievement of justice and peace. Thus, our work necessarily has involved trying to ferret out the truth of an issue or incident that impacts the achievement of just deeds and just legislation and the success of peaceful ventures in times of conflict. What President Dwight Eisenhower identified as the military-industrial complex has grown far more powerful since his administration and has become, in truth, the military-industrial-media complex, designed to make each war appear to be a "necessary" war.

Some of the things I spent much of my life doing, as recorded in this book, may have resulted in achievements for justice and peace. I don't know. I guess the point is that I, a sinner under God's mercy, joined with like-minded people in trying to do God's will to make peace and protect

---

4. These are often very similar to those being promoted by progressives in our own country.

the poor and vulnerable in our world. We are all God's children. We belong to each other.

I'm grateful to my wife Helen for her comments on reading the last draft of this book and for suggesting needed corrections. I also wish to thank the following kind friends who have agreed to review the book and offer up their comments: Paul Magno, former Business Manager at Witness for Peace, and currently a member of the National Council of the Fellowship of Reconciliation, among others; and, Tom Ricker, Program Associate at the Quixote Center and Associate Adjunct Professor teaching international human rights and politics at the University of Maryland. My thanks also go to Ray Torres and Gil Ortiz, former steering committee members of WFPMA, for reviewing the chapter "Witness for Peace Mid-Atlantic." Ray Torres also was kind enough to give me three of the photos appearing in this book.

Andrew Mills
December 31, 2022
Lower Gwynedd, Pennsylvania

Slavery and Civil Rights

The Wisdom of Cornelia Van Blake

Cornelia Van Blake

ABOUT TWENTY YEARS AFTER the Selma to Montgomery march led by Martin Luther King, I met Cornelia Van Blake, who gave me an education about the Black family as well as about civil rights. She had started to come to the Plainfield Friends Meeting (Plainfield, New Jersey) as an attender. She had lived in Plainfield for many years, raising her family including nine children. She had decided to return after years away because one of her children, Clare Roberts, lived in Plainfield and her ex-husband Seymour Van Blake's cousin, Donald Van Blake, and his family lived there. She and I became friends.

I have taken the liberty of looking up Cornelia on Ancestry.com. In those documents, she is alternatively listed as "Black," "Mulatto" or "White." She was born as Cornelia Montrose Ward in Harrisburg, Pennsylvania, on

January 16, 1919. Her father, Rev. Beverly Ward, and her mother Julia E. Holmes Ward were married in May 1916 in Plainfield, New Jersey. Cornelia's father was the pastor of the Capital Street Presbyterian chapel in Harrisburg. He hailed from Virginia while Cornelia's mother's people were from North Carolina. After shepherding the church in Harrisburg, the family moved to Rochester, New York, where he also served as a pastor. At the time of his death in December 1931, he was serving as the pastor of the Faith Presbyterian Church in Germantown, Pennsylvania.

Cornelia married Seymour Van Blake, Jr, and they had nine children. Seymour was an upholsterer for Segal's in Millburn, New Jersey, for 20 years. He died at age 71 in January 1991.

Cornelia's grandfather on her father's side is believed to be Thomas M. Ward. There is a record on ancestry.com indicating that he served in the confederate army in the Civil War from March through July 1862. Thomas and his wife Matilda had been slaves of Mr. William Ward of West Creek farm. Thomas is said to have been taken away by the Union army during the Civil War because he wouldn't tell where his master's money and jewels were hidden.

* * *

For many years, Cornelia served as a real estate administrator under the federal Department of Housing and Urban Development (HUD), and also lived in Los Angeles for a time. As a long-time resident of Plainfield, New Jersey, she was well known as a child advocate and had participated in several civic and fraternal organizations.

Several former members of Plainfield Meeting remember her fondly from her presence at the meeting in the late 1980s and early 1990s. Barbara Andrews, former head of First Day School, remembers how active Cornelia was in the FISH food distribution program run by Anita Hoynes, a member of the meeting. The program distributed groceries to needy people in the Union and Middlesex Counties area. Mary Capron, former office secretary of the meeting and now a UCC pastor, remembers her as being a warm and determined woman. Mary remembers that she started and ran a thrift store near the Plainfield Meeting house.

I was taken with a display Cornelia put up in the Meeting house for a couple weeks showing large-type printed stories of former slaves in the South. I was drawn to her because of this. She shared with me many of these printed stories which she had obtained as photocopies from the Los Angeles public library.

In the course of our friendship, Cornelia explained to me the depth to which slavery had affected, and still affects, Black families. One of the most profound effects was the intentional separation of slave family members— wives from husbands and children from their parents. This prevented the essential bonding of the biological members of a family. It also prevented the development of cultures unique to each family. Men didn't feel the benefits and discipline of belonging to a life-long wife. Cornelia also explained how slaves, as slaves, very rarely had the opportunity to learn the basics of household economy, as simple arithmetical skills, such as would flow naturally to the children of a non-slave family. This paucity of rich content in the skills and obligations of operating a family unit tended to continue through several generations for at least many family lines. The unsavory heritage and legacy of slavery have been very long-lasting.

* * *

The African-American artist Cecil Fergerson spoke about Cornelia in an interview by a UCLA art history staff member in July 1991.[1] Cecil had the following remembrance of meeting her:[2]

> "I know one time I was riding down the street, and I saw all these old people in this big old yard having a barbecue—you know, like senior citizens, black people. So I stopped and joined the party. Because I had gotten to the point where I knew that a lot of history and stuff was in the minds of elderly black people, and that's how you learn, because there weren't any books. You get into conversations with people, right? And this lady was sitting down at the table, and I went over to her and introduced myself. Her name was Cornelia Van Blake . . . She almost looked white. We got to talking, and in the conversation she said, 'I know you, Mr. Fergerson.' 'Oh, yeah?' I said. She said, 'Well, I don't know you personally, but I've often been to events where you spoke.' And she said, 'I always wanted to meet you, because you seem a fascinating man.'
>
> "Of course, that is a compliment coming from somebody twenty years older than me. She was an elderly kind of woman. And she said, 'I often hear you speak about the black family and the importance of the black family and the extended black family and why we have to get back to that. You touch on that

1. Fergerson, "Interview," tape 6, side 2, 266-69.

2. Courtesy of Center for Oral History Research, Charles E. Young Research Library, UCLA.

every time you talk.' And she said, 'I'll bet you that your folks are from Louisiana or Texas, and then they probably migrated to either Saint Louis or Oklahoma.' You know, she was right! And I was saying, 'Oklahoma.'

"And she said, 'The reason you're so family oriented'—this is her talking now—she said, 'is because many black people after the Civil War, aggressive black people, left the South, and they left and kept their families intact. A lot of slaves didn't leave the plantation. They were too afraid to venture away from the plantations.' She said, 'So you have a long history of family. You've heard stories about your family. But a lot of kids that you talk to, they have no idea what you're talking about, because they never had a family.' She said, 'You could ask them what the definition of a family was, and they couldn't tell you. So they really don't know what you're saying.'

"I thought about that for a minute, and I said, 'That's impossible' in my own mind. So then I started adding that to my speeches. 'What's your definition of a family?' It's a simple definition: mother, father, grandparents, uncles, aunts, cousins, nephews, nieces, you know. And then the extended family: the man down the street and next door, the preacher, people at church."

* * *

Appendix A represents a collection of a few of the stories and recollections of former slaves in the United States. I compiled these stories in 1992 from photocopies of the typewritten originals, and I entered the text into a word processor on my computer. Cornelia gave me copies of these stories; she obtained them from public libraries, mainly from the Los Angeles public library.

This appendix begins with a page displaying quotations from the Quaker John Woolman (1720–1772) of Mt. Holly, New Jersey, one of the strongest voices against slavery in the 18th century. He traveled through the American frontier, primarily through the southern colonies, to preach Quaker principles and advocate against slavery and the slave trade. He would meet and stay overnight with Quaker slaveholders and would urge them to free their slaves; he was successful in some cases.

The ex-slaves, whose voices are "heard" in Appendix A, were interviewed in the 1930s by people under the pay or contract with the Works Progress Administration (WPA), a federal job agency during the great depression. The project under the WPA was known as the "Federal Writers' Project."

As part of this project, between 1936 and 1938, federal authorities organized teams of interviewers in 17 states who took down the recollections of over 2,000 former slaves.[3] The documents from which these narratives were taken were typewritten, quite possibly personally by each interviewer. They were then collected into relatively large volumes, one for each of the 17 states. I am told that this material is available in the larger public libraries. In addition, microfiche of the typescripts for each state have been available in the Library of Congress for many years. Finally, in 1972 and later in 1978, the Greenwood Publishing Company published the entire typescript in what turned out to be a total of 31 volumes.[4] Appendix A represents a small sample of all the WPA slave narratives I took from photocopies Cornelia made of the original typed documents in the Los Angeles public library.

The WPA interviewers were obviously instructed to faithfully record both the content as well as the speech forms of the interviewees. I tried to preserve the phonetic forms the interviewers used to convey the pronunciation of each person interviewed. I did, however, attempt to standardize certain of the phonetic forms.

In Appendix A, you'll learn about the conditions of a few of the slaves during slavery and afterwards. You'll learn what their masters were like, and equally as important, about the overseers of their work and about the "patrollers" who checked on and abused slaves when they went off their plantation; the slaves had to have passes permitting them to be off.

Many slaves were whipped bloody on a routine basis. The overseers and patrollers were usually members of the poor white class, who were looked down upon by the plantation owner class. You'll also learn from Appendix A about the ex-slaves' later experience with the Ku Klux Klan, which gained significant membership in the late 19th century and in the 1920s. Taken together, one comes away with a strong sense that reparations are long overdue.

Much of our country's economic prosperity was built off the forced labor of millions of Black people, who were subjected to regular beatings, sexual assault, and family separation. In January 2019, Rep. Sheila Jackson Lee from Texas introduced a bill, HR 40, to examine slavery and discrimination from 1619 to the present and to study and develop reparations proposals for African Americans.

3. Escott, *Slavery Remembered*.
4. Rawick, ed., *American Slave*.

Cornelia has helped me to see that it is nearly impossible to understand the situation of African Americans in this country without first understanding the nature of slavery in the 18th and 19th centuries. For the roots of many of our present problems can be traced to the institution of slavery in this country.

Overview of the 1965 March from Selma to Montgomery[1]

The March from Selma to Montgomery, Alabama, in March 1965 took place to gain full voting rights for our Black and minority citizens, particularly in the Deep South. The 15th Amendment to the U.S. Constitution of 1870 just wasn't enough, though its meaning couldn't have been clearer.[2]

> Section 1. *The right of citizens of the United States to vote shall not be denied or abridged by the United States or by any State on account of race, color, or previous condition of servitude.*
>
> Section 2. *The Congress shall have power to enforce this article by appropriate legislation.*

The problem was that the amendment as passed and ratified in 1870 prohibited neither literacy tests nor poll taxes. In fact, soon after its ratification, White supremacists, such as the Ku Klux Klan (KKK), used paramilitary violence to prevent blacks from voting. The so-called Enforcement Acts were passed by Congress in 1870–1871 to authorize federal prosecution of the KKK and others who violated the amendment. However, as Reconstruction neared its end and federal troops withdrew from the South, prosecutions under the Enforcement Acts dropped significantly. Congress further weakened the Enforcement Acts in 1894 by removing a provision against conspiracy.

In 1877, Republican Rutherford B. Hayes was elected president after a highly contested election, receiving support from three Southern states in exchange for a pledge to allow White Democratic state governments to rule without federal interference. As president, he refused to enforce federal civil rights protections, allowing states to begin to implement racially discriminatory Jim Crow laws.

And that's pretty much the way voting rights stood for several decades. For example in 1961, the population of Dallas County, Alabama (Selma being the county seat) was 57 percent Black, but of the 15,000 Blacks old enough to vote, only 130 were registered (fewer than one percent). And

---

1. Wikipedia, "Selma to Montgomery Marches."
2. Wikipedia, "Fifteenth Amendment to the United States Constitution."

Lowndes County, immediately east of Dallas County, was 81 percent Black and 19 percent White, but not a single Black was registered to vote.

In the early 1960s, two groups committed to nonviolence began registering Black people in the South. These were Martin Luther King's organization, the Southern Christian Leadership Council (SCLC), and the Student Nonviolent Coordinating Committee (SNCC), which from 1962, with the support of the Voter Education Project, had committed themselves to the registration and mobilization of Black voters in the Deep South.

The Alabama Governor at the time, George Wallace, was a notorious opponent of desegregation and civil rights, and the local sheriff of Dallas County had stridently opposed Black registration drives. In spite of this, SCLC and SNCC volunteers had been working to register Black people in Dallas County for a few years, even though their efforts were often thwarted by local police and county officials.

The March[1]

Leading up to the march, there were numerous protests and actions by activists all over the country, particularly in the South. There were so many smart and brave Black leaders who orchestrated protest events with respect to voting rights. All of these together set the tone for the march and the ultimate acceptance and passage of the Voting Rights Act in the summer of 1965.

Civil rights activist Jimmie Lee Jackson was among more than 200 people participating in a peaceful night voting-rights march on February 18, 1965 in Marion Alabama, 26 miles northwest of Selma. He was brutally beaten and shot by Alabama State Trooper James Fowler. He died eight days later from his wounds while in Selma's Good Samaritan Hospital. His death sparked the Selma to Montgomery marches. These marches, three in total, were organized as part of the voting rights movement.

The first attempted march to Montgomery began on March 7, 1965, when an estimated 600 civil rights marchers headed southeast out of the town of Selma toward Montgomery on U.S. Highway 80, a distance of 54 miles. John Lewis of SNCC and the Reverend Hosea Williams of the SCLC led the march. The protest went according to plan until the marchers attempted to cross the Edmund Pettus Bridge, where they encountered a wall of state troopers and county posse waiting for them on the other side, who attacked the marchers brutally. That stopped the march in its tracks.

Amelia Boynton, who had helped organize the march as well as marching in it, was beaten unconscious. Another marcher, Lynda Blackmon Lowery, age 14, was brutally beaten by a police officer during the march, and needed seven stitches for a cut above her right eye and 28 stitches on the back of her head. John Lewis, later the well-regarded congressman from Georgia, suffered a skull fracture and bore scars on his head from the incident for the rest of his life. In all, 17 marchers were hospitalized and 50 treated for lesser injuries. That day soon became known as "Bloody Sunday." That evening, Martin Luther King, Jr. sent off a blitz of telegrams and public statements "calling on religious leaders from all over the nation to join us on Tuesday in our peaceful, nonviolent march for freedom." On March 8th he

---

1. Wikipedia, "Selma to Montgomery Marches."

sent out this plea: "... it is fitting that all Americans help to bear the burden. I call therefore on clergy of all faiths to join me in Selma for a ministers' march to Montgomery." King subsequently expanded the appeal to "people from all walks of life" to join the demonstration.

On the morning of Tuesday March 9th, the marchers regrouped and were ready to attempt what would be the second march. Martin Luther King, Jr. led more than 2,000 marchers out on the Edmund Pettus Bridge and held a short prayer session before turning them around back into Selma. Though there was an angry dispute about this among the marchers, King did this to obey a court order preventing them from making the full march at least until March 11. Had the marchers disobeyed the court order it could have resulted in punishment for contempt, even if the order were later reversed. They did not want to alienate one of the few southern judges, Judge Johnson, who had displayed sympathy for their cause, by violating his injunction.

That evening, three White Unitarian-Universalist ministers who had come to Selma for the march were attacked on the street and beaten with clubs by four KKK members. The worst injured was Reverend James Reeb from Boston. Fearing that Selma's public hospital would refuse to treat Reeb, activists took him to Birmingham's University Hospital, two hours away. Reeb died on March 11 at the University Hospital.

A week after Reeb's death, on Wednesday March 17, Judge Johnson ruled in favor of the protesters, saying their First Amendment right to march in protest could not be abridged by the state of Alabama:

> "The law is clear that the right to petition one's government for the redress of grievances may be exercised in large groups . . . These rights may . . . be exercised by marching, even along public highways."

Judge Johnson had sympathized with the protesters for some days but had withheld his order until he received an iron-clad commitment of enforcement from the White House. President Johnson had avoided such a commitment in sensitivity to the power of the state's rights movement, and he attempted to cajole Governor Wallace into protecting the marchers himself, or at least giving the president permission to send troops. Finally, seeing that Wallace had no intention of doing either, the president gave his commitment to Judge Johnson on the morning of March 17, and the judge issued his order the same day. To ensure that this march would not be as unsuccessful as the first two marches were, the president federalized the Alabama National Guard on March 20 to escort the march from Selma.

On Sunday, March 21, close to 8,000 people assembled at Brown Chapel A.M.E. Church in Selma to begin the final march to Montgomery. This time they crossed the Edmund Pettus Bridge safely, guarded by the Alabama National Guard. Most of the March participants were Black, but some were White and a few were Asian and Latinx. Spiritual leaders of multiple races, religions, and creeds marched abreast with Reverend King.

In 1965, the road to Montgomery (U.S. Highway 80) was four lanes wide going east from Selma, then narrowed to two lanes through Lowndes County and widened to four lanes again at the Montgomery County border. Under the terms of Judge Johnson's order, the march was limited to no more than 300 participants for the two days they were on the two-lane portion of Highway 80. At the end of the first day, most of the marchers returned to Selma by bus and car, leaving 300 to camp overnight and take up the journey the next day.

On March 22 and 23, 300 protesters marched through chilling rain across Lowndes County, camping at three sites in muddy fields. On the morning of March 24, the march crossed into Montgomery County and the highway widened again to four lanes. All day as the march approached the city, additional marchers were ferried by bus and car to join the line (including our group!). By the time the marchers reached Montgomery it was late afternoon. And there were approximately 20,000 Black and White people, comprising the marchers and their supporters who had gathered in the city.

That night in Montgomery on a makeshift outdoor stage at The City of St. Jude, an inter-racial Catholic complex on the outskirts of Montgomery, the "Stars for Freedom" rally was held and attended by over 15,000 people. The star singers Harry Belafonte, Tony Bennett, Frankie Laine, Peter, Paul and Mary, Sammy Davis, Jr., Joan Baez, Pete Seeger, and Nina Simone performed there.

The next day, Thursday March 25, approximately 25,000 people marched from the City of St. Jude campus to the steps of the State Capitol Building, where King delivered his speech "How Long, Not Long." He said:

> "The end we seek is a society at peace with itself, a society that can live with its conscience.... I know you are asking today, How long will it take? I come to say to you this afternoon however difficult the moment, however frustrating the hour, it will not be long."

After delivering his speech, King and the marchers approached the entrance to the capitol with a petition for Governor Wallace, asking him to ensure the right to vote for Blacks. But a line of state troopers blocked the door. One announced that the governor was not in. Undeterred, the marchers remained at the entrance until one of Wallace's secretaries appeared and took the petition.

The happy outcome to the march was the enactment of the Voting Rights Act that summer. It was signed by President Johnson in an August 6, 1965 ceremony attended by Amelia Boynton and many other civil rights leaders and activists. This act prohibited most of the unfair practices used to prevent Blacks from registering to vote and provided for federal registrars to go to Alabama and other states with a history of voting-related discrimination to ensure that the law was implemented by overseeing registration and elections. But one notable discouraging thing was that the federal government never prosecuted either Jimmie Lee Jackson's murderer or Reverend Reeb's murderer.

Perhaps the most definitive description of the march is found in Renata Adler's "The Selma March" appearing in the April 10, 1965 issue of the *New Yorker*.[2] It described in great and flourishing detail the many participants and aspects of the march, as only an article in the *New Yorker* can do.

---

2. Adler, "Selma March."

We Davisites Prepare to Join the March

I didn't know at the time how much Dewey's sermon would affect me and others. It must have been Sunday March 14, 1965. Dewey (Rev. Dwayne Proett) spoke of receiving an urgent invitation from Rev. Martin L. King, Jr. for him as a fellow pastor to come and participate in the march from Selma to Montgomery, Alabama. Rev. King had put out a nationwide call for members of the clergy to join him in Alabama after the March 7th brutalities on the marchers were nationally televised. The aim of what turned out to be the successful march was to protect and enhance the voting rights of Black people in America. Dewey made it clear in the sermon that he was inclined to accept Martin Luther King's invitation to participate in the march and thereby support his fellow minister's call.

Dewey was the senior-most minister of the three pastors of our church, the Davis Community Church, the local congregation of the United Presbyterian USA denomination in Davis, California. I was thrilled that Dewey was considering participating in the march and I wanted to support him. A friend of mine, also a member of the church, Richard (Dick) Holdstock, was also keen on supporting Dewey. Dick was a deacon of the church and attended a deacons' meeting that week in which Dewey presented his desire to participate in the march. Dick supported Dewey entirely, but Dewey didn't get much support from Dick's fellow deacons. Then the next day the matter came to a meeting of the *session*, the governing body of the church. I sat in on the session meeting when Dewey presented his case for going to Montgomery, Alabama. It wasn't a slam dunk. There were a couple of members of the session who were not thrilled to be sending their minister to Alabama, and for a questionable purpose, they felt. So Dewey had to do some explaining of the Christian basis for participating in the march. I spoke briefly in the session meeting about the importance of sending Dewey to Alabama for the march.

In the end, Dewey won the approval of the session, not only him, but they also approved of Rev. Bill Case, the most junior minister of the church, going on the march as well. That left the associate minister to mind the store while the other two were away also doing God's will!

Dick and I knew we both wanted to be part of the march and to join Dewey and Bill on the trip to Montgomery. We felt it was our duty as

Christians and as members of the church to accept Martin Luther King's call.

Until then, I had not been particularly active in the civil rights movement. My last effort in the movement had been 12 years earlier, in 1953, when my first wife Jane and I joined the local CORE group in Columbia, Missouri, where I was a graduate student in Rural Sociology at the University of Missouri.

CORE stands for Congress on Racial Equality, and was founded in Chicago, Illinois, in March 1942 by James L. Farmer, Jr. and others. The inter-racial group evolved out of the pacifist Fellowship of Reconciliation, and sought to apply the principles of nonviolence as a tactic against segregation. The group's inspiration was Mahatma Gandhi's teaching of non-violent confrontations. At the time of CORE's founding, Gandhi was still engaged in non-violent resistance against the British rule in India. CORE believed African Americans could also use nonviolent civil disobedience to challenge racial segregation in the United States.

Our CORE group in Columbia met monthly. We were a mixed group, including local Black people, university Whites, and the local Jewish rabbi. James Hunter led the group, a teacher in the city's Black-only Douglas High School, which would be desegregated just a year later and ultimately closed as a consequence of the Supreme Court's ruling in May of 1954 prohibiting segregation in public schools.

Our CORE group aimed to open up local restaurants to both Black and White patrons. We tried sit-ins in local restaurants. Twice at lunch time, I met up with Tom Walker, a Black senior in high school, and we entered a diner on the main street in town. We sat down at the counter and asked to be served. We were not served, but we were not threatened either. Columbia at that time was not at all ready to be integrated.

* * *

Back to Davis in 1965, Rev. John Pamperin assumed the leadership role for the bus trip to Montgomery. He was the assistant minister at the Cal Aggie Christian Association, a campus ministry serving the University of California at Davis and the community. As an ordained minister, John had received the same plea and invitation from Martin Luther King that Dewey had. Dick Holdstock met with John Pamperin and others at the Cal Aggie House to begin planning the trip.

Right after Dewey and Bill Case received approval from the church to participate in the march, Dick and I got together and planned how we would recruit members of our church. Dick and I were referred to as the "lay leaders" for the trip in an article in the *Davis Enterprise*.[1] We wanted as many members as possible to participate in the last day of the Selma to Montgomery march.

My personal aim was to fill the bus with only members of the Davis Community Church. Following numerous phone calls by Dick and me, we found that was not to be. So we spread the net a little wider and made phone calls to members and pastors of other churches in Davis. Still, the bus didn't come close to filling up. So we started phoning people unassociated with local churches who were members of groups supporting civil rights. It was not easy getting people to give up an entire week with almost no advance notice, considering their job requirements and family obligations.

I even called up faculty members in my own Irrigation Department, where I was a graduate student at the time. I didn't know anything about how they stood on civil rights. One of the professors I called was Ted Strelkoff, a professor of hydraulics in the department. I'd never taken a course from him, and he had no association with any church, but he said "yes!" (It turned out that he and I sat next to each other on the bus on the way to Montgomery.)

The local paper, the *Davis Enterprise*, advertised the bus trip, and so did the *Daily Democrat*, the newspaper in nearby Woodland. Before long, we had filled up the bus; the last people to sign up were in the Sacramento area, so the bus had to go north to pick those folks up before we could head southeast toward Alabama. All the preparations happened within four days.

A day or two before our departure, we leaders assigned each other different responsibilities. John Pamperin was to be in charge of communication with MLK's March coordinators in Alabama so we would know where to go once we got to Montgomery and so they would know our progress on the road. Gerald Friedberg, an assistant professor of political science, would monitor developments with the march on his transistor radio.

I was assigned the job of shepherding the people on the bus to and from Montgomery. That meant I was the one who at a minimum did a head count whenever the bus stopped for a meal or rest stop and when we were ready to proceed on our way again. It turned out to be not much harder than herding sheep. It was particularly challenging when we were in Montgomery and set to come back to our hosting church from an event.

1. Davis Enterprise, "Davisites Board Bus."

The Davis ministers who went on the bus were Ministers Dave Burnight and John Pamperin (assistant) from the Cal Aggie House (Christian Campus Ministry) and Pastors Dewey L. Proett and Bill Case (assistant) of the Davis Community Church. Pastor Phil Walker[2] of the Davis Methodist Church decided to take the train to Montgomery a day or two earlier, but he returned with us on the bus. The Sacramento area religious community was represented by the Reverend Leon King, pastor of the AME church in North Highlands near Sacramento, and Reverend Anton Pollard, a Catholic priest who brought a few members of his parish with us on the bus.

The Rev. Robert Senghas, pastor of the Unitarian Universalist Church in Davis, did not go on the bus as he had already been to Selma, Alabama, and had just returned to Davis. But Senghas helped our group plan our trip, and, keenly aware that one of his fellow Unitarian pastors (Reverend James Reeb) had just been beaten to death in Selma, he advised our group regarding the risks we could face.

We wound up recruiting 28 people from the Davis area and seven from the Sacramento area. Our 35 passengers included seven clergy members and many others who were religiously affiliated—Protestant, Catholic, and Jewish. There were ten women (seven of whom were "housewives"), six UCD students (including me), three professors, lab technicians, a rancher, a chemist, and three from the *Cursillo de Christiandad*[3] in Sacramento. Our group included three African Americans, one Asian American, and two Mexican Americans.

Dick's wife at the time, Jacque, made the arrangements with Greyhound to charter the bus and driver; it would cost each rider about $50. The cost to charter the bus was $3,200. Gratefully, other people were generous enough to make up the difference between $3,200 and 35 riders x $50, or $1,750. In particular, the Cursillo de Christiandad in Sacramento was the largest donor, who made it possible for us riders to pay only the nominal amount to travel to Alabama and back.

A significant support group stayed behind in Davis, which attended to logistical details, coordinated volunteers, and kept up communications between the bus passengers and the MLK headquarters in Alabama. Jacque Holdstock played a key role in coordinating the support group.

---

2. I remember on the way back on the bus, Rev. Phil Walker told us that he went to Montgomery because God had given him his life and it was time to risk it for God's children. "I only have one life to give," he said.

3. A successful program to spread Christian faith for the Spanish-speaking community.

Everyone had to sign a pledge of nonviolence before boarding the bus. In a 2013 documentary about the trip,[4] Terry Turner, a young Black biochemistry lab technician at the university who came with us, said that he agreed to the nonviolence pledge at his mother's insistence, with decidedly mixed feelings, but stuck with the pledge once he'd made it.

Before the departure of our bus, Terry Turner's mother told John Pamperin: "You don't have a clue what you're doing." In the 2013 documentary, Terry himself said, "It was obvious this was not going to be an easy trip. I knew that, more than probably John and Dick did, because I knew those people [in the South]. And I knew that those people are crazy. They'll shoot you."

And in retrospect, John later said, he could see how young, idealistic and perhaps "cocky" he was at the time, thinking that issues of racial equality and voting rights could be addressed with a degree of success within a few weeks or months. "I didn't understand how vicious hate can be, and how painful it is to watch people's civil rights being denied."

---

4. In 2013, local filmmakers Ben Bruening and David Martin made a 23-minute documentary video about the 1965 bus trip, "To March with Martin." The film includes interviews with Richard Holdstock, John Pamperin and Terry Turner (who died shortly after the film was made). It can be seen online at *www.imdb.com/video/wab/vi1572253977/*.

On the Road to Montgomery

Our bus departed Davis at about 4 pm on Sunday March 21st, the same day that the third, and successful, march from Selma started, protected by Alabama National Guard forces that President Lyndon Johnson had ordered under federal control.

Once on the bus, John reviewed with the group strategies for self-defense in nonviolent protests. We discussed the potential dangers we might face. There were lighter moments too, when Dick Holdstock with his guitar would lead us in songs. And Dewey's singing voice sounded out better than most of ours.

We traveled all the 2,000 miles without night stopovers. We had, as I remember, at least three drivers on the way and the same on the way back. We made pit stops, as well as stops for meals, refueling, and little else. I didn't sleep much at all, even though we traveled through the nights of March 21st, 22nd, and 23rd. I wanted to stay awake to make sure the drivers weren't nodding off.

I was excited before and during the trip. It was invigorating to be with so many people on the bus who saw the rightness of the march led by Martin Luther King and other Black leaders and wanted to participate in it. I felt fearful only a couple of times, but mostly I was just excitedly satisfied that I had decided to do the right thing. I had little need to feel afraid on the march itself, as it was so well protected.

As the bus entered the Deep South, we passed several Confederate flags displayed along the road. Once as we were traveling through Mississippi, our driver noticed cars going by, checking out our bus. He got nervous and started driving kind of wild and fast down the highway. He warned us not to show ourselves in the windows. This was the same driver who was a Southerner and who expressed some animosity toward us "northerners" for interfering in the South's business.

Our interracial group encountered the challenge of dining at segregated diners and restaurants, which either refused us service or gave us very icy service. At one stop, we succeeded in moving two tables together at the demarcation line between the "black dining area" and the "white dining area," at which point the restaurant served everyone—reluctantly.

In Montgomery

We arrived in Montgomery around 5:00 am the morning of March 24th. We stopped at the agreed-upon meeting place in town. John Pamperin was the first to get off the bus. John later related the following story.[1] A Black shoeshine "boy," who had to be around 70, approached him!

The man said to him, "Need a shoeshine, sir?"

John replied, "A shoeshine is the last thing I need!"

"But, sir, I want to give you a shoeshine free," the man insisted.

So John gave in, and the man started to give him a shoeshine. While working on John's shoes, the man never looked up but said, "You're to call 220-2467. They'll tell you where to stay." To which John replied, "Are you kidding?" The man said, "No, this is serious." So John made the call and got directions to our host church, a Black church (The Lily Baptist Church), and we were taken there in our bus.

When we arrived at our host church, the parishioners gave us an early breakfast. Some of us were then taken in parishioners' cars out to where the march was. Others of us were taken there via shuttle bus. In any case, we joined the march at about 10 am that day when it was about 10 miles west of town. I remember that I started walking alongside two Black women who were carrying in their arms their winter coats, still moist from a rain shower the previous day. One of them kept saying over and over, "I want my freedom. I'm going to get my freedom!"

---

1. Bruening and Martin, "To March with Martin."

Part of the march on the highway to Montgomery, AL March 24, 1965
(Courtesy of Hattie Weber Museum of Davis History; Photo by Gerald Friedberg)

For us it was more like a walk in the park—nothing akin to the first "Bloody Sunday" march on March 7th. Now we and the other marchers had the protection of the federalized Alabama National Guard, who guarded us the whole day until we reached Montgomery. And there was always the comforting sight and sound of the army helicopters overhead and army jeeps along the road. It was nothing like what the marchers endured on March 7th.

All along the way, the men who were monitors of the march from the Southern Christian Leadership Conference were active moving along the shoulder of the road. They were making sure that everyone stayed in line, that there were no gaps, and checking whether or not anyone on the march needed emergency care. I spotted Andrew Young as one of the monitors as he passed us along the side. He was a close confidant of Martin Luther king, Jr. I met Andrew when he was a student in 1954 at Hartford Theological Seminary in Hartford, Connecticut.[2]

During the march, White supremacists shouted insults and spat on a few of us. Dewey Proett later told us that some people had spat on him.

2. I was attending the seminary at the same time in preparation for my first term as an agricultural missionary to South India under the Congregational Churches through the American Board of Commissioners for Foreign Missions. In 1977, Andrew Young became the U.S. Ambassador to the United Nations, and in 1981 he became Mayor of Atlanta. He was jailed for his participation in civil rights demonstrations, both in Selma, Alabama, and in St. Augustine, Florida. Andrew was with Martin in Memphis, Tennessee, when MLK was assassinated in 1968.

He and other pastors were singled out because they were wearing their clerical collars. These agitated Whites along the road were just aching to attack us marchers. As one member of our group told it, "They were ready to rip us apart." And State troopers cruised by with Confederate flags on their bumpers. But there were also groups of Black people along the road shouting joyfully and cheering us on!

Part of the march inside Montgomery, AL March 24, 1965 (Courtesy of Hattie Weber Museum of Davis History; Photo by Gerald Friedberg)

By the time we marchers reached Montgomery it was late afternoon. By that time, there were about 20,000 Black and White people, made up of the marchers and their supporters, who had entered the city.

Soon after we returned to our host church, the parishioners presented us with the most delicious southern fried chicken dinner I have ever had. It was simply delicious and wonderful. And afterwards both the bus riders and the parishioners sang hymns. Dewey Proett's playing of the piano and singing the hymns wowed everybody.

Then we got ready to go to the Catholic St. Jude's campus where the evening entertainment, "Stars for Freedom Rally," took place. It was so thrilling for me to be in the crowd a mere 50 feet from the makeshift stage and watch and listen to Harry Belafonte, Joan Baez, Odetta, Pete Seeger, Billy Eckstine, Peter, Paul & Mary, and other artists singing their hearts out. It was a complete delight despite its raining lightly on us most of the evening.

After the show, our group returned in our bus to our host church. We spent that night sleeping in the sanctuary of the church, either on the pews or on the carpeted floor. That night, the brave Black deacons of the church stayed awake all night outside the church guarding us against potential white extremist attacks. We heard them walking around and around the church in the night. I will never forget their bravery and their kindness to us, risking their lives for us.

The next day, Thursday the 25th, was a little more laid back. Around noon time we had lunch in a downtown restaurant. As we were leaving, I remember having a brief conversation with a local educated White man in his 40s. He tried to assure me that Southerners didn't want to deprive Blacks of any of their rights. "We don't have any intention of doing that," he said. I didn't argue with him, but I felt he was trying to cover up the history of the evil perpetrated on Blacks during and after slavery.

After lunch, we were taken on our bus to St. Jude's campus, where the march to the State Capitol was to begin. Our crowd of marchers swelled to 25,000 by the time the march reached the capitol building. We gathered in front of the building to hear King and other speakers, including Ralph Bunche (winner of the 1950 Nobel Peace Prize), address the crowd. "No tide of racism can stop us," King proclaimed from the building's steps in a thrilling speech, as viewers from around the world watched on television.

After the speeches, John Pamperin decided to temporarily separate from the group and take a cab to a florist shop. He wanted to buy a flowering plant for the women of our host church as thanks for their hosting us. The taxi took him to a White florist shop. As he said in a 2013 video,[3] when he entered the shop and approached the back of the shop to purchase the plant, he noticed that everybody in the shop stopped talking. He had an eerie feeling, and thought "I'm in deep danger because not one person here is talking." So he threw $25 for the plant down on the counter and carried his purchase swiftly out of the shop. He was lucky to find a cab outside; it was a Black cabbie who said to him, "Get in!" The cabbie basically reamed him out for being so stupid as to put himself at such a risk, not just for himself but for his hosts as well. The cabbie took him back to the church where the rest of us were waiting, having returned from the rally on our bus.

After John showed up and had given a few of the women of the church the flowering plant from us, we all got back on our bus according to plan and headed home to Davis. Going down the road (out of Montgomery), we heard via radio that some people in other groups had been shot at. At one point, our driver noticed lights in and around a farmhouse near the

3. Bruening and Martin, "To March with Martin."

road. This prompted him to hit the accelerator while yelling for us to duck down so the bus would appear empty.

As we proceeded west on U.S. 80, we learned about Viola Luizzo's murder on the radio. Viola Liuzzo was a 39-year-old White mother of five from Detroit who had come to Alabama to support voting rights for Blacks. She was assassinated that night by KKK members while she was ferrying marchers back to Selma from Montgomery. Ten minutes after her murder, we learned that it happened at a location very near where our bus had just passed. So it was a scary ride until we got west of Selma.

Once we felt safe on the trip back, we began discussing what we could do for social justice in Davis and elsewhere, a discussion which would lead each of us to different volunteer actions. After that, the ride was uneventful, and there was not near as much talk. We arrived back in Davis a little before midnight on Sunday March 28th.

Our bus riders at a rest stop in Arizona on the road back home, March 1965. (Courtesy of Richard Holdstock; photo by Gerald Friedberg)

Back Home

Once we got back to Davis, we were interviewed by reporters from *the Davis Enterprise, the Sacramento Bee, the Daily Democrat,* and the UC Davis *California Aggie*. Five days after we got home, April 2nd, six of us participants described our impressions of the march to over 300 people who had crowded into the junior high school multipurpose room in Davis. I served as moderator of the meeting and said that we, the participants, had not solidified our impressions entirely but that sharing our experiences preliminarily could be beneficial. The others who spoke at the meeting were Rev. Robert Senghas, Rev. Dewey Proett, Ted Strelkoff, Terry Turner, and Marilyn Mohrmann.

A day or two later, another Davis marcher, Eugene Martin, and I accepted an invitation to speak at a Black church in Sacramento. We were royally received and happy to talk to the parishioners and answer their questions. That was a very happy day.

One of our bus riders described our participation in the march as being "exhausting and exhilarating, frightening and triumphant." This sounded like an apt description to me.

Dick Holdstock later said the trip to Alabama "colored my entire life" in the following decades. "I don't like to brag about having done it," he said. "I like to hope that I can live my life in a way that emulates the idea of trying to make life better for others."

John Pamperin later told Dick that Dewey (Rev. Dwayne Proett) began to have doubts about his going on the march a day or two before our bus left, but he stuck to his promise and joined us.

Dewey wrote these notes about the bus trip for his upcoming sermon on the Sunday after we got back, April 4th:[1]

> "I did not want to go! I felt deeply sensitive to the members of the Church who for reasons of place of birth or upbringing could not sympathize with the trip and who would be deeply hurt by my participation . . . but, quite unexpectedly, was the overwhelming support that came from members who, up to now had not revealed such a tremendous concern for the world . . . Many have

1. Dahlin, "DCC at 150."

since told me that this has now strengthened the church. They thought people had the false image of [the]Community Church being that large, comfortable church at Fourth and C that would not be moved to active participation in the cares of others. But when the pastor went—the image was changed."

In the sermon, Dewey described the friendships we had forged on the long ride.

Bus Passengers from Davis and nearby Woodland: (28) Bob Balla, Rev. Dave Burnight, Rev. Bill Case, David Chapman, Frankie Cheney, Dr. and Mrs. Gerald Friedberg, Steve Gillman, Richard Holdstock, Judy Iltis, Kathryn Johnson, Barbara Johnson, Gene Laskowski, Eugene Martin, Melvin Miller, Andrew Mills, Merilyn Mohrmann, Alan Karasaki Ota, Rev. John Pamperin, Dr. Malcom Polk, Rev. Dwayne Proett, Dr. Ted Strelkoff, Peggy Thomas, Roger ('Terry') Turner, Rev. Phil Walker, Larry Wenzle, William Wemple, and Anita Whipple.

Bus Passengers from Sacramento and Vicinity: (6) N. Briblescas, Alicia Jimenez, Rev. Leon King, Jonah Parker, Rev. Anton Pollard, and Charles Vecovitch.

Bus Passenger from Auburn, California: (1) Barbara Minor.

The experience in Alabama led several people who made the trip into further activism. John Pamperin got involved in demonstrations against the war in Vietnam, and in the environmental movement.

Terry Turner and Dick Holdstock were subsequently major actors in a group they created in April 1966, the Davis Human Relations Council, which launched a campaign to fight housing discrimination. As Dick said later, "Every house in Davis at that point came with a restrictive covenant prohibiting sale to people of color and Jews. I opened up my pile of paper, relating to the purchase of my home, and there it was." The Davis Human Relations Council was also active in a number of other local civil rights issues. Dick served on the Davis City Council during the 1970s, and Terry would become a professor of arts and humanity at the Woodland Community College, a position he held for 35 years.

Fellow bus rider, Eugene Martin, and I started the Davis Vietnam Peace Committee in June of that year. For nearly two years, we organized several local actions to educate the town's people about the war and why it was important to end it.

One unfortunate impact of the Davisites' participation in the march was the firing of Rev. Dave Burnight from his position as senior campus minister at Cal Aggie House. Rev. John Pamperin, ordained as a United

Church of Christ minister, was not fired, but Dave was. Pamperin[2] later said it was because Dave was an ordained Presbyterian minister and the Presbyterians at that time were providing significant funding for Cal Aggie House. Apparently, they thought that Dave had demonstrated by his participation in the march that he and his ministry were "too far out," John said.

2. Bruening and Martin, "To March with Martin."

Long-Term Impact of the March

On March 17, 1965, even as the Selma-to-Montgomery marchers were pleading for the right to carry out their protest, President Lyndon Johnson addressed a joint session of Congress, calling for federal voting rights legislation to protect Black people from the barriers that prevented them from voting.

That August, Congress passed the Voting Rights Act of 1965, which guaranteed the right to vote (earlier awarded by the 15th Amendment) to all Black people and Native Americans. Specifically, the act banned literacy tests as a requirement for voting, mandated federal oversight of voter registration in areas where tests had previously been used and gave the U.S. Attorney General the duty of challenging the use of poll taxes for state and local elections.

Along with the Civil Rights Act, the Voting Rights Act was one of the most expansive pieces of civil rights legislation in American history. It significantly reduced the disparity between Black and White voters in the U.S. and allowed greater numbers of African Americans to participate in politics and government at the local, state, and national levels.

Since its enactment, Congress passed major amendments to the Act[1] in 1970, 1975, 1982, and 2006. Each amendment coincided with an impending expiration of some or all of the Act's special provisions. Originally set to expire by 1970, Congress repeatedly reauthorized the special provisions in recognition of continuing voting discrimination. Congress extended the coverage formula and special provisions tied to it, such as the Section 5 pre-clearance requirement, for five years in 1970, seven years in 1975, and 25 years in both 1982 and 2006.

Section 5 and most other special provisions applied to jurisdictions encompassed by the "coverage formula" prescribed in Section 4(b). The coverage formula was originally designed to apply to jurisdictions that engaged in egregious voting discrimination in 1965, and Congress updated the formula in 1970. Coverage was further enlarged in 1975 when Congress expanded the meaning of "tests or devices" to encompass any jurisdiction that provided English-only election information, such as on ballots, provided the

---

1. Wikipedia, "Voting Rights Act of 1965."

jurisdiction had a single-language minority group that constituted more than five percent of the jurisdiction's voting-age citizens.

The following graphic[2] shows the statewide coverage in the act (in black) and those states partially covered (in dark gray). The states of New Mexico and Alaska were included mainly because of ongoing voting rights discrimination against Native Americans.

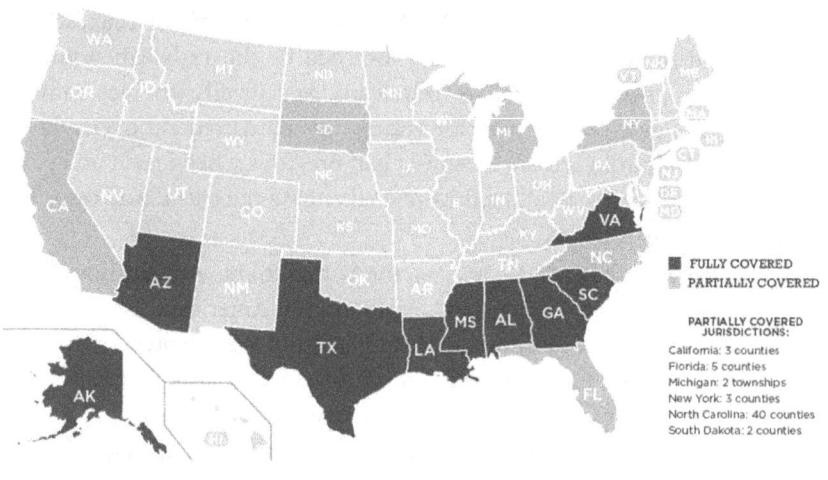

Map of Covered Jurisdictions of Section 5 of the Voting Rights Act

These expansions brought numerous jurisdictions into coverage, including many outside of the South. To ease the burdens of the reauthorized special provisions, Congress liberalized the bailout procedure in 1982 by allowing jurisdictions to escape coverage by complying with the Act and affirmatively acting to expand minority political participation.

On June 25, 2013, in a 5–4 decision in *Shelby County v. Holder*, the Supreme Court effectively annulled Section 5 of the Voting Rights Act, which required states and local governments to clear with the federal

2. Lawyers Committee for Civil Rights under Law, https://lawyerscommittee.org/wp-content/uploads/2015/06/LCCRUL-Sec5-flyer.pdf

government in advance of any voting rule changes if those states had a history of discrimination with regard to voting rights. The court struck down the coverage formula of Section 4(b) as unconstitutional; it did not strike down Section 5 per se, but without a coverage formula, Section 5 was unenforceable. The court reasoned that the coverage formula violated the constitutional principles of "equal sovereignty of the states" and federalism, because its disparate treatment of the states was, they said, "based on 40-year-old facts having no logical relationship to the present day." The big question regarding the court's decision: "Had the states and other jurisdictions covered by the act changed substantially regarding attitudes toward minority voting rights?"

It would seem not. After the 2013 court decision, several states that were fully or partially covered—including Texas, Mississippi, North Carolina, and South Carolina—implemented laws that had been previously denied under the pre-clearance requirement. Research has shown that the coverage formula and the requirement of pre-clearance had substantially increased turnout among racial minorities, even as recently as 2012, the year before the court's decision. Some jurisdictions that had previously been covered by the coverage formula increased the rate of voter registration purges after this decision by the court.

And now in October 2022, 57 years after the Voting Rights Act was first enacted, America is facing state governments' refusing to fully protect the right to vote. States are bringing forth legislation that discourages Black people, Native Americans, and poor people from voting, in the name of keeping elections honest. State legislatures in many states are trying to make voting harder in several ways, including imposing shorter hours at polling places and limiting the number of vote-by-mail drop boxes.

On July 2, 2021, in response to states' effectively trying to make it harder to vote, the Supreme Court ruled in *Brnovich v. Democratic National Committee* that two new Arizona voting restrictions could stand in spite of Section 2 of the 1965 Voting Rights Act. The case concerned a pair of voting restrictions: one that required election officials to discard ballots cast at the wrong precinct and another that made it a crime for most people to collect ballots for delivery to polling places, a practice that critics call "ballot harvesting." Democrats argued those rules end up disproportionately affecting voters of color, therefore violating Section 2 of the Voting Rights Act of 1965, while the Attorney General of Arizona defended the laws as necessary protections against threats to election integrity, such as voter fraud—which is essentially nonexistent.

Justice Elena Kagan speaking for the minority,[3] wrote in her dissent regarding the 7/2/2021 decision, which was joined by the two other liberal justices, "What is tragic is that the court has damaged a statute designed to bring about 'the end of discrimination in voting.'" Two professors in law schools (Harvard Law School and the Maurer School of Law at Indiana University) concluded[4] from the conservative majority's ruling that the court has declared that voter fraud, *not* racial discrimination, is the threat to the American system of representation.

For voting rights activists, this latest Supreme Court decision creates a need to more strongly support the congressional push to enact at least one of two voting laws that would effectively prevent states from limiting access to the ballot: For the People Act, a sweeping overhaul of federal election and campaigning laws, and the narrower John Lewis Voting Rights Advancement Act, which would restore Section 5 of the Voting Rights Act.

In a recent article in the *New Yorker*, Jane Mayer[5] writes that well-funded conservative groups are taking advantage of the fear that many Whites have of Black and Brown people's gaining more rights and power in the country. The groups' strategy is to fund programs that would presumably protect voting from fraud in every state in America, while at the same time making it harder for poor people of color to vote, thereby increasing the chances of conservative victories at the polls. But the consensus among nonpartisan experts is that voting fraud, particularly in major races, is negligible. In Arizona, for example, an Associated Press investigation[6] found that, in 2020, one hundred and eighty-two of the 3.4 million ballots cast in Arizona were problematic. Only four of these ballots led to criminal charges, but to date no one has been convicted. One nonpartisan expert stated that voters rarely cast fraudulent ballots, for the same reason counterfeiters don't manufacture pennies—it doesn't pay. Dark-money-funded conservative organizations like the Heritage Foundation, ALEC,[7] and the Federalist Society are at the center of trying to limit the voting rights of Black and Brown people in the name of stopping fraudulent voting.

Many of us who marched in March 1965 naively thought that the federal act to protect voting rights, expected as a result of protests and the march, would take care of the problem forever. But we've learned that

---

3. Bokat-Lindell, "Did the Supreme Court Just Kill."
4. Charles and Fuentes-Rohwer, "Court's Voting-Rights Decision."
5. Mayer, "Big Money behind the Big Lie."
6. Christie and Cassidy, "AP: Few AZ Voter Fraud Cases."

7. ALEC is the American Legislative Exchange Council, a corporate-funded nonprofit that generates model laws for state legislators.

prejudice and racism are deep within the human soul, not easily excised from any of us. Neither is political greed that's blind to the need to protect voting rights for all. So if we think we see clearly and want to stand up for every person's civil rights, we must dedicate ourselves to being activists until we die. We're on a new march now that will continue well past the end of our lives. Because we know that God wants us to nurture everyone with love and thereby help fight the racism and greed in ourselves and in the society we live in.

Martin's Vision of Peace in Vietnam and Mine

As early as March 2, 1965, Martin Luther King asserted that the war in Vietnam was "accomplishing nothing" and called for a negotiated settlement. This was in response to press questions after he had addressed an audience at Howard University.[1] Martin was the premier believer and leader in nonviolence. This came out in his opposition to the war and in his policies for organizing and demonstrating to obtain the civil rights legislation we all wanted. However at that time, considering the status of civil-rights bills then in the U.S. Congress, he felt he had to avoid condemning the war outright, as he didn't want to damage his relationship with President Lyndon Johnson and therefore put at risk the voting-rights legislation then before Congress.

But in August 1965 at the annual meeting of the Southern Christian Leadership Conference (SCLC), Martin called for a halt to the bombing of North Vietnam and urged[2] that the United Nations be empowered to mediate the conflict, and he told the attendees that "what is required is a small first step that may establish a new spirit of mutual confidence . . . a step capable of breaking the cycle of mistrust, violence and war." Later that year, Martin framed the issue of war in Vietnam as a moral issue: "As a minister of the gospel," he said, "I consider war an evil. I must cry out when I see war escalated at any point." But at the same time he was fearful of being labeled a Communist for fear it would diminish the impact of his civil rights work. So he tempered his criticism of U.S. policy in Vietnam through late 1965 and 1966, while his wife, Coretta Scott King, took a more active role opposing the war.

But in 1967, Martin became more strident in his opposition to the war, in spite of many people in the civil-rights movement distancing themselves from his stance on the war.[3] On April 4, 1967, Martin gave a sermon in the Riverside Church on the upper west side of Manhattan that may be the most prophetic speech anyone has ever made about U.S. foreign policy. In it, he said:[4]

1. Martin Luther King, Jr Research and Education Institute, "Vietnam War."
2. Martin Luther King, Jr Research and Education Institute, "Vietnam War."
3. National Association for the Advancement of Colored People, for example, issued a statement against merging the civil rights and peace movements.
4. Martin Luther King, Jr Center for Nonviolent Social Change, "MLK: Beyond

"The war in Vietnam is but a symptom of a far deeper malady within the American spirit, and if we ignore this sobering reality, we will find ourselves organizing 'clergy and laymen concerned' committees for the next generation. They will be concerned about Guatemala and Peru. They will be concerned about Thailand and Cambodia. They will be concerned about Mozambique and South Africa. We will be marching for these and a dozen other names and attending rallies without end, unless there is a significant and profound change in American life and policy." And "We must rapidly begin the shift from a thing-oriented society to a person-oriented society. When machines and computers, profit motives and property rights, are considered more important than people, the giant triplets of racism, extreme materialism, and militarism are incapable of being conquered."

In early 1968, Martin worked with Dr. Benjamin Spock to create a "Vietnam Summer" that aimed to increase grassroots peace activism in time for people to want to vote for peace in the upcoming 1968 elections. In speeches around the country, Martin described the three problems plaguing the nation: racism, poverty, and the war in Vietnam.

In his last Sunday sermon, delivered at the National Cathedral in Washington, D.C., on March 31, 1968, Martin said[5] that he was "convinced that the war in Vietnam was one of the most unjust wars that had ever been fought in the history of the world." He saw clearly that the war was not only taking lives, many of them Black, but the money spent on it was depriving programs aimed to uplift the poor of our country.

But Martin paid the price for his outspoken assertions against the war; he was murdered in Memphis on April 4, 1968. He was in Memphis to support the striking sanitation workers in that city. The official story was that the killer was James Earl Ray, a drifter, small-scale criminal, and escaped fugitive, who was subsequently prosecuted for the crime and sentenced to 99 years in prison. But the King family believed there had been a conspiracy involving the government that resulted in Martin's death. Finally in 1999, they brought a civil suit in Memphis against another man, Loyd Jowers, and others, the "others" referring to U.S. intelligence agencies and the Mafia. After four weeks of testimony and over 70 witnesses, the twelve jurors[6] reached a swift unanimous verdict on December 8, 1999, namely that

---

Vietnam."
5. Martin Luther King, Jr. Research and Education Institute, "Vietnam War."
6. Yellin, "Memphis Jury sees conspiracy in Martin Luther King's Killing."

Martin was assassinated not by James Earl Ray but as a result of a conspiracy involving Jowers, the Mafia, and government agencies.

At the time of the Court's verdict, Coretta Scott King, Martin's wife, expressed her gratitude to the jury,[7] saying:

> "There is abundant evidence of a major high level conspiracy in the assassination of my husband, Martin Luther King, Jr., and the civil court's unanimous verdict has validated our belief . . . It is important to know that this was a SWIFT verdict, delivered after about an hour of jury deliberation. The jury was clearly convinced by the extensive evidence that was presented during the trial that, in addition to Mr. Jowers, the conspiracy of the Mafia, local, state and federal government agencies, were deeply involved in the assassination of my husband."

Several people have come forward to comment on that jury's findings. There have been complaints that the case overlooked much contradictory evidence that never was presented. But there was plenty of horrifying evidence indicating some government participation in Martin's assassination.

It doesn't take much imagination to realize there were powers in the government that wanted Martin removed from the public scene. These powers desperately wanted to continue the war, and they saw Martin's leadership in the peace movement as a significant threat to the public support they needed for the war. They had their way, and we lost one of the best American leaders who ever lived. And so the war ground on for seven more years, resulting in the deaths of tens of thousands of American service members and several hundred thousand Vietnamese people.

* * *

Gene and I did not face the weight of the U.S. intelligence agencies and the military-industrial complex, as Martin had, when we ran the Davis Vietnam Peace Committee from June 1965 until early 1967. Eugene Martin, a lab technician at the University of California at Davis, was on the bus with me when 35 of us went to Montgomery, Alabama, in March 1965 to take part in the last day of the march from Selma to Montgomery. Gene and I spoke to local churches about the march in the Davis and Sacramento area. We soon found we both agreed with Martin Luther King on the need to end the Vietnam War, and we decided to form a peace group

---

7. Savali, "Did You Know?"

in Davis dedicated to ending the war in Vietnam. Thus, in June of that year we started the Davis Vietnam Peace Committee.

Gene and his wife were kind enough to offer their house as a meeting place, right next to the campus of the University of California at Davis (UCD). I was a graduate student there working toward my Ph.D. in Soil Science. We used to meet every Monday night at 7 pm at Gene's house, but the membership of the committee never exceeded six people.

In our meetings, we would discuss how to get the facts about the war to people in the Davis area. The starkest set of points we emphasized was the mounting death toll of Vietnamese people and U.S. service men and women. On nice Saturday mornings, we manned a literature table in downtown Davis where we discussed the need to end the war with passersby. Most weekends, I was part of the two or three people manning the table. One Saturday, I was sitting at the table with another UCD student, and someone warned us that one of the workers at the local lumber yard was angry and was coming to confront us. Presently he appeared carrying a four-foot long 2 by 4 in his right hand. He came up to the table and menaced me. Somehow or other, I kept my cool and stood up to him. I told him we had the right to oppose the war and asked him what he thought of the war. At that point, he relaxed his grip on the 2 by 4, and decided he didn't want to be violent after all. A few minutes later he decided he needed to go back to the lumber store, which he did.

Most of our committee members participated in writing letters to the editor, in which we tried to give compelling reasons to oppose the war. I was particularly active in writing letters opposing the war every month or two to the Davis Enterprise, our local weekly newspaper. One night during that time at two in the morning, when my family and I were sleeping, our telephone rang. I woke up immediately and picked it up. The caller said after a pause, "Hi Red," in a very menacing tone. That was it. I never got a similar call again. The caller wanted to make me feel fearful, which it did in a way. But not enough for me to give up my peace activities. That intimidating call was nothing compared to the death threats Martin Luther King and other stalwarts for peace experienced for many years.

One project that the Davis Vietnam Peace Committee undertook was a scientific survey of the Davis population's opinions about the war in Vietnam. One of our committee members, Ron Clifford, was a sociology professor at UCD and he was well versed in designing scientific polls. Using telephone listings, he was able to select a small random sample. Once the sample participants were identified, we split up the list among five of us. And we started to do a house-by-house interview of each of our selected participants. It took us a couple of weeks to complete the survey, and then Ron analyzed the data.

The main finding of the survey was surprising to us. Only approximately 35 percent of those polled opposed the war. This was almost exactly what the polls across the country were saying in 1966. We expected a higher number for our college town. As the war wore on, the country became less and less enamored with the war and by 1971 the number of people opposing the war had risen to about 60 percent. But despite this, it took our political leaders four more years to end the war.

Our committee continued trying to do our best after September 1966 and into 1967. Still, at that point, only a small number of people were interested in stepping up to demand the end of the war. I graduated in June of 1967, and the following month my family and I were off to India for another term of service under the United Church Board for World Ministries.

Nicaragua Connection

MUCH OF MY LIFE since August 1985, when I made my first visit to Nicaragua, I've been involved in trying to understand and promote the truth about that country. This meant, among other things, untangling the official untruths about the Sandinista government and confirming Nicaraguans' right to choose a path different from what my own country, the United States, has tried to impose on this small country of 6.7 million people.

Their story is similar to the stories of many other Latin American countries, where popular leftward experiments in the mode of governing and wealth distribution have usually been thwarted by my own country through outward conflict and the promotion of lies or half-truths in the mainstream media. But the struggle continues. *La lucha continua.*

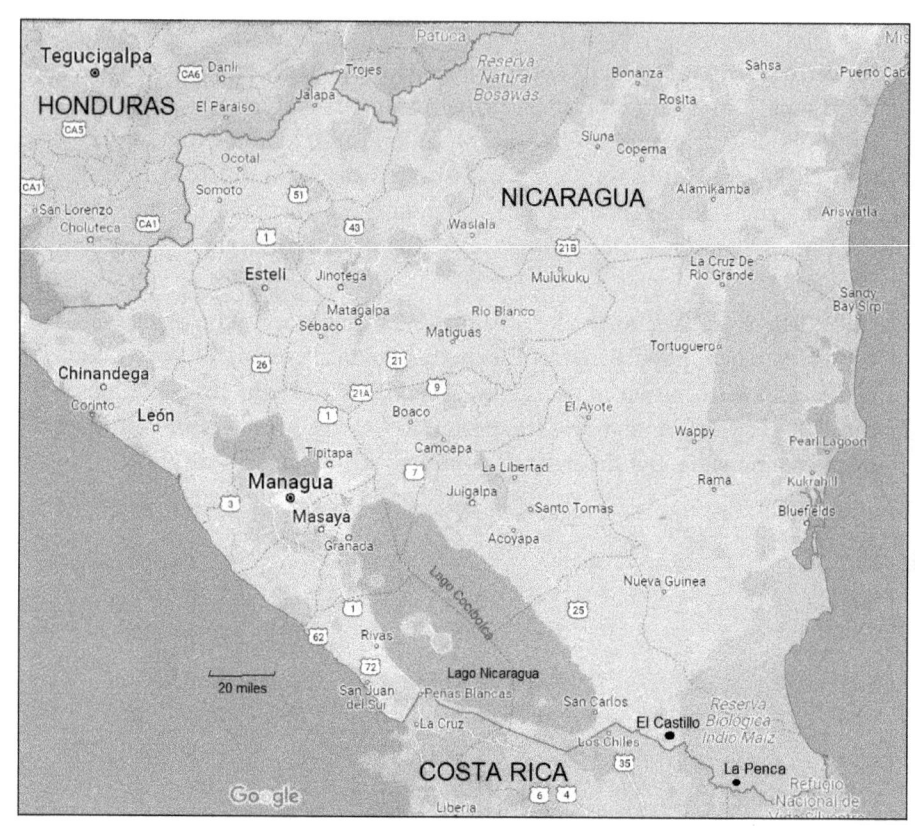

Map of Nicaragua (Courtesy of Google Maps)

Introduction to Nicaragua

Nicaragua has been known for the last 100 years as the second poorest nation in the Americas after Haiti. This statistic has hung around regardless of the decade or the economic policies of the country's different governments. Nicaragua's current population is 69 percent Mestizo, 17 percent white, 5 percent Indigenous, and 9 percent Black and other races, although its demographics have changed with migration.[1] Mestizos in Nicaragua are mixed-race people, believed to be approximately one-half European, one-third African (Black), and one-sixth indigenous by applying a methodology developed by chromosomal research at the University of Zaragoza, Spain.[2]

The modern history of Nicaragua began with the Spanish conquest of the country. By 1529, the Spaniards had completed their conquest over the indigenous population. Many Indians were soon enslaved to develop and maintain "estates" there.[3] Others were put to work in mines in northern Nicaragua, but the great majority was sent as slaves to Panama and Peru for significant profit to the newly landed Spanish aristocracy.

Nicaragua gained independence from Spain in 1821. She became a part of the United Provinces of Central America in 1823 and became an independent republic in her own right in 1838.[4] Complete jurisdiction over the indigenous Miskito people on the Atlantic coast was not established until the presidency of Jose Santos Zelaya, who headed the government from 1893 to 1909.

Zelaya, though a dictator, was a committed nationalist.[5] He promoted plans for Central American reunification and refused to grant the United States trans-isthmian canal-building rights on concessionary terms, thus encouraging the United States to choose Panama for the project. This, plus Zelaya's attempt to control foreign access to Nicaraguan natural resources as well as rumors that he planned to invite Japan or Germany to build the

---

1. Britannica, "Nicaragua."
2. World Population Review, "Nicaragua population."
3. Wikipedia, "Pueblo Nicaraguense."
4. Britannica," Nicaragua."
5. Wikipedia, "History of Nicaragua."

coveted waterway, caused the United States to urge Zelaya's Conservative opposition to stage a revolt.

In 1910, U.S. Marines landed in Bluefields on the east coast and Corinto on the west coast.[6] And from 1912 to 1933, U.S. Marines were stationed in Nicaragua largely to enforce the Bryan-Chamorro Treaty signed in 1914, which gave the U.S. control over any proposed canal through Nicaragua. The Marines left in 1933 partly because of General Augusto Cesar Sandino's fighting an effective guerrilla war against them and partly because of the Great Depression. But before they left, the U.S. set up the *Guardia Nacional* (National Guard), a combined military and police force trained and equipped by the Marines, designed to be loyal to U.S. interests. Anastasio Somoza Garcia, a close friend of the United States government, was put in charge. Fearing future armed opposition from General Sandino, Somoza invited him to a meeting in Managua in February 1934, where the National Guard assassinated Sandino.

Following the death of Sandino, Somoza's National Guard executed hundreds of men, women, and children. Using these troops,[7] Somoza took total control of the country by 1937 and destroyed any potential armed resistance. The Somoza family ruled as a cruel and violent dictatorship in Nicaragua until the Sandinista revolution of 1979. Franklin Roosevelt said of Somoza, "He might be a son of a bitch, but he's *our* son of a bitch."

From 1945 to 1960, the U.S.-owned Nicaraguan Long Leaf Pine Company (NIPCO) directly paid the Somoza family millions of dollars in exchange for favorable benefits to the company, such as not having to reforest clear-cut areas. By 1961, NIPCO had cut down all the commercially viable coastal pines in northeast Nicaragua.[8]

In 1961, a young student, Carlos Fonseca, turned back to the historical figure of Sandino and founded the Sandinista National Liberation Front (FSLN) with the aim of overthrowing Somoza's dictatorship.[9] The FSLN was a tiny party throughout most of the 1960s, but Somoza hated it, and his repressive treatment of anyone suspected to be a Sandinista sympathizer was well known.

Martial law was declared in 1975, and the National Guard began razing villages suspected of supporting the Sandinistas in the jungle. Human rights

---

6. Wikipedia, "History of Nicaragua."
7. Wikipedia, "History of Nicaragua."
8. Wikipedia, "History of Nicaragua."
9. Wikipedia, "History of Nicaragua."

groups condemned the actions, but U.S. President Gerald Ford refused to break the U.S. alliance with Somoza.

A nationwide protest strike in 1977, including labor and private businesses, demanded an end to the dictatorship. At the same time, the Sandinistas stepped up their rate of guerrilla activity. Several towns, assisted by Sandinista guerrillas, expelled their National Guard units. Somoza responded with increasing violence and repression.[10] When León became the first city in Nicaragua to fall to the Sandinistas, he responded with aerial bombardment, famously ordering the air force to "bomb everything that moves until it stops moving."

In May 1979, another general strike was called, and the following month the FSLN staged its final offensive. City after city fell to the insurgents, backed by tens of thousands of local civilian combatants. On July 17, Somoza resigned and fled the country; two days later the Sandinistas entered Managua and accepted the surrender of what was left of his army, ending the long years of Somoza rule.[11]

The new government inherited a devastated country. About 500,000 people were homeless, more than 30,000 had been killed, and the economy was in ruins.[12] In July 1979, the Sandinistas appointed a five-member Government Junta of National Reconstruction.

United States President Jimmy Carter, who had cut off aid to Somoza's Nicaragua in 1979, initially hoped that continuing American aid to the new government would keep the Sandinistas from forming a far-left government aligned with the Soviet bloc. However, it turned out that U.S. aid to the Sandinista government was very little, and the Sandinistas had to turn to Cuban and Eastern European assistance to build a new army.

FSLN leaders were intent on creating a socialist-oriented economic system that would meet the basic needs of the majority. Still, they did not regard the Soviet Union, Eastern bloc countries, or Cuba as appropriate economic models. Sandinista Nicaragua was to be a new socialist experiment, allowing for individual ownership and private enterprise.[13] The Sandinista policy of developing a mixed economy (about 60 percent private and 40 percent public) resulted in growth from 1980 through 1983.[14] But the United States declared a trade embargo on Nicaragua in 1985, which

10. Wikipedia, "History of Nicaragua."
11. Britannica, "Nicaragua."
12. Britannica, "Nicaragua."
13. Williams, "Central America Wars, 1980s."
14. Britannica, "Nicaragua."

along with the human and economic costs of fighting the war against the Contras led to major economic problems.

The key large-scale programs of the Sandinistas included a National Literacy Crusade from March to August 1980. Nicaragua received international recognition for gains in literacy, health care, education, childcare, unions, and land reform.[15] In 1981, the government enacted the Agrarian Reform Law, which formalized what could be done with Somoza's vast property.[16] This included offering free land titles to peasants and other state supporters in exchange for government service or for establishing agricultural cooperatives.

However, Nicaragua was criticized for a few reported human and civil rights abuses against the Miskitos and other indigenous groups on the Atlantic coast. In the early years after the revolution, some leaders of the indigenous groups, such as Steadman Fagoth and Brooklyn Rivera, attempted to set up a government independent of the Sandinistas in the northern Atlantic region.[17] The government of Nicaragua resisted this.

As early as 1981, guerrillas calling themselves Contras—from a contraction of the Spanish word for counterrevolutionaries— had started operating in Nicaragua with the help of Argentina's rightist military regime. Gradually the Argentine advisers gave way to sponsorship by the Central Intelligence Agency (CIA), and by 1983, the United States was supplying the Contras with a steadily increasing stream of arms. The Contras, many of whom had been members of the former National Guard under Somoza, began by making incursions from Honduras into Nicaragua. They attacked clinics and schools that the new government had set up in the northern part of the country. They used brutal and gruesome methods to spread fear among the rural population, including kidnapping civilians, beheading or raping them, or cutting out the tongues of the victims. Often children had to watch as their mothers were raped and their fathers mutilated.

As early as 1983, the Contras had begun to establish a similar presence in the rural areas of the central and southern parts of the country. This is what the Sandinistas faced while trying to bring the economy out of the recession inherited from the Somoza regime.

The Contra army grew to about 15,000 soldiers by the mid-1980s.[18] Eventually, the Nicaraguan government also expanded its military forces, acquired crucial equipment such as assault helicopters, and implemented a

---

15. Wikipedia, "History of Nicaragua."
16. Britannica, "Nicaragua."
17. Prevost, "'Contra' War in Nicaragua," 8.
18. Britannica, "Nicaragua."

counterinsurgency strategy and tactics, which enabled it in the late 1980s to contain and demoralize the Contras but not defeat them.

Notwithstanding U.S. propaganda, the Sandinista government developed an electoral system modeled on European multiparty systems and held national elections on November 4, 1984. Despite the ongoing war, the Sandinistas won this national election, garnering 67% of the vote. The election was certified as "free and fair" by the majority of international observers.[19] Daniel Ortega won the presidency easily.

U.S. pressure against the Nicaraguan government escalated throughout 1983 and 1984; the Contras began a campaign of economic sabotage and disrupted shipping by planting underwater mines in Nicaragua's port of Corinto.[20] On May 1, 1985, Reagan issued an executive order that imposed a total economic embargo on Nicaragua, which remained in force until March 1990, soon after the UNO party won the national election over the FSLN.

In 1986, Nicaragua won a historic case against the U.S. at the International Court of Justice. The Court ordered the U.S. to pay Nicaragua $12 billion in reparations for violating Nicaraguan sovereignty by supporting and financing Contra attacks against the country. The alleged violations included: attacks on Nicaraguan facilities and naval vessels; the mining of Nicaraguan ports; the invasion of Nicaraguan air space; and the training, arming, equipping, financing, and supplying of forces (the Contras) seeking to overthrow Nicaragua's Sandinista government.

In its ruling, the Court identified U.S. attacks on Nicaraguan territory during 1983-1984, including attacks on Puerto Sandino on 13 September and 14 October 1983, an attack on Corinto on 10 October 1983; an attack on Potosi Naval Base on 4/5 January 1984, an attack on San Juan del Sur on 7 March 1984; attacks on patrol boats at Puerto Sandino on 28 and 30 March 1984; and an attack on San Juan del Norte on 9 April 1984.

The United States withdrew its acceptance of the Court, arguing the Court had no authority in matters of sovereign state relations. The United Nations General Assembly passed a resolution to pressure the U.S. to pay. Only Israel and El Salvador voted with the U.S. against the resolution.

The International Court of Justice decision called the nature of the conflict in Nicaragua one of aggression directed by a foreign power against Nicaragua.[21] In a twelve-to-three vote, the Court's summary judgment against the United States stated that by:

---

19. Wikipedia, "History of Nicaragua."
20. Wikipedia, "History of Nicaragua."
21. Wikipedia, "History of Nicaragua."

... training, arming, equipping, financing and supplying the contra forces or otherwise encouraging, supporting and aiding military and paramilitary activities in and against Nicaragua, the United States has acted, against the Republic of Nicaragua, in breach of its obligation under customary international law not to intervene in the affairs of another State.

In 1991, under the administration of President Violeta Chamorro, Nicaragua dropped its claim from the International Court. When Nicaragua dropped its claim, it stated in a letter that it "had decided to renounce all further rights of action based on the case and did not wish to go on with the proceedings." The International Court subsequently issued an order removing Nicaragua's case from the court's list.

The 1990 general elections were held under careful international observation. On February 25, 1990, the U.S.-endorsed and U.S.-financed National Opposition Union (*Unión Nacional Opositor* or UNO) coalition and its presidential candidate, Violeta Chamorro, won an upset victory. Chamorro won with 55 percent of the presidential vote compared to Ortega's 41 percent. Of 92 seats in the National Assembly, UNO won 51, and the FSLN won just 39.

A peaceful transfer of administrations took place on April 25, 1990. The fact that a peaceful transfer of power happened then is a testament to the dedication of the Sandinistas to the principle of democracy. The victory of the UNO party can be understood as the result of two factors: (i) the financial backing of the UNO candidates by the U.S.;[22] and (ii) the war-weariness of the population as they believed that the U.S. would stop the Contra attacks if UNO won.

With the transfer of power in Nicaragua, the Bush administration called off the war. The war's costs were substantial: approximately 31,000 Nicaraguans killed; thousands more maimed and wounded; 350,000 internally displaced; and roughly $9 billion in economic damages.[23] "By any measure," wrote sociologist Lynn Horton, "Nicaragua's armed conflict of the 1980s took a devastating human and economic toll." To Latin Americanist historian Thomas Walker, the Contra War was "one of the greatest human tragedies of the second half of the twentieth century."

---

22. In October 1989, the U.S. Congress approved $9 million to support the UNO political campaign.

23. Williams, "Central America Wars, 1980s."

Witness for Peace

Witness for Peace was started in 1983 when Christians in Nicaragua, the Protestant relief and development agency in Nicaragua (CEPAD), and some Catholic clergy in Nicaragua called on U.S. churches for help. They wanted us Christians in the U.S. to send delegations to Nicaragua to see what death and destruction Contra rebels were causing to ordinary citizens in Nicaragua. Almost every Contra attack involved violence, torture, rape, and other atrocities against unarmed Nicaraguans. They wanted us to demand that our government stop funding all such attacks.

In April 1983, Gail Phares, leader of the Carolina Interfaith Task Force on Central America (CITCA), gathered a group of 30 North Carolinians representing ten religious denominations. The group visited Nicaragua that month. They went to three border towns in Nicaragua near Honduras. When the group arrived, one of those towns was actually under attack by Contras. The Contras stopped shooting as soon as the Gringos arrived. Gail said she thought,[1] "We have got to stop President Reagan from destroying the Nicaraguan revolution, as the U.S. had done in Guatemala in 1954." On the way back to Managua, the group discussed having a vigil with a large group of U.S. citizens in the Nicaraguan war zone. They discussed this possibility with CEPAD leaders in Managua, who discussed the idea with Sandinista leaders. The latter finally agreed, provided the vigil would be held at a place where the *Norteamericanos* (North Americans) would be safe.

---

1. Peace, *Call to Conscience*, 103.

Gail Phares, on the right, with Sharon Hostetler. The latter would later become Executive Director of WFP (2008 to 2014)

Gail Phares got real busy as soon as she returned home; she enlisted the help of other supporters in CITCA. They made hundreds of phone calls to activist representatives of many Protestant denominations and Catholic communities in the U.S. CEPAD staff in Nicaragua also contacted people they knew in the U.S.

The result was that on July 2, 1983, a delegation of 157 U.S. citizens from 31 states and Puerto Rico arrived in Managua.[2] From Managua, they went by bus to the northern town of *Jalapa*, and when one bus broke down, those folks had to complete their journey in the back of pickup trucks. They were accompanied by government military vehicles as Contras were known to be in the area. In the next few days, the visitors heard many stories about Contra attacks on the townspeople. The highlight of the trip was a vigil on July 6th when the guests and their hosts held hands standing across a field.

On the last day, when the group was in Jalapa, about 20 people out of the group met together. They discussed plans to make the kind of witness they had experienced in Jalapa permanent in Nicaragua. A month later, leaders from CEPAD and David Sweet, a Latin American history professor, secured the Sandinista government's approval for a permanent witness

2. Peace, *Call to Conscience*, 103–8.

program involving delegations of U.S. citizens. Finally, Witness for Peace (WFP) was formally established by twenty people meeting in Philadelphia during October 8–10, 1983. They named a steering committee of six and selected Yvonne Dilling of the Maryknoll community at age twenty-eight to be the national coordinator.

An early draft of a Witness for Peace recruitment advertisement stated:[3]

> WANTED: Non-violent Christian men and women, immoderate in opposition to militarism and foreign intervention, for peace mission to Nicaragua-Honduras border. Must speak fluent Spanish, have previous rural living experience in Third World, be of sound mind and body, and be prepared spiritually to stand and if necessary risk death alongside a people threatened with armed invasion by forces trained and outfitted in the U.S. Subsistence salary. Must be over 21.

The founding group agreed that WFP would be dedicated to nonviolence and nonpartisanship regarding the political parties in Nicaragua, and it would be Biblically based. It did not require volunteers to be Christian but allowed Jews and others to join, as long as each participant was comfortable with WFP's actions based on prayer and the Bible. The first press release of the organization on November 17, 1983, stated the purpose of the group was first to "establish a human shield to protect the people of Nicaragua from the violence of the U.S.-backed counterrevolutionary forces," and second, to generate U.S. public opposition to "the covert war being waged by the U.S. government against the people of Nicaragua."

Witness for Peace offices were set up in Washington, DC, Durham (North Carolina), and Santa Cruz (California). On October 27, 1983, four long-term[4] volunteers arrived in Jalapa, followed five weeks later by the first short-term[5] delegation. Thus began, said Gail Phares,[6] "the longest non-violent presence in an active war zone in history."

After a few months had passed, the number of long-termers in Nicaragua began to increase and they branched out from Jalapa, establishing a presence in *Ocotal, Somotillo, San Pedro Del Norte, Jinotega, Matagalpa,* and *Paiwas,* in the north, and *San Juan del Sur* and Bluefields in the south. As the Contra attacks spread geographically, those areas of

---

3. Griffin-Nolan, *Witness for Peace*, 23.
4. Volunteers who had made one- to two-year commitments
5. Generally a two-week long delegation
6. Peace, *Call to Conscience*, 106.

conflict were where the long-term teams tried to go. By August 1984, there were 18 long-termers in Nicaragua.[7] The two primary responsibilities of the long-termers were: (1) to host the short-term delegations and (2) to document Contra attacks in village areas where they worked and the impacts of the attacks on Nicaraguan citizens. Their reporting also expanded to cover various developments in Nicaragua, including the relationship between the Sandinista government and the churches and the Nicaraguan electoral process in 1984 (interviewing different political party leaders about their freedom to organize and campaign).[8]

Usually, two long-termers would be assigned to each short-term delegation, and it was their job to arrange for the short-termers' lodging, meals, and transportation, in addition to setting up meetings with the villagers and informational meetings in Managua. They were the leaders and counselors of the delegation once the latter arrived in Nicaragua.

In 1984, Witness for Peace sent an average of two short-term delegations to Nicaragua every month. Most of these delegations were made up of 18 to 20 people. Each short-term delegate had to pay for her/his flight to Nicaragua and also paid a set amount to offset the in-country expenses of their delegation. Each short-term delegation stayed for a few days with Nicaraguan families in conflict areas; some also worked in the fields or coffee plantations with them.

One term, *accompany*, is important to understand as it is used frequently to describe the way WFP International Team members (Long-termers) and short-term delegates interact with the people they've come to help. In *accompanying* the people of a particular locality, delegates stay with them, physically stand with them, and in some sense protect them from attacks by the powerful who resist their demands for peace and justice.

For a few days of the two weeks, the short-term delegations would attend meetings in Managua with newspaper editors, human-rights organizations, representatives of various political parties, and diplomats in the U.S. embassy. All this so that delegates could take home a complete range of information about the country and the ongoing Contra attacks. Delegates were urged to speak to audiences back home and to Congressional representatives about the war to end U.S. support of the Contra war. I took this obligation very seriously after I returned from my delegation in August 1985.

Witness for Peace during 1983–1990 was an organization that took actions based on prayer and belief in God's guidance. Consistent with its

---

7. Griffin-Nolan, *Witness for Peace*, 111.
8. Peace, *Call to Conscience*, 106.

name in Spanish, *Accion Permanente Cristiana por la Paz* (Permanent Christian Action for Peace), Witness for Peace delegations took action in opposing the Contras, who were fighting a brutal U.S. proxy war against the people of Nicaragua.

This action policy took a bolder form in November 1984 when a U.S. Navy destroyer was sighted in Nicaraguan waters not far from the Pacific port of Corinto, Nicaragua. It seems that a Soviet ship was about to be unloaded at the port, and Reagan claimed that there were Soviet MIG fighters in crates aboard the ship. This turned out to be about as true as a later claim of weapons of mass destruction in Iraq in 2002–03. At any rate, the WFP long-term team not only brought two short-term delegations to Corinto to camp out on the beach and pray for peace, but they also rented a shrimp boat. They loaded the boat with some long- and short-termers and headed out to sea to confront the U.S. destroyer. When they were within voice range of the ship, the designated long-termer, Stuart Taylor, a Presbyterian minister, yelled out[9] in his Southern drawl, "Y'all go home!" over and over. "You're not wanted here! Go home!"

The U.S. navy decided it was best for public relations at home for the destroyer to turn tail, which it did. There were no MIGs, and, best of all, there was no invasion. WFP believes that its policy of non-violent action was one factor that persuaded the Reagan administration not to invade Nicaragua.

Witness for Peace operated in Nicaragua with the permission of the Sandinista Nicaraguan government. There was necessarily some degree of coordination between the two, as WFP volunteers and delegates set up shop, as it were, in areas of military conflict. Many on the long-term team favored the revolution, as they knew the oppression Nicaraguans had lived under in the Somoza regime up to 1979. And they saw the steps the Sandinistas had taken to improve education and health care in the country's rural areas. But a few short-term delegates felt that the long-term team was all too ready to accept favorably whatever the Sandinistas did. It was well known that the Sandinista government had acted unfairly and aggressively in some cases against the Miskito Indians and other minorities living along the Caribbean coast in eastern Nicaragua. So there *were* things one could say unfavorably about the Sandinistas.

Daniel Erdman, a Presbyterian pastor from New Mexico, recalled that by the end of his July 1984 short-term delegation to Jalapa, he had "come away with the impression that WFP was a pro-Sandinista organization." Because of political differences that emerged among the short-term

9. Griffin-Nolan, *Witness for Peace*, 12–26.

delegates, WFP found it impossible to adopt any kind of policy statement on the Nicaraguan revolution. Opposition to U.S. policy remained the unifying issue.[10] As William Sloan Coffin said:[11] "You don't have to agree with everything the Sandinistas are doing to disagree with everything our government is doing in Nicaragua."

10. Griffin-Nolan, *Witness for Peace*, 122–23.
11. Pastor of the Riverside church in the Morningside Heights neighborhood of Manhattan, New York City

Kidnapped by Contras

That day when Brooks Smith spoke at my Meeting (the Plainfield Friends Meeting in New Jersey), I didn't know anything about Nicaragua. In fact, my knowledge wasn't too far removed from sounding like some friends who would ask: "Isn't Nicaragua in Africa?" That was November 14, 1984. Brooks was then the pastor of the North Plainfield Presbyterian church and had recently returned from a two-week delegation to Nicaragua sponsored by Witness for Peace (WFP).

Brooks spoke fervently and enthusiastically about his delegation experience in Nicaragua. As with all such WFP delegations beginning in July 1983 until mid-year 1990, the purpose of his delegation was as Americans to accompany Nicaraguans living near the northern border with Honduras. By "accompany," they meant "be present with them" and thereby minimize attacks on them by Contras, who had begun to cross the border to attack and commit atrocities on Nicaraguans living in communities on the Nicaraguan side of the border.

When the organizing group of U.S. church leaders came to the border town of Jalapa in July 1983, they noticed that as long as *they* were there, the Contras didn't come to attack the Nicaraguan civilians. Their CIA handlers told the Contras that risking killing Americans in any attack was to be avoided at all costs. So as long as the Americans stayed with the Nicaraguans, the latter were safe. Witness for Peace was organized to provide an uninterrupted succession of short-term delegations to accompany the people who were the targets of Contra attacks.

Brooks's two-week delegation of 15 Americans went to Jalapa, Nicaragua, a town close to the border with Honduras; a chaplain from Rapid City, South Dakota, led the delegation. The delegation helped the local people pick coffee beans on common lands for a week. His group spoke to the Nicaraguans about recent Contra attacks in the area. The remaining week in Nicaragua, they were in Managua meeting with human rights groups, representatives of the opposition newspaper *La Prensa*, the U.S. ambassador to Nicaragua, and many others. While they were in Jalapa, a Nicaraguan army contingent nearby shot down a made-in-the-US helicopter flown by Contras. The delegation was very concerned this might precipitate a counterattack from the Contras and a possible invasion by U.S. forces. But luckily, that didn't happen.

I was impressed with what Brooks said so eloquently about the Christian spirit of Witness for Peace, so much so that I attended another talk he gave the following February (1985) at a local Presbyterian church. He repeated descriptions of his experiences on the WFP delegation. It all seemed to me to be such compassionate and spirit-filled actions by WFP. I committed myself to sign up to be a part of a short-term WFP delegation to Nicaragua.

I decided to go in August of that year to fit in with my family's schedule. I applied to the headquarters of WFP in Washington, DC. No delegations were scheduled to leave from New Jersey in August, so I decided to sign up with a delegation from New York State that was scheduled to leave that month. My family accepted my decision to be part of the delegation, and I arranged for time off from my work at the environmental engineering firm Dames & Moore. One person in my Friends Meeting in Plainfield, New Jersey, opposed my going, as she thought it was too dangerous for me, but she did not stand in my way.

There were specific requirements of participants in WFP delegations. It was considered best to be fluent in Spanish, although this was not required. I was only at the beginner level of speaking Spanish. As part of the application, I had to submit an essay indicating why I wanted to be part of the two-week WFP delegation. People had to agree with the organization's faith-based foundation and were expected to represent a church or synagogue. And participants needed to be committed to non-violence.

In mid-June, I learned that I had been accepted to join the New York delegation. Soon after, I heard from the delegation coordinator, Rev. Lloyd Duren, who informed me that the delegation folks planned to meet at his church close to Poughkeepsie, New York, on a Saturday in June. Lloyd was pastor of the Trinity United Methodist church seven miles from Poughkeepsie. This was to be a pre-delegation get-together and non-violence training event. On the appointed day, I drove up to Poughkeepsie and met at Lloyd's church with the 18 other delegation members—14 from New York State, two from Vermont, one from DC, and one from Pennsylvania. I was the only one from New Jersey.[1] I was impressed with how bright and how dedicated they were to protecting the Nicaraguan people. Along with

---

1. There were an additional two men from California who were recruited later as they had had expertise in river boating, which it turned out we would need on the river at the border between Nicaragua and Costa Rica. They would meet up with us in Managua.

discussions, eating lunch together, and an in-depth session on non-violence training, we prayed for the success of our delegation.

Lloyd and WFP staff instructed me on the day and time we would all meet in Miami and what flight we needed to schedule to get from Miami to Managua. After the meeting in Poughkeepsie, the time seemed to fly by. On Sunday August 4th, I left for Miami with bare personal essentials, my sleeping bag, a water canteen, and a 35 mm camera. I also brought a water purifying kit consisting of purifying iodine tables and a water-filtering device operated by a hand pump. The group had designated me as the one to oversee drinking-water supply and purification during our upcoming travels in Nicaragua.

In Miami, I met up with the rest of the group hailing from the East Coast, and we boarded a plane to Managua. It was in Miami where we were told that we would not be going to towns near the border with Honduras after all. All the previous WFP short-term delegations had gone to the north of the country. Instead, we were scheduled to go to the south on a barge as a "peace flotilla" down the *Rio San Juan* (St. John's River) separating Nicaragua and Costa Rica. That was indeed a sudden turn of events. It turned out that the border between Nicaragua and Costa Rica had become a real war zone. The Contras had made several attacks on at least two border towns on the Nicaraguan side and occupied one of them, where they constructed an airfield to receive their supplies by air. They pretty much held sway in those days over any traffic on the river.

The purpose of our peace flotilla was to pray for peace on the river and to support any initiatives that could maintain peace in that border region. WFP wanted to support Nicaragua's offer to negotiate an internationally supervised demilitarized zone on the border. Such a demilitarized zone would block U.S. plans to increase the number of Contra camps in Costa Rica. Clearly, for the Contras to be victorious over the Sandinistas in Nicaragua, they would have to complement their forces in Honduras with increased forces attacking from the south, from Costa Rica. WFP announced to Costa Rican officials and peace groups in that country that their peace flotilla would soon be voyaging down the Rio San Juan to serve as an embryonic peace-keeping force on the river.

When we arrived in Managua Sunday afternoon, several members of the WFP long-term team welcomed us. They took us by bus to the WFP office in the city which included a large dormitory room containing many bunk beds. So that was our home for the next two nights. That evening we discussed the trip and peace flotilla we were about to embark on. We spent one hour on non-violence training.

Soon after we arrived in Managua, our group heard that Eden Pastora, head of ARDE, the Contra group that operated out of Costa Rica, had issued a threat against the upcoming peace flotilla. He announced that "the armed men of ARDE . . . have the order to fire on wolves in sheep's clothing. We will not be responsible for the lives of Communists disguised as Sandinistas or for the lives of politicians disguised as shepherds of peace." Our delegation prayed about the risks we were about to undertake. We felt God's spirit led us to proceed with our mission despite the threat.

In response, the Witness for Peace office said in a statement read in part during a news conference:

> "For centuries, Christian theologians have justified the risking of lives to wage war. In Nicaragua today, we are called to take risks for peace . . . We ask for the prayers and support of peace-loving people of Costa Rica, Nicaragua, and the United States."

Later that day, WFP submitted a formal press release: "Witness for Peace will continue to work for reconciliation in Nicaragua despite this threat. We will pray for Eden Pastora and the men he leads, but we will hold President Reagan and those members of Congress who voted for Contra aid responsible for any injury which the Contras may inflict on our group."

We left by bus for Grenada with 10 WFP long-termers on Tuesday morning. But first, each of us donned our yellow T-Shirts identifying us as Witness for Peace members. The T-shirt said *Accion Permanente Cristiana por la Paz* (Permanent Christian Action for Peace).[2]

Grenada is 25 miles south of Managua and at the northern end of *Lago de Nicaragua* (Lake Nicaragua), a fresh-water lake that is the tenth largest in the Americas. It's of tectonic origin, and there are stunning volcanic mountains on its western side. In particular, the largest island on the lake, Ometepe, has two beautiful volcanic mountains. The lake drains to the Caribbean Sea via the *Rio San Juan*, historically making the lakeside city of Granada an Atlantic port, although Granada (as well as the entire lake) is closer to the Pacific Ocean geographically. On the southeastern tip of the lake is the town of San Carlos, where the *Rio San Juan* begins its journey eastward, ultimately discharging to the Caribbean.

At the lakefront in Grenada, we all boarded a speed boat/yacht with a large cabin. We headed to San Carlos, a distance of about 50 miles. It took us about three hours to cross the lake north to south going at top speed, or so it seemed to us, finally reaching San Carlos at 5 pm.

---

2. 'Witness for Peace' does not directly translate very well to Spanish.

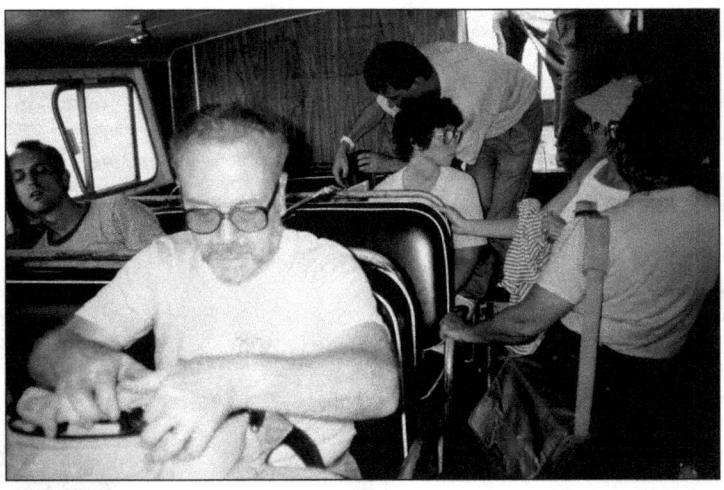

View inside the yacht's cabin. Lloyd Duren is in the foreground.

During the voyage, the view of the lake and the mountains on the west was fabulous, particularly when we sailed past Ometepe Island containing two volcanic mountains.

When we disembarked at San Carlos, a small crowd of people met us, and then we attended a short ceremony at a ball field in town, complete with a few speeches in Spanish. Then we all paired off to meet our hosts for the night. Rev. John Paarlberg from Syracuse, New York, and I were taken to the home of the Rodrigues family, with whom we stayed the night. Gabriel, the father, and his wife Olivia had two grown children, Miguel and Emilia. The night we stayed with them, Emelia was with them, as was her baby girl Elena. Gabriel and Miguel were on active duty in the Nicaraguan army and seemed content to be serving their country. The family had to live quite simply, but they cheerfully invited John and me to their dinner table. Conversation with us around the dinner table was limited, as John's and my knowledge of Spanish was poor.

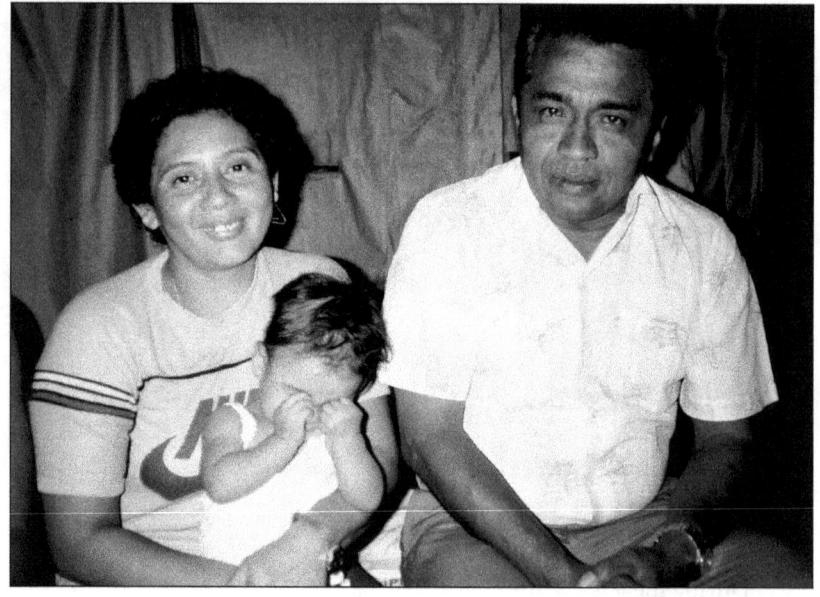

Gabriel and Olivia Rodrigues and grandchild

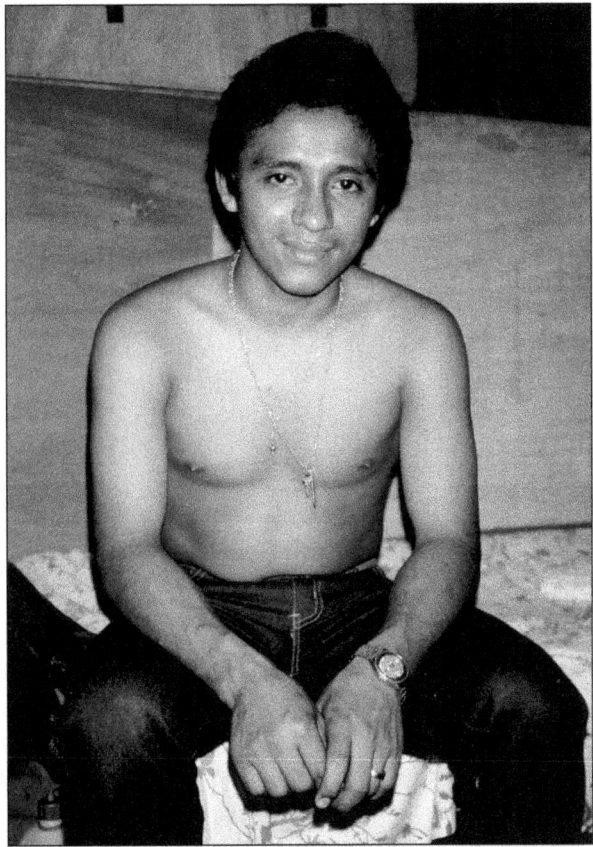

Miguel Rodrigues

The next day John and I got up early and joined our group at the lakefront. The long-termers had arranged for speed boats to take all of us part-way down the *Rio San Juan*, which began its downstream course at San Carlos. There were six of us in each speed boat, plus the driver/pilot.

One of our speed boats with members of our delegation. Sr. Anita Von Wellsheim from Albany NY is in the foreground

About two hours and 27 miles later, we arrived at the little Nicaraguan town of El Castillo along the river, where we would transfer ourselves and our meager belongings from the speed boats to a barge pulled by a tug boat. The townspeople had turned out in force for us and started to serenade us by singing lustily accompanied by guitar and fiddle, as shown in the photo. This town had suffered four Contra attacks in the previous two years.

Celebration of our visit by El Castillo townspeople

After the welcoming event, we began to board the barge. By that time, some 16 members of the media had appeared and were ready to board the barge with us. In addition, two Nicaraguan women and a tiny baby, who lived on the barge, were with us, as well as the Nicaraguan pilot of the tug boat, Dom Enrique. He showed us the bullet holes on his tug boat from three previous ambushes by the Contras. So we were 51 people on the barge, over its capacity, no doubt, considering we all would have to sleep on the barge that night.

This is how we fit inside the barge

Tug boat is in the front; it's preparing to pull the barge

Some members of the New York delegation, more energetic and artier than me, had prepared a beautiful flag that we hoisted on a pole at the back of the tug boat. It was a white flag with lettering saying "Witness for Peace New York." When we were in Managua, we had all signed our names in different places on the flag. In addition, we put up large white banners on the sides of the barge with wording in Spanish indicating we were seeking peace along the border.

Our New York delegation WFP flag

Along the way, Geralyn McDowell of Troy New York led us in song, and a long-termer, Julie Beutel, accompanied with her guitar. One of the songs we sang the most was "We are the Boat" (*Somos El Barco*), made a favorite by Pete Seeger. We even learned to sing it in Spanish. It was apropos as we were, after all, in a boat; well, barge.

When everyone had boarded, we set off downstream. Before very long, we passed by the community of *Las Tiricias* on the Costa Rican side, where we saw three or four Civil Guard[3] officers on the Costa Rican side. We pulled the boat up to the shore, and Ed Griffin-Nolan, the WFP Nicaragua Coordinator with us, and another long-termer got out to speak to them. As a group, we presented them with a flower bouquet and prayed with them for the Costa Rican Civil Guards who had been killed that May at nearby *Las Crucitas* in an exchange of fire with Nicaraguan soldiers. The Nicaraguan soldiers had been involved in a campaign to attack Contra bases on both sides of the river.

Our destination for the day was a place on the river known as *La Penca*, Nicaragua, which the Nicaraguan army had recaptured from the Contras in May. The Contras had earlier built an airstrip there soon after they captured it. The Contras used the airstrip to receive supplies by air from Honduras and El Salvador. After about eight hours of travel, we arrived at *La Penca*.

---

3. Instead of an army, Costa Rica has a Civil Guard corps, which means it is not set up, nor does it intend, to invade any other country.

We had come about 45 miles as the crow flies and about three-fifths of the distance along *Rio San Juan* from *Lago de Nicaragua* to the Caribbean. It was almost dark. About twenty bemused Nicaraguan soldiers were there to greet us on the Nicaraguan side. They sang to us, and we in turn sang to them. We prayed with them for peace on the river.

Then we turned around and headed back west toward *El Castillo*. But it was getting late, so our pilot found a mooring place on the Nicaraguan side of the river, about a mile from *La Penca*. So we spread out our sleeping bags on the floor of the barge. There was very little wiggle room. Some of the news reporters took their sleeping bags up on the tin roof of the barge and slept there. It was a peaceful night.

At 6:00 am the following day, we set sail for *El Castillo*. But at about 7:30, we heard gunshots from the Costa Rican side. Then we realized someone was there shooting guns in the air over our heads and over the barge. It was a small contingent of Contras, and they yelled at our pilot to bring the barge to the Costa Rican side, which he did. Then we saw the Contras, seven of them, each with a rifle in hand. They told us all to get out of the barge, which we did. Then we stood in a line in the wooded area by the river, hand in hand, waiting for what would happen next. I didn't feel fearful; I felt like I was in a movie. It wasn't yet a real-enough feeling for me to be afraid.

Kidnapped: Contra fighter in foreground; we're in the back standing in a line

Meanwhile, the WFP staff who stayed in Managua were trying to contact us by radio. Our radio was left on the barge when we had to vacate the barge under gunpoint. The long-termers on board had left the radio on "transmit" so the Managua folks could hear anything happening within the microphone range. While we were exiting the barge, the folks in Managua heard via the radio what sounded like sporadic bursts of gunfire. But it turned out that this sound of gunfire had been caused by the crew dragging poles and ropes across the corrugated tin roof of the barge as they secured the boat to the shore. So there was fearful concern in the Managua office that there may have been massive bloodshed.

After about ten minutes, we got orders from the head of this Contra contingent, William, that we were to follow a path away from the river up a hill. We started up and kept on walking and walking. It must have been about two miles, not the easiest for an 80-year-old man who was a member of our delegation. We finally reached our destination, an opening in the forest where there was a tiny one-room wooden shack devoid of any furniture.

So that's where we hung out for about seven hours. One time when two Nicaraguan helicopters appeared and started to fly close to us, the Contras made us take cover quickly in the shack or under trees so the Nicaraguan pilots wouldn't see us.

Kidnapped and under guard at the shack

By that time we were all pretty muddy as it had rained recently. There were no macadam paths or concrete sidewalks, no building with comfortable chairs or baths where we could bathe and change clothes. So we just looked a mess. But that was the least of our worries. We had no idea what the Contras were planning for us. We didn't know what their chief (Eden Pastora?) wanted to do with or to us.

While we were waiting, a few of the Spanish-fluent long-termers of our group started to talk to individual Contra fighters. The lead Contra, William, said he knew nothing of Eden Pastora's threat against us but that he had stopped the boat because he didn't have any orders to let us pass. By talking to the Contras, we could listen to their stories—why they joined the Contras and more personal things about their families, etc. These fighters were as valuable human beings to us as were our Nicaraguan friends supporting the Sandinista government. If we had any enemies, it was our own CIA who had encouraged and organized the Contras to prey on innocent Nicaraguans who were just trying to support their government and live their lives.

Ed Griffin-Nolan, on the left, with two contras. William is next to Ed

One of the Contras, Israel, spoke extensively with Mary Dutcher, a long-termer from St. Louis. He was a Miskito Indian. He and his people hail from the east coast area of Nicaragua. Israel said that one of his brothers was also a Contra, and another had served in the National Guard under

Somoza[4]. Regarding the Contra army structure in Costa Rica, he said that William was the head of more than 50 Contras, sort of like an army company, and that Daniel was in command of over 300 Contras, including William's group. Daniel was like a commander of a battalion. He said that Eden Pastora commanded Daniel's group and 17 other "battalions" similar to Daniel's. Israel said that the Costa Rican Civil Guard just ignored them (the Contras) and left them alone.

Mary Dutcher speaking with the Contra Israel, when we were back in the boat

Ed Griffin-Nolan had an informal interview with William. He said that his father had been in the National Guard under Somoza. William said he had owned quite a bit of property and felt things were much better under the Dictator. He claimed the Sandinistas were starving the people by making the male family members go off to fight them (the Contras)! He said he had met Eden Pastora several times, and it was Pastora who had armed him when he William joined ARDE three years before.

---

4. The pre-1979 dictator of Nicaragua. Many of his National Guard soldiers later became Contras.

Most everyone had brought some food and water with them. So we were okay for lunch. But we started to run out of drinking water. I had brought a jug with me that held filtered river water I had treated with iodine tablets. But now I needed to refill it. One of the long-termers, probably Ed Griffin-Nolan, talked with William around 10 am about the drinking-water issue. He reluctantly agreed to allow three of us (not me), including Ed, to go back to the barge under guard to get more water and to communicate with the WFP office in Managua.

So it happened, and the radio we had brought from Managua was still on the barge and was operational. At about 10:45, Ed, now on the barge, spoke via radio in Spanish to Sharon Hostetler at the WFP office in Managua to assure her (and the world, it turned out) that we were all okay. With an armed Contra guard standing by, Ed said in Spanish: "We are being held by our brothers from ARDE who are treating us well." The other message to Sharon, in English, was that we did *not* want any military intervention or "rescue." The three WFPers, accompanied by the Contra armed guards, came back with several jugs of river water.

Around 4:00 pm, our captors began acting a little anxious. They didn't know what to do with us during the coming night. It appeared they were not going to kill us, at least not that day. William said they couldn't release us because they had not yet heard back from their group's superior officer. He wouldn't tell us who his superior officer was. Then Ed Griffin-Nolan negotiated with William to allow the entire group to return to the barge for the night, as it would have been impossible for us all to bed down in the small hut, let alone on the muddy ground.

The walk back to the boat was not easy, as it had rained more and was even muddier on the trail than when we hiked up that morning. As we hiked down, several armed Contras accompanied us. Then a couple of the media photographers in the lead chose the wrong path at a Y in the trail. That really irritated William when he realized we were in unfamiliar territory and had to backtrack. By the time we finally reached the boat it was after sundown. William was in the boat and in a rage, mostly brought on by the fact that he had allowed us to get lost and thereby had lost face with his men. He demanded that we all get out of the barge and march back up the hill in the darkness.

But then Geralyn McDowell from Troy, New York, became the focus of attention. She was exhausted, collapsed on the ground, covered with mud, and her feet bleeding. She was sobbing. It was a frightening moment for all of us. Fortunately, William relented and resumed control over the situation to save face. He ordered us all to get *on* the barge, but we had to keep all the lights off and not make any noise. He allowed us to make a brief radio call to our Managua office.

So we bedded down for another night on the barge, this time much muddier and sweatier than we were the night before. Before we went to sleep, I did some work filtering the river water and disinfecting it with iodine tablets to fill our jugs. We were under guard all night.

We awoke at about 6:00 and rolled up our sleeping bags. We had granola and water for breakfast. Then sitting in our barge under guard, we waited . . . and waited. William told us he couldn't release us unless the Contra battalion commander Daniel came. So we had to stay in the barge until Daniel arrived. We kept our spirits up by praying and singing, led by Geralyn McDowell. *Finally,* at noon Daniel came and commanded us to get off the boat and to meet him in a nearby cacao grove, which we did, including the Nicaraguan pilot and the two Nicaraguan women. We stood in a circle, and at the head of the circle was Daniel. During this time, Contra soldiers guarded us all.

Daniel told us in Spanish that we hadn't been badly treated and that it could have been much worse, for we were in a war zone after all. He said he didn't belong to the southern Contra group ARDE but managed an independent anti-communist Contra group. Daniel seemed to talk on and on. *Finally,* he said that he was releasing all of us. We could return to our boat and resume sailing up the river to *El Castillo.* At that point, we all held hands, including the hands of the Nicaraguans with us. We walked back to the boat hand in hand, to make sure that none of the Nicaraguans would be held back by the Contras to face likely brutality and death. When we were *all* back on the boat, we breathed a big sigh of relief and said a heartfelt prayer of thanks to God. The long-termers on the barge radioed Managua that we were okay and were heading home. We had been held captive for 29 hours. Meanwhile, the pilot had started the engine and we were off to *El Castillo.*

Later we learned that "Daniel" was actually Noel Boniche, a fugitive from justice in Nicaragua. It seemed he had joined ARDE after being accused of stealing 120,000 cordobas from a government agency in 1983.

An hour and fifty minutes after leaving, a helicopter full of armed Costa Rican Civil Guardsmen landed on the Costa Rican side of the river. They demanded that we pull over to their side. Ed Griffin-Nolan and Fr. Tom Fenlon from Newburgh, New York, got off the boat and spoke with a Colonel Lesmer Chavez, who asked several questions. He said that they had been looking for us for two days. Then he gave us permission to continue our voyage. Later on the barge we heard a Costa Rican radio news broadcast saying that we had not returned from La Penca earlier because we had had engine troubles! That was supposedly based on Colonel Chavez's report.

Costa Rican Civil Guard officers with Ed and Tom

Two hours later when we were passing by Las Tiricias, another Costa Rican Civil Guard ordered our pilot to pull the boat over to the side. He instructed us to wait there because a U.S. Consul was expected to arrive soon. We didn't think we could wait more than a few minutes because our pilot was worried that we might not reach El Castillo before nightfall. After many minutes had passed and the Consul had still not shown up, we told the guard we had to leave. But the guard insisted on detaining us under orders from his Chief of Staff. Finally, after waiting for an hour and ten minutes, the guard said he had been authorized to release us.

We proceeded on to El Castillo just as the sun was getting close to setting. Out of the blue, we were suddenly "attacked" by a few speed boats coming downriver toward us. The boats held more people from the press, and as soon as they reached our boat, several of them just leaped onto the barge. We had to make way for them or be crushed. I never knew until then just how rude and aggressive members of the press could be. They immediately started to quiz each member of our delegation and the long-termers. Five minutes later we could see the lights of El Castillo. What a grand welcoming the townspeople gave us! They kept chanting *Queremos la paz!* (We want peace). When we landed, there were songs and prayers of thanksgiving all around. That night we bedded down in the local church.

In the morning, after a light breakfast, I busied myself with getting potable water available for us. The long-termers helped me obtain water from town sources that was better than river water, and I disinfected it with iodine tablets.

Then we proceeded by speed boats to San Carlos. The original 19 of our delegation continued with our planned itinerary, while eight of the long-termers returned to Managua by helicopter. That afternoon, my short-term delegation visited a resettlement cooperative near San Carlos; it was about the hottest day I remember on that trip. The cooperative community had suffered a Contra attack just eight days earlier. Then we went by motor boat to the island of *Solentiname* in Lake Nicaragua to pray for peace in a little church, where children of the town sang beautiful songs for us.

We returned to San Carlos, and on Saturday the 10th I was with a small group who returned to Managua by helicopter instead of by boat. The Contras had eliminated the possibility of our returning by bus, as the main road on the east side of Lake Nicaragua was closed due to a recent Contra ambush there. In Managua, we stayed once again at the WFP office in the city. We had a busy schedule from Monday the 12th through Thursday the 15th.

Two of the long-termers, Mary Dutcher and Nancy Eckel, who shepherded our delegation throughout our two weeks in Nicaragua, had made several appointments for us. We visited and had interviews with two human-rights groups, one independent and one favoring the opposition to the Sandinistas ruling party. We also paid a visit to the editor of *La Prensa*, which seemed to be operating quite freely and effectively as the opposition press. The editor didn't have anything good to say about the Sandinista government.

We tried to visit the U.S. Embassy but failed because the embassy staff said no officials would be available until the following week. We desperately wanted to express our strong moral opposition to the U.S. funding the Contras and to the CIA's organizing the Contras in the first place. But on the street opposite to the embassy building, American ex-patriots[5] living in Nicaragua had created and maintained a large sign facing the embassy. The sign in Spanish gave the content of a telegram that the Nicaraguan

5. Many of the American expatriates living in Nicaragua formed the Committee of U.S. Citizens Living in Nicaragua (CUSCLIN), who held weekly Thursday-night vigils in front of the U.S. embassy as a "permanent witness to their rejection of U.S. policy toward Nicaragua."

freedom fighter A. C. Sandino[6] had sent on July 12, 1927, to U.S. Captain G. D. Hatfield, commander of the U.S. Marine contingent. Hatfield was demanding that Sandino and his troops surrender to the marines. Sandino's telegram in Spanish to Captain Hatfield said:

Sign directly across from U.S. Embassy erected by U.S. expats

"I received your communication yesterday and I understand it. I will not surrender, but I wait for you here. I want freedom for my country or death. I do not fear you. I count on the patriotic ardor of those who fight with me."

Throughout our tours around the city, we noticed large, durable election signs for different opposition parties still standing in several parts of the city, remnants of the November 1984 election, which the Sandinistas won handily at 67 percent, with a 75 percent turnout. The political sign shown here says: *La Solucion Somos Todos!* (All of us are the solution!). Our delegation had two interviews with representatives of opposition parties.

---

6. The ruling party, Sandinista, takes its name from the Nicaraguan hero Sandino.

Election campaign sign for the Social Christian Party for the 1984 election

The Latin American Studies Association (LASA), made up of academics whose primary interest is Latin America, sent a special delegation from the U.S. to Nicaragua before and during the 1984 elections to observe and report on the elections. Their extensive report concluded that the elections were free and fair despite minor flaws.

On one of the days we were in Managua, Miguel D'Escoto, the Sandinista government's Foreign Minister, invited our delegation to his home. He had arranged for a delicious lunch for us in his backyard. We were able to have a leisurely talk with him and other guests, and everyone expressed thanks to God for our safe return.

Miguel D'Escoto with two women of our delegation

Born to Nicaraguan parents in Los Angeles, Miguel D'Escoto spent his childhood in Nicaragua. As a young man, he studied religion in the United States and in 1961, became a Catholic priest of the Maryknoll Missionary Society. Later in the mid-1970s, he moved to Nicaragua. As a believer in liberation theology, he joined the Sandinista movement because he became convinced that they would bring justice and vastly improved conditions to the poor of the country. In that way, he was a product of Vatican II, Peruvian priest Gustavo Gutiérrez the author of the theological concept of 'liberation theology', and Pope Leo XIII's 1891 statement that the church should include "an option for the poor" in its approach to the world.

On July 7, 1985, a month before we arrived, in a poor neighborhood of Managua, Miguel D'Escoto, the Nicaraguan Foreign Minister, resigned from that post temporarily and began an indefinite period of total fasting and prayer to denounce the Reagan administration's policy toward his country. He had been a tireless emissary of Nicaragua's desire for peace. He took this profound decision only after seeing every diplomatic effort matched by the obstruction of the U.S. government. He ended his 30-day fast on the day my delegation started eastward down the *Rio San Juan* in speed boats.

The evening of Tuesday the 13th there was a big ecumenical service of thanksgiving for our safe return at a large church in the city. It was sponsored by Protestant pastors, the Protestant relief and development agency in Nicaragua (CEPAD) and Catholic clergy. Children from areas that had suffered Contra attacks brought baskets of flowers which they distributed to our delegation and the long-termers attending.

Our delegation: ready to leave Nicaragua

We all left Nicaragua on Friday, August 16th, leaving Managua on an American Airlines flight. This time, we had one stopover in Belize City rather than in Tegucigalpa, Honduras, where we had stopped on our flight *to* Managua. Belize is a tiny nation that borders Guatemala and Mexico on the west and the Caribbean on the east. We had no idea that we would be at the Belize airport for a long time. We thought perhaps a half an hour, at most. We were eager to get home and be reunited with our families. But no, it would not go as quickly as we wanted.

We must have waited there for at least three hours until finally about 6 or 7 pm we were informed that the flight had been given the go-ahead for takeoff. So instead of arriving at LaGuardia airport on Long Island at 5 or 6 pm, we arrived around 8 or 9 pm. We believe that U.S. government officials may have given American Airlines orders for our flight to stay in Belize for a long enough time so that our arrival in the States would be too late to be covered on the six o'clock evening news.

I have no memory of how I got myself from LaGuardia airport to my home in Scotch Plains, New Jersey. It was all just a blur. But it was wonderful to be back with my family and at home. We delegation members had our 15 minutes of fame. There was even an article about me in the Newark *Star-Ledger*. Over the next few months, I gave talks on my experience at churches and at several rotary clubs in the area. But then it all just petered out. Reagan's policy in pressing forward with the Contra war continued, if anything, at a faster pace. But some people believe that Witness for Peace's actions, including our peace flotilla, may have played a big part in the U.S. stopping short of invading Nicaragua.

Unfortunately, our being kidnapped didn't affect the frequency of Contra attacks in the north of the country. Three days after Daniel, the Contra, released us from his battalion in the southern Contra force (August 11th), a northern Contra contingent entered several hamlets surrounding Achuapa, a small town in the Department (State) of Leon.[7] The Contras tortured and killed 13 civilians, 11 of whom neither owned nor carried guns. On August 17th, their bodies were found. All the remains showed signs of torture: cut-out tongues, stab wounds, empty eye sockets, severed fingers and toes, castration. Most of the dead had been tortured so badly that they were difficult to identify. Despite the horror of that attack, the major U.S. media never covered it.

I returned to Nicaragua in 1990 on a non-WFP delegation from the Chicago area. Our mission was to help monitor the February 25, 1990, national elections there, which we did at several polling stations on the southern side of Managua. Everything seemed to be in order, and in fact, everyone deemed the entire election fair, with the win for the UNO party and their candidate Violeta Chamorro winning the presidency by 14 points.

Except, people said it wasn't *exactly* fair, as the U.S. Congress in October 1989 had given $9 million to help UNO's campaign against the Sandinistas. The $9 million was equivalent to $2 billion worth of political intervention by a possible foreign power in a US election at the time. And leading up to the election, the George H. W. Bush administration funneled $50 million of "non-lethal" aid to the Contras.

I still remember the night before the election when the FSLN sponsored a huge rally in *Plaza de la Revolución* (Revolution Square) at the

---

7. Witness for Peace Documentation Project, *Kidnapped*, 33.

center of Managua. I was present in the crowd, and it was massive. Some have estimated there were at least 300,000 people there. Seeing this, I firmly believed the Sandinistas would win big the following day.

A portion of the crowd rallying the evening before
election day on February 25, 1990

Many of us were crushed by the election results, knowing that the victors almost assuredly would not continue the policies of the Sandinistas that were helping people improve their lives. The thing was that the people were just totally war-weary, not the way the U.S. has been war-weary with regard to our preemptive wars. No, they were war-weary because they themselves were the targets and victims of ongoing Contra attacks all over the country. Yes, that kind of war-weariness. So they understandably voted for peace, for the U.S.-sponsored candidates.

New Jersey Peace Mission

When I returned from my delegation to Nicaragua in August 1985, I felt I must do everything I could to stop Congress from funding the Contras any further. I didn't know just what I could do in that regard, but I was driven to do something.

U.S. aid to the Contras began in 1981 when CIA operatives started recruiting and financing the guerrilla fighters in camps along the Nicaraguan-Honduran border by covertly channeling money and arms to the recruits, many of whom formerly belonged to Somoza's National Guard. In 1983 Congress approved some legal military aid to the Contras but it put limits on it: no more than $24 million could go to "the Central Intelligence Agency, the Defense Department . . . which would have the effect, of supporting, directly or indirectly, military or paramilitary operations in Nicaragua by any nation, group, organization, movement or individual." Later, after a legislative battle of more than two years, President Reagan in 1986 persuaded Congress to renew military aid to the Contras. This fiscal 1987 appropriation marked the first time since mid-1984 that the U.S. would be legally allowed to give weapons, ammunition, and other military supplies to the 10,000 to 15,000 Contras, who were then in camps along the Nicaraguan-Honduran border.

For several years, I had been going to Washington DC at least annually to lobby against Congress's continual funding of the Pentagon for its neverending preparations for war. I would often do lobbying in conjunction with the Friends Committee on National Legislation (FCNL), the Quaker lobbying group in DC. I would visit the FCNL office, which is very close to Capitol Hill, to get tips on how to approach my congressional representatives. They would also give me handouts addressing some of the wars we were waging or some of the shiny new weapons being developed.

Usually, I would start my annual foray to DC by first announcing in April at my Friends Meeting in Plainfield, NJ, that I would be making my annual "cherry-blossom" lobbying tour of DC in a couple of weeks. It was the time of year when Congress started to appropriate money for the Pentagon and other departments for federal programs. I would invite any Friends who were so moved to accompany me. One year, 1975 I think it was, Dorothy Hutchinson, a long-time member of the Meeting and a retired physical education teacher, volunteered to come with me. I remember I took my youngest son Jeremy at age 15 with us. Dorothy was in remarkable shape for a woman over 80. In her sneakers, she ran the socks off Jeremy and me in the Cannon House Office building and the Russell Senate Office Building while lobbying our Representative and Senators, respectively, and in walking to Union Station near where I had parked my car. It was a blessing to have her with us; she sparked any dimming spirit I may have had at the time.

In August and September 1985, I tried to interest other members of my Nicaragua delegation that summer in joining me in lobbying against Contra aid in Congress. That didn't yield much fruit, except for Sister Kathy Maire, who joined me on one lobbying trip to DC. Sister Kathy's regular work involved serving a Hispanic parish in the Bronx. I kept up my visits to DC every three or four weeks to beg my representatives to stop all aid to the Contras. That's all I could do, considering I had a full-time job and family responsibilities at home in Scotch Plains, New Jersey. This continued into and through 1986. Finally late in October of that year, I realized that my lone-ranger approach to lobbying to end Contra aid wasn't working very well.

I had heard about a special kind of peace mission that had been established in a couple of other states to lobby Congress for peace. Each used a collection of peace groups across its state to take turns lobbying about specific peace issues. I heard that a Rob Evans had formerly been active in the Rhode Island Peace Mission. I called him up and invited him to come and meet with a small group of us at the New Jersey SANE[1] office in Montclair, New Jersey. He came, and we were so happy to hear what Rob had to say to us. It didn't sound too complicated. We just had to find out what peace groups in different parts of the state might be interested in my proposed group's coordinating lobbying visits to DC concerning Contra aid.

New Jersey SANE already had a salaried person on staff, Barbara Appelbaum, dedicated to Central American issues, particularly the Contra war in Nicaragua and the death-squads attacks on civilians in El Salvador that the ruling conservative party, ARENA, supported. Barbara and I decided to start the New Jersey Peace Mission (NJPM) in December 1986. It was to be dedicated to lobbying Congress to stop the killing and the wars in Nicaragua and El Salvador. El Salvador was a little different from Nicaragua, as El Salvador was an ally of the United States. The U.S. supported the ARENA

---

1. Statewide office for the Committee for a SANE Nuclear Policy. In 1993, this peace organization's name was changed to 'Peace Action.' It continues its work preventing the deployment of nuclear weapons in space, thwarting weapons sales to countries with human-rights violations, and promoting a new United States foreign policy based on common security and peaceful resolution to international conflicts.

government with arms and military training even though the government was primarily responsible for the frequent death-squad attacks on civilians.

Our first task was collecting a list of local peace groups in New Jersey, which turned out not to be hard, thanks to Barbara and several other NJ SANE members who soon joined us in the committee that would run the New Jersey Peace Mission. We decided to meet every Monday evening at the SANE office in Montclair. I served as chair of the committee. Barbara, Elizabeth Huberman, and Bill Donnelly were the regular committee members, often joined by a couple of other peace friends from the area. Elizabeth and Bill were long-term peace activists who lived in the northern part of the state.

I made the initial contacts with in-state peace groups via telephone, as there were no emails or text messages then. I found that ten local peace groups in Jersey were eager to work with us in scheduling their lobbying visits to DC. During the Monday committee meetings, we discussed not only the scheduling but also the up-to-date news about conditions in Nicaragua and El Salvador that needed to be conveyed to the group scheduled to do the lobbying the next week. During the week following the Monday meeting, I would send letters to the next group's leaders conveying what we believed they should emphasize in the upcoming lobbying visit.

During the first year of operation in 1987, I remember we succeeded in sending some peace group from New Jersey to do the lobbying nearly every week of that year; probably about 42 lobbying visits that year. One weekday in April of that year, we arranged to send several busloads of people to DC to take part in a large statewide lobbying effort to end aid to the Contras. I went on one of the buses. Soon after arriving in DC, people visited their own congressional representatives in the House office buildings. Then a large group of us met with U.S. Senator Bill Bradley in his office on Capitol Hill.

We must have impressed him, and his aides would vouch for it, because we sent groups at least every two weeks to lobby him and Senator Lautenberg to vote against Contra aid. I believe that our persistent lobbying of Bradley was at least partially responsible for his changing his vote for supporting Contra aid from "Yea" to "Nay." God be praised.

An article in the New York Times on February 9, 1988, was headed *Washington Talk: Congress: Bradley About-Face on Contras Proves Intriguing*. On February 5, 1988, the Senate voted 51 to 48 to approve Contra aid, including military aid. So Senator Bradley's vote against the aid was not enough to tip the scales. Fortunately, the day before, the House had voted (219 to 211) to stop aid to the Contras, so the aid package was dead in the water. But the Times article noted the following: "Senator Bill Bradley has long been known as a maverick. Last week the New Jersey Democrat enhanced that reputation again: When the Senate gave President Reagan a surprise victory by voting in favor of assistance for the Nicaraguan rebels on Thursday, Mr. Bradley, who had strongly defended aid to the contras in the past, abruptly changed his mind."

Unfortunately, the following year on April 14, 1989, Congress approved a $49.7 million package of aid to the Nicaraguan rebels with little trace of the partisan rancor that marked congressional debate on such issues in the previous eight years. The vote was 309 to 110 in the House and 89 to 9 in the Senate. The bill was designed to meet only the "humanitarian" needs of the Contras, so the vast majority was comfortable voting for it. Not so, for those few legislators who saw it as continuing support for terrorists attacking Nicaraguan civilians.

During the time I was working on the New Jersey Peace Mission, I participated in a demonstration against the CIA on April 27, 1987, because of the CIA's role in directing the Contra war against Nicaragua and the CIA's role in South Africa. Among an estimated 75,000 people demonstrating with me were the Rev. Jesse Jackson, folk singers Peter, Paul and Mary, actor Ed Asner, and Dr. Benjamin Spock. We nearly surrounded the CIA headquarters building in Langley, Virginia. About 1,500 of us committed civil disobedience by refusing to remove ourselves from federal property near the end of the rally. It was slow processing us. While waiting, we were made to sit in buses with hands handcuffed behind our backs. I remember how I pleaded with a police officer who came on the bus to loosen my handcuffs as they were hurting me. He didn't oblige. After about two excruciating hours of sitting on the bus that way, we were led out of the bus to a building where a group of U.S. Park Service police officers was processing us. I don't remember my being charged with anything besides a minor misdemeanor; I had to pay a fine, and then they released me. I think it was $100. According to the *Los Angeles Times*, 538 of those committing civil disobedience at the end of the demonstration were arrested, and 90 were put in jail.

Later in the year, a few of us from Congressman Matthew Rinaldo's district met outside his office in Montclair, New Jersey, and would demonstrate with banners and songs to protest his voting for Contra aid. One time in August of that year, we were milling around outside Rinaldo's office with our banners. Suddenly a car pulled up along the curb right in front of the office, and three burly men got out and confronted us. They made threatening gestures and then took photos of us. Then they got back in the car and drove off. We surmised that they were probably first-generation Cuban refugees, as there were many Cuban exiles in nearby Elizabeth. I had no idea what they were going to do with the photos they took of us. No doubt they believed they had to resist anyone being soft on the "communism" they saw operating in Sandinista Nicaragua. Our protests sadly failed to persuade the congressman to change his vote from "Yea" to "Nay" on Contra aid, so the Cuban-Americans' threatening us wasted their time.

In late 1988, I handed over the leadership of the NJPM to a friend in my Quaker Meeting, Plainfield Friends Meeting, named Toby Riley. I had become depressed over a major issue between my wife Jane and me. I believed I could not do a good job as leader of the NJPM until I felt significantly better. However, I continued to do my daytime work as a groundwater hydrologist for an environmental engineering firm in Cranford, NJ. So I approached Toby, and he was willing to take it on provided he understood what was required of him. Toby was a computer salesman and computer systems technician; he operated independently. He took over from me in the latter part of 1988, but I sensed that he lacked the fire, perseverance, and sense of urgency that I had for the cause of stopping the war in Nicaragua. But as far as I could tell, he did a satisfactory job as its head until we had to leave New Jersey for Iowa in 1989. When I recently talked to him at age 90, Toby couldn't remember exactly what happened to NJPM before it folded sometime late in 1989.

In November 1989, my wife and I moved to Manson, Iowa, in response to a call my wife Jane received from a United Church of Christ (UCC) congregation there. She had completed her seminary training at Princeton Theological Seminary in 1983 and was ordained in the Plainfield (NJ) UCC church just before we moved to Iowa. In late November that year, she began assuming her duties as pastor of both the Manson UCC congregation and the nearby Moorland UCC congregation. We started living in the parsonage in Manson that the congregations provided for us.

For the two and a half years I lived in Iowa, up to May 1992, I did little to try to end the Contra war, other than write letters to the editor. Peace people in Iowa, particularly those who felt an urgent calling to stop the war in Nicaragua, lived long distances from Manson. But I did join a delegation to Nicaragua in February 1990 from the Chicago area; it was not a delegation sponsored by Witness for Peace. I discuss this experience in the preceding chapter, "Kidnapped by Contras."

Witness for Peace After 1990

In 1989, Witness for Peace (WFP) discussed the possibility of having long-term teams in one or two Latin-American countries in addition to Nicaragua. The WFP Board decided to move forward with that. By 1990, there were four long-termers in Guatemala and two in Mexico accompanying Guatemalan refugees in southern Mexico.[1] WFP's approach in these countries was necessarily different from that in Nicaragua. In Guatemala, the poor faced the oppressive regimes of near-dictators who received U.S. aid for their police forces and their military, but no aid earmarked to effectively improve the people's lives. Long-termers there documented violations of the human and civil rights of the poor. They also reported on the impact on the poor of the complicated neo-liberal economic policies involving so-called *structural adjustment* that the U.S., through the World Trade Organization (WTO) and the International Monetary Fund (IMF), was imposing (promoting) on poor countries. These policies prevented the vast majority of the poor in these countries from improving their lives. Sometimes the policies had the opposite effect, i.e., making poor farmers even poorer.

The modus operandi (MO) of WFP in Guatemala and southern Mexico became the MO for the Nicaragua team also after the national elections held there in February 1990. With the victory of the conservative UNO party, the Sandinistas stepped down and the Contras stopped their attacks. Thereafter, in addition to reporting on civil and human rights abuses (no longer Contra attacks and torture/abuses), the long-term team (now called the "International Team") reported on the impact on the Nicaraguan poor of the structural adjustment policies that the U.S. through the WTO and the IMF began to promote in Nicaragua.

In 1992, at the height of the coup that ousted President Aristide and murdered thousands of Haitians, the Haitian religious community called for an international presence to stand by their people in crisis. In response, WFP began sending delegations to Haiti.

In 1998, WFP opened its Mexico office in response to the Acteal massacre in Chiapas, and increased concern about the effects of NAFTA on the country and a desire to focus attention on the root causes of migration.

---

1. Griffin-Nolan, *Witness for Peace*, 220.

And in 1999, WFP established a delegations program in Cuba. Since then, WFP and thousands of delegates have worked to expose the human costs of the U.S. embargo against Cuba and to end it. In 2000, WFP opened its Colombia office to shine a light on the human, social, and environmental effects of the US-sponsored 'Plan Colombia', a multi-billion-dollar military and counter-narcotics funding package for the Colombian armed forces.

By 2008, the 25th anniversary of Witness for Peace, the organization had extended its mission to include in-country presence and solidarity with the people of Guatemala, Mexico, Colombia, Haiti, and Venezuela, as well as Nicaragua. The delegations to Cuba were discontinued from 2005 to about 2009 because the Bush administration canceled travel licenses to thwart solidarity activism, among other things. Soon after the Obama administration began, the licenses were reinstated. WFP was able to have a long-termer stationed in Havana, and the delegations to Cuba resumed.

In 2015, WFP discontinued its presence in Nicaragua. The decision was tied to the fact that a right-wing military coup had taken place in neighboring Honduras in 2009 under the watchful eye of President Obama's Secretary of State, Hillary Clinton. Witness for Peace wanted a presence there to accompany the poor and monitor the human-rights situation under the new conservative/right-wing rulers. When the issue was raised in 2013, the International Team and the WFP Board thought they could have a presence in both Nicaragua and Honduras. But it soon became evident that with the limited resources available, WFP couldn't be present in both countries, and in 2014 they picked Honduras. In 2015, WFP closed its office in Managua and opened its Honduras office in El Progreso in response to the critical need for human rights accompaniment and solidarity resulting from the US-supported coup in that country.

In any case, as related to me by Sharon Hostetler, former Executive Director of Witness for Peace and leader of the International Team in Central America, the last Witness for Peace short-term delegation to Nicaragua was a teen delegation led by Ron Garcia-Fogarty and coordinated by Sharon during July 3–12, 2017. She didn't know when the last member of the WFP International Team left Nicaragua, as she resigned from WFP in 2014. It was probably sometime in 2015 that the last International Team member left the country. Sharon had done an excellent job as Executive Director for Witness for Peace from her home and office in Managua beginning in 2008. She continued to assist Witness until mid-2017 as a freelance delegations consultant.

In the fall of 2014, the Board tried and failed to engage the services of an Executive Director to replace Sharon. So in early 2015, the Board authorized a new administrative structure called the "Group of Five," in which five members constituted the management group. The group consisted of representatives from each of the five sectors of the organization: the Board, Regional Organizers, Regional Councils, Steering Committees, and International Teams. This Group of Five served the functions of Executive Director and directed the organization from 2015 to 2018.

2018 was a challenging year for Witness for Peace. Beginning in March 2018, the Board decided to search for a new Executive Director to replace the Group of Five. I understand that, for some reason, they were unable to select a new Executive Director. At the beginning of 2018, there were 17 or 18 Board members. Because of disagreements between some members of the Board and the International Team and a generally a low morale among the Board members and staff, by the end of 2018 fifteen Board members had resigned. By the end of the year, the few remaining Board members decided to lay off all the International Teams and the national staff in DC. This was mainly because of declining financial resources and the consequent feeling of the remaining Board members that continuing WFP's historic mission was no longer possible.

Soon after that, however, most of the laid-off staff making up the International Teams and the regional organizers communicated urgently with one another. And then, WFP teams from Colombia, Cuba, Honduras, and Mexico convened in Minnesota with regional and national colleagues from around the U.S. The participants engaged in a week of visioning and building, and they drafted, finalized, and signed a "Workers Statement" to reflect their central values and beliefs. In January 2019, the WFP Solidarity Collective (WFPSC) was founded, apart from the National WFP Board, by a group of former WFP national and international staff, board members, regional organizers, and volunteers. These founders committed themselves to a new vision of horizontal solidarity with their international partners and within their own internal governance.

In the new WFPSC, decisions are made collectively based on weekly calls which include international team leaders and regional organizers. In January 2021, the WFPSC selected a new national board that had more of an advisory function than before. However, the new board can approve budgets and voice opinions and concerns about the policies being carried out in the field.

The Solidarity Collective's website emphasizes: "We work with grassroots activists and community organizations dedicated to pursuing justice in Latin America. Our accountability begins with these partners. The Solidarity Collective delegates seek to change U.S. policies and work for justice in our own communities. Therefore, we are accountable to disenfranchised communities in the U.S. and the movements for justice of which we are part. Our delegations honor the call by Latin American Civil Society for an end to U.S.-led militarism and extraction. We affirm the political self-determination of all Latin American and Indigenous Peoples, including the right to resist injustice through collective struggle. The Solidarity Collective actively promotes civil, political, and human rights for all people. Therefore, we honor and support social movements across the Americas and beyond."

Witness for Peace Solidarity Collective continues the original work of WFP effectively in accompanying and supporting local vulnerable groups in Latin America in their pursuit of justice through the presence of its International Teams and short-term delegations. It's a young organization in more ways than one. By January 2022, the oldest member out of 17 core collective members was 40 years old!

Nicaragua after the Sandinistas' Electoral Defeat in 1990

In the elections of February 25, 1990, Violeta Chamorro and her party UNO defeated Daniel Ortega and the FSLN. To the surprise of the Sandinistas, she won 55 percent of the votes compared to 41 percent for Ortega, the Sandinista leader. Her victory relied almost exclusively on the United States' promise to end the deadly Contra War and lift its economic sanctions.[1] Under the tutelage of policy advisors from the U.S., President Chamorro ushered in several neoliberal policies, which focused on lowering trade barriers, reducing taxes, and cutting spending within the public sector. Her government slashed spending for education and healthcare, laid off thousands of state workers, and used free-trade zones to entice multinational companies to set up shop around the country.

Chamorro's administration replaced Sandinista-era textbooks with new ones paid for by the U.S. Agency for International Development (USAID). Her government's use of austerity and structural-adjustment programs reduced or eliminated most government welfare for Nicaragua's impoverished citizens, leading to increased homelessness and crime.[2]

The administrations of those who immediately followed Chamorro, Presidents Arnoldo Aleman (1997–2001) and Enrique Bolaños (2002–2006), continued her policies. With the war years in the past and U.S. sanctions lifted, businesses began to return, and the national economy jumped back to life. Between 1991 and 2006, GDP grew by an average of 3.4% per year.[3]

However, as the neoliberal economy expanded, Sandinista loyalists and other working-class people were largely left out. It was the working class that overwhelmingly supported the Sandinista government during the 1980s.

I joined a short-term WFP delegation to Nicaragua in July 1995 when UNO governed the country under President Chamorro. We observed the level of poverty and the increased threat of crime compared to when I was

---

1. Waddell, "Nicaragua: Better the Devil you know."
2. Britannica, "Nicaragua from 1990 to 2006." in "Nicaragua."
3. Waddell, "Nicaragua: Better the Devil you know."

there in 1990, mainly caused by UNO's strict adherence to the World Bank's structural adjustment policies that oppose social programs for the poor.

During my 1995 delegation, a fellow delegate, Tom Ricker, and I stayed a couple of nights with a poor family in Matagalpa.

Our Matagalpa family and me July 1995 (photo by Tom Ricker)

Tom's experience in the delegation had a life-changing effect on him, and he subsequently devoted his life to international solidarity programs. He is presently Program Associate at the Quixote Center and teaches international human rights and political science at the University of Maryland part-time. Based in Maryland, the Quixote Center is a multi-issue social justice organization rooted in building a more justly loving world. They work with partners at the grassroots level in Haiti and Nicaragua to enact lasting systemic change. They serve under-represented groups, such as the poor and people in rural communities.

* * *

In the 2006 presidential elections in Nicaragua, the FSLN and Daniel Ortega returned to power after defeating conservative candidate Eduardo Montealegre.[4] Ortega won with 35 percent of the votes, which was a plurality. The primary reason for the FSLN's victory in that election was that the opposing parties were at odds with one another and couldn't form any kind of unified front as they had done under the UNO party in the 1990 elections.

The Sandinistas have stayed in power since 2006. They won much more impressively, in the 2011 and 2016 elections, and recently in the 2021 elections, obtaining significant majorities of the votes for the presidency and the National Assembly. Most experts believe that whatever electoral flaws there may have been, the FSLN party would have won the 2011 and 2016 elections handily.

However, some commentators believe that the 2021 elections were not honest, mainly because the Sandinista government didn't allow outside groups to monitor the elections. The government also arrested seven "presidential hopefuls," they say, from the right-wing opposition in the summer before the November 2021 elections. But Sandinista supporters point out that not a single one of those arrested was a registered candidate. Moreover, the seven were reported to have been arrested on charges of conspiring with a foreign government (the United States) to take millions of dollars from Washington in a sizeable money-laundering scheme that appeared to be directly connected to the violent uprising (or coup attempt) in 2018.[5] So there seems to be a valid law-and-order reason for their arrest and jail time. And one must bear in mind the likelihood that the international media had been primed by opposition media outlets in Nicaragua and by U.S. media reports that the Nicaraguan government was nothing short of a dictatorship.

As soon as Ortega and the FSLN party won their electoral victory in 2006, the predictable enemies of the Sandinista revolution began sounding off via the opposition media in Nicaragua. This was expected, but few in the international press paid much attention. At least not until April 2018, when the six-month uprising (or attempted coup) began. The uprising was

---

4. Britannica," Nicaragua."
5. Norton, "Debunking myths about Nicaragua's 2021 elections."

the watershed event that seems to have established the international media's negative opinions of the post-1980s Sandinista government. During the uprising and thereafter, every international media outlet from the BBC and *The Guardian* to *Der Spiegel*, from the Associated Press and NPR to Democracy Now! editorialized against Daniel Ortega and the FSLN government. It was as if someone turned on a switch in a worldwide media power station. The main reasons for this were likely the one-sided reports by Amnesty International and by Human Rights Watch accusing the government of brutish behavior against the "peaceful" protestors. The United Nations Human Rights office was slightly easier on the Ortega government, as in their report they presented the government figures on the victims of killings as well as those given by the protestors and aligned groups.[6]

Who to believe?

The situation in Nicaragua since 2006 has been extremely complicated. Even more complicated than what has been a very complicated history of this nation. 2006 was when the Sandinistas began to successively win the national elections. First of all, we have the post-1980s Sandinista government, which fosters a mixed economy and supports neoliberal policies to some degree, including belonging to the CAFTA-DR group, while at the same time instituting and maintaining programs to improve the lives of the poor. It has reached agreements with the Catholic Church partially through acceptance of a total ban on abortions passed by the assembly just before the 2006 national elections, and yet many, many clergy somehow feel threatened by the FSLN and its members.

It is also complicated by the many diverse political and media actors. The loudest voices are either avidly pro-Sandinista or angrily anti-Sandinista. Some opposition media do exist and are allowed to operate fairly freely in the country. Protests are permitted, provided they don't aim to overthrow the government. Elections are still free and mostly fair, despite the opposition politicians' claims.

And then there is the so-called uprising that occurred from April through September of 2018. My goodness, then it becomes really, really complicated. The protestors, some of the clergy, the opposition politicians, the in-country human-rights organizations, and most of the international media all claim that it was the protestors who were beaten and killed by the national police and by pro-Sandinista mobs. At the same time, the

6. OHCHR, *Human Rights Violations and Abuses*.

Sandinista supporters and many observers paint a more nuanced picture of the uprising (or attempted coup) and say that the majority of the victims of the violence were police and Sandinista supporters at the hands of the protestors.

So, dear Reader, you get your pick. Just pay your money and make your choice. For information and opinions by the near-worldwide media against the government, especially regarding the conflicts that took place during 2018, please see the following (ANTI) references:

1. Amnesty International's October 2018 report *Instilling Terror: From Lethal Force to Persecution in Nicaragua*.

2. Office of the United Nations High Commissioner for Human Rights (OHCHR). *Human Rights Violations and Abuses in the Context of Protests in Nicaragua 18 April – 18 August 2018*.

3. Waddell, Benjamin. "We may be witnessing the rise of fascism in Nicaragua." HuffPost (July 30, 2018).

4. Robinson, William. "Nicaragua: Chronicle of an election foretold." NACLA (November 9, 2021).

5. Francis, ed., *A Nicaraguan Exceptionalism? Debating the Legacy of the Sandinista Revolution*, Institute of Latin American Studies, University of London.

6. Alvarez, Maximillian. "Nicaragua presents a challenge to the international left." therealnews.com (November 11, 2021).

For information and opinions about the government and the 2018 violent clashes by in-country independent reporters and generally pro-Sandinista commentators, please see the following (PRO) references:

1. Nicaragua Notes, afgj.org. *Live from Nicaragua: Uprising or Coup?* A Reader. Alliance for Global Justice, 2019.

2. Nicaragua Notes, afgj.org. *Dismissing the Truth: Why Amnesty International is Wrong about Nicaragua*. Alliance for Global Justice, 2019. [An evaluation and response to the Amnesty International report "Instilling Terror: from lethal force to persecution in Nicaragua"]

3. Perry, John. "After 2 Months of Unrest, Nicaragua Is at a Fateful Crossroads." *The Nation* (June 22, 2018).

4. Norton, Ben. "Debunking myths about Nicaragua's 2021 elections, under attack by USA/EU/OAS." MR [Monthly Review] Online (November 13, 2021)."

5. Ricker, Tom. "Update on Nicaragua: Interview about Situation in Masaya." Quixote Center: (June 6, 2018) https://www.quixote.org/update-on-nicaragua-interview-about-situation-in-masaya/

6. Luna, Yorlis Gabriela. "The Other Nicaragua, Empire and Resistance." COHA Nicaragua, Council on Hemispheric Affairs (October 2, 2019). https://www.coha.org/the-other-nicaragua-empire-and-resistance/.

Having read both the ANTI and PRO references, as well as many others, I tend to believe those voices which generally defend the actions of the Sandinista government during the 2018 violent conflicts and point out the often violent actions by the protestors. This is because the PRO arguments and the happenings they describe are much more detailed and just ring truer. And because recent history teaches us of the U.S.'s undying attempts at regime change in countries to the south of us who have opted for socialist elements in their government. The facts indicate that the U.S. played a major role in planning and funding at least a portion of the protests of 2018.

Summary of the major happenings during the protests of April to September 2018

The protests began on April 18, 2018. The nominal reason for the protests was a small decrease in social security payments, which the government had just introduced. However, the reductions were much less than the Nicaraguan business association (COSEP) had insisted the government apply. During the first two days, protests took place on the campus of the public university UPOLI (Polytechnic University of Nicaragua) in Managua. And on the 19th night, there were conflicts in several Nicaraguan cities as people started to throw stones at police and attack the INSS (Social Security) buildings. In some locations, the police used live ammunition to try and control the protests. Three people died that day, although there are different opinions about who those people were.

A vigorous disinformation campaign fooled many students and others into joining the protests by misrepresenting the details of the government's social-security proposals. But the students leading these protests were soon joined by those with the much wider agenda of attempting to bring down the Ortega government.

After the second day, the protests spread further throughout the country and became more violent. The major questions were: (1) were the victims who died largely protestors, or were they mostly Sandinista supporters? And (2) what weapons did the protestors use against the police and Sandinista supporters, if any? The protestors insisted that they were the primary victims of oppression, while the Sandinista supporters gave figures showing that more of those killed were Sandinista supporters than protestors. In terms of weapons, the protestors insisted they only had stones and homemade mortar guns, which shoot balls of gunpowder. But there is evidence that they started using ordinary guns fairly early in the protests. So there were gun battles between the police and the protestors. Evidence shows that protestors sometimes used rifles, pistols, and even AK-47 weapons.

Max Blumenthal[7] reported that in late April 2018, Ortega ordered his police forces (the National Police) to stay in their police stations as a condition of the National Dialogue he had initiated with the opposition. For at least 50 days, the national police were not out in the streets to confront the protestors or any common criminals, so the populace, particularly the Sandinista supporters, had to fend for themselves against these often violent elements.

Something else happened near the end of April—the number of students involved in the protest started to diminish. They were replaced by older adults, many of whom, the Sandinista supporters claim, were paid by the organizations[8] backing the protest. Some observers noted that the older non-students began to call for the FSLN regime to step down, but few of the students were interested in protesting for regime change.

On May 7th, the protestors entered UNAN (National Autonomous University of Nicaragua), a public university in Managua, and attacked students and teachers in an attempt to take it over. The protestor group was there for many weeks. When the National Police finally entered the university on July 14th to free it from the protestors, they found that the protestors had stored weapons there and had abused and damaged some of the university buildings.[9]

In early May, the protestors started building roadblocks or barricades across roads and streets, both in the cities and in the countryside. The protestors built the roadblocks of rocks or bitumen pulled up from the roads and were commonly four to six feet high. Where they appeared, they extended completely across each road. In some cases on vital highways, they simply

---

7. Blumenthal, "How Washington and Soft Power NGOs Manipulated," 195.

8. COSEP, the Nicaraguan business association; right-wing political parties such as MRS; NGOs supported with U.S. funds; certain elements of the Catholic Church; and, local human-rights organizations such as CENIDH and ANPDH known to be opposed to the government.

9. Nicaragua Notes, "Dismissing the Truth: Why Amnesty International is Wrong about Nicaragua," 37.

consisted of piles of metal or burning tires. In the less populated parts of the country, the highway roadblocks were bigger and had stricter rules for those vehicles and pedestrians who wished to pass through. The purpose was to disrupt car and truck traffic and monitor the people walking down the street or road. Sandinista supporters have stated that whoever tried to pass by the barricades was often badly treated. People were being asked for their papers at the barricades by masked youths carrying homemade mortar guns; they were having their bags searched. Anything linking them to the government or police meant they wouldn't get past—or worse.[10]

Needless to say, the protests didn't have much popular support, so Sandinista supporters believe the protestors had to resort to hiring criminals to man the armed roadblocks, particularly at night.

At first before the roadblocks became armed, there were cases in which women and merchants organized and pushed the roadblocks out of the way. But the roadblocks were put back up and the protectors of the same armed themselves with heavier weapons. The most ferocious roadblocks were set up in the city of Masaya,[11] guarded by armed gangs who would extort motorists and terrorize the local population.

According to the authors of "Dismissing the Truth,"[12] there were at least 1,200 roadblocks set up in the cities by early June and approximately 125 on the main transport routes of the country, covering the entire western half of the nation. In the Masaya Department alone, there were around 600. These city roadblocks prevented most traffic movement for weeks, apart from motorcycles and people on foot. Because of the roadblocks on the main roads and those in the cities, the country became paralyzed, significantly impacting economic activity. The official Truth, Justice and Peace Commission (CVJP)[13] calculated that at least 150 deaths occurred at these roadblocks; the vast majority of these were murders by armed members of the opposition.

According to Blumenthal[14], the first major counteroffensive of the government was on June 19th, two months after the beginning of the protests, when the police liberated all the roads leading into the city of Masaya. After

10. Ricker, "Update on Nicaragua: Interview about Situation in Masaya."

11. Blumenthal, "How Nicaragua defeated a right-wing US-backed coup," 70.

12. Nicaragua Notes, "Dismissing the Truth: Why Amnesty International is Wrong about Nicaragua," 7–8.

13. Truth, Justice and Peace Commission set up by the National Assembly of Nicaragua.

14. Blumenthal, "How Nicaragua defeated a right-wing US-backed coup," in Nicaragua Notes, "Live from Nicaragua: Uprising or Coup?" 72–3.

that, slowly across the country, police started taking out the remaining roadblocks. According to Sandinista supporters, the national police were heroes because they were the ones who finally removed the barricades, which enabled Nicaraguans to return to normality and peace. But outside the country, this is all presented by the major media as total repression against nonviolent protesters. However, the government would never have been able to remove the hundreds of barricades the opposition erected if they hadn't had popular support to do so. In what other country would building and defending roadblocks be regarded as exercising a constitutional right to protest, which is what the protesters claimed? In what other country would the police not arrive in force within a couple of days to remove the barricades and arrest those holding the weapons?

During 2018, the major media seemed to follow only the protestors who were supposedly innocent students who didn't want the social security benefits of the government to be lowered. Sandinista supporters believe that the campaign to overturn the government included what appeared to be fake videos and false reports. Facebook posts reported that public hospitals were refusing to treat injured protesters. There appeared to be fake videos of "injured" students being treated in universities and at the Catholic Cathedral of Managua.

According to Nicaragua's Truth, Justice and Peace Commission (CVJP), 22 officers of the national police were killed during the crisis. And, as photos and videos publicly displayed show, a number of these officers were tortured and mutilated, dismembered, and set on fire. These were not the acts of "peaceful" demonstrators. But it is also true that the opposition had peaceful marches at various stages. However, several protests ended in violence against police, bystanders, or those believed to be government sympathizers.

While those media and organizations backing the protests insist that a total of 350 people were killed during 2018, most all of whom were pro-testors, the CVJP estimated that, in total, 253 individuals were killed as a consequence of the crisis-related violence.[15] Of these, 22 were police, 48 were Sandinista activists, 31 were opposition activists, and 152 deaths lacked sufficient information. However, the CVJP believed that most of these 152 deaths occurred at the opposition roadblocks, and those responsible were primarily people manning these roadblocks. In short, as far as the CVJP could determine, the Sandinista and pro-government forces, including police, were at least as much victims of the violence, if not more so, than the opposition forces. Along with the deaths, many cases reported

15. Kovalik, "Human Rights in Nicaragua," 191–2.

torture and hate crimes mostly against Sandinista supporters or passersby, including setting the victims on fire.

The study, "Monopolizing Death," demonstrates[16] how partisan local NGOs probably conflated all deaths that occurred in April 2018, including accidents and the murders of Sandinistas, with killings by government forces. Washington seized on the bogus death count to drive the case for sanctions and intensify pressure for regime change.

Concerning the human-rights accusations against the FSLN government in 2018, it has come to my attention that the human rights organizations, e.g., Amnesty International (AI) and Human Rights Watch, which we all from babyhood have trusted implicitly, turn out to be not deserving of that trust in several important instances. With regard to the protests of 2018, both of these international organizations just took the "fully-documented" reports of the two human-rights organizations in Nicaragua (CENIDH and ANPDH), which were known to be siding with the opposition. The CENIDH itself is largely funded by foreign donations.

Dan Kovalik in the 'Conclusion' chapter in *Live from Nicaragua: Uprising or Coup?* quotes well-respected human-rights professor and former board member of Amnesty International (AI), Francis A. Boyle.[17] Professor Boyle relates, for example, how AI itself aided and abetted the deadly military and economic campaign against Iraq waged by the United States and " . . . that genocidal war waged by the United States, the United Kingdom and France, inter alia, during the months of January and February 1991, killed at a minimum 200,000 Iraqis, half of whom were civilians. Amnesty International shall always have the blood of the Iraqi People on its hands!"

Kovalik also reminds readers that the chief human rights organizations such as AI "played a treacherous role in spreading lies about the Gaddafi government which helped pave the way for his brutal ousting in 2011 and the consequent destruction of Libya in the process." Kovalik concludes, "Even when human rights groups like AI, and Human Rights Watch are not openly cheerleading Western imperial crusades in developing countries, these groups have made it clear that it is not within their purview to oppose military and other interventions in other countries." Finklestein in his *Gaza* states[18] that that while Human Rights Watch did issue at least one report on the human-rights devastation the Israeli government visited on Gaza during its 2014 attacks, Amnesty International itself whitewashed the Israeli

---

16. Hendrix, "Monopolizing death."
17. Nicaragua Notes, "Live from Nicaragua," 267.
18. Finklestein, *Gaza*, 238–39.

attacks,[19] obscuring "the yawning gap separating the magnitude of suffering inflicted on Gazan as compared to Israeli civilians."

In general, the major questions concerning the allegations AI made about the 2018 conflicts relate to:

- AI's reporting being based solely on discussions with the anti-government protestors.

- AI's reporting that essentially all the deaths caused in the conflicts were of protestors, while less biased references indicate that more of the deaths involved Sandinista supporters and the police than protestors.

- AI's reporting that the protestors were only protesting peacefully and had as weapons only the occasional homemade mortar gun. Less biased references show that in many instances, the protestors had and used regular guns, set policemen on fire, and burned down police stations and other government buildings, the homes of Sandinista supporters, and a newspaper office.

- AI's assuming that most of the people on the protest side were students and other concerned citizens. Less biased references show how the student portion of the protests diminished significantly after a week or two from the beginning on April 18th. They further indicate that the barricades set up on many streets and roads throughout the country by the protestors in May and June were manned and defended, violently in most cases, by older adults, some of whom may have been paid criminals.

It was instructive for me to review and compare Amnesty International's second report, *Instilling Terror*, and the Nicaragua Network's *Dismissing the Truth*, which was a response to *Instilling Terror*. In my view, the actual data and cases presented in AI's report did not come even close to confirming, in their words:[20]

> " . . . that the government made widespread and conspicuous use of pro-government armed groups with whom it coordinated violent actions against protesters in order to increase the capacity for repression and for use of lethal force, as well as to instill terror in the population."

19. What a contrast to the report AI released in February 2022 saying that Israel has imposed apartheid policies on the Palestinian people ("Israel's Apartheid Against Palestinians: Cruel System of Domination and Crime Against Humanity")!

20. Amnesty International, *Instilling Terror: From Lethal Force to Persecution in Nicaragua*, 46.

It's likely they came to this conclusion by simply accepting at face value what in-country human-rights groups told them. As stated in *Dismissing the Truth*,[21] "Amnesty International relies to a considerable extent on the work of "human rights" bodies in Nicaragua [CENIDH and ANPDH], which have a dubious track record, are hostile to the government and completely biased." Most notably, in their recording of human rights abuses, AI completely ignored the sizable number of deaths (and incidents of torture) inflicted on Sandinista supporters by protestors during this period. In *Dismissing the Truth*, the authors present considerable evidence contradicting the anti-government slant for many specific cases mentioned by AI where the names of the individuals were given.

Also, one other thing I noticed in AI's report was their attitude toward the removal of the roadblocks by the national police. It was as if forcibly removing the blockades was somehow a violation of the rights of protestors. I think it's safe to say that no other country in the world would allow any roadblock erected by protestors to remain more than two to three days, whatever force it might take to remove it.

Since the 2018 conflicts, Nicaragua has recovered to a large degree, but those conflicts and having to fight the COVID pandemic soon after have weakened the economy.

* * *

Just as I was in the midst of the final editing of this book, a news item showed up on August 19, 2022, telling of an event reflecting the tug-of-war between the FSLN government and certain Catholic clergy. It relates to the bishop of the Matagalpa Diocese, Bishop Rolando Álvarez. He was very active in supporting the protestors during the uprising/coup in 2018 while at the same time serving on the Episcopal Conference team as a presumably unbiased mediator in the first national dialogue of that year between the Nicaraguan government and the opposition.

Early in August 2022, the Nicaraguan government launched an investigation into the bishop, accusing him of inciting violent actors "to carry out acts of hate against the population." Since August 3rd, authorities had confined Bishop Álvarez to the episcopal complex in Matagalpa where he lives; they prevented him from leaving his diocesan offices.

On August 19, 2022, the national police carried out a pre-dawn raid of the bishop's quarters as Nicaraguan authorities accused him of "organizing

21. Nicaragua Notes, "Dismissing the Truth: Why Amnesty International is Wrong about Nicaragua," 44.

violent groups" and inciting them "to carry out acts of hate against the population." The police then took the bishop to Nicaragua's capital, Managua, where they placed him under house arrest in his family home.

The Archdiocese of Managua has expressed support for Álvarez. UN Secretary-General Antonio Guterres has expressed his grave concern over the "serious obstruction of democratic and civil life" in Nicaragua. And so have the media worldwide. According to the Associated Press and the main-line press, all Álvarez was calling for was profound electoral reform to "effectively achieve the democratization of the country." But it is likely to have been more than that.

For almost two weeks in August 2022, the Vatican was publicly silent about the investigation of Álvarez. And Pope Francis has not been eager to criticize the Nicaraguan government about Bishop Alvarez's arrest. Finally, on Sunday August 21st, Pope Francis said:[22] "I am following closely, with concern and sorrow, the situation in Nicaragua, which involves both people and institutions . . . I would like to express my conviction and my hope that, through open and sincere dialogue, the basis for a respectful and peaceful coexistence can still be found."

Pope Francis seems to understand the complicated situation between the church and the government in Nicaragua and seems to understand to some extent that Alvarez backed the often violent protestors. At the time of the uprising in 2018, the pope called for a peace dialogue. And he summoned Bishop Alvarez and Cardinal Leopoldo Brenes (Archbishop of Managua) to a private meeting in the Vatican, setting off rumors that he may have scolded the Nicaraguan monsignors for their obvious involvement in the conflict they were officially mediating.[23]

The last thing Daniel Ortega and the FSLN need is more bad press. They have no reason to oppress or persecute the church simply because some of the clergy have voiced opposition to the government. Quite the opposite: they want and need peace with the church. There has to be something to their accusations against the bishop.

The story of MRS

One political party in Nicaragua that has been highly influential in turning liberals or left-leaning people in the U.S. and Europe against the FSLN

---

22. Independent Catholic News, "From: Nicaragua: Pope, world leaders concerned at growing crisis."
23. Zeese and McCune, "Correcting the record," 117.

government is the MRS, the Movement for the Renovation of Sandinistas. Recently they reformed themselves into what is called UNAMOS.

Chuck Kaufman in his blog in July 2018,[24] summarized the creation and evolution of the MRS party well:

> "The Sandinista Renovation Movement (MRS) was formed in May 1995, blowback from the divisive 1994 FSLN Party Congress, which I had the privilege to attend as an observer... the Congress itself was very conflictive over issues of internal democracy and transparency of the party's economic holdings. Treatment by the party leadership of what we then called the Sandinista dissidents was intense... As a result, a number of high profile heroes of the Revolution and former party and government leaders split off from the FSLN and formed their own party.
>
> "Comandante Henry Ruiz (Modesto), who led much of the guerilla war against Somoza in the mountains; Monica Baltodano, the only woman to lead a guerilla column and the primary contact for sister city groups in the US and elsewhere; Dora Maria Tellez, one of the leaders of a daring action that took hostage Somoza's legislature and Supreme Court justices and who later became Minister of Health; Sergio Ramirez, former vice president and world-renown author; Gioconda Belli, former guerilla and renowned poet; much later, in 2006, Victor Hugo Tinoco, number three in the Foreign Ministry who was well-known in the US to Nightline viewers during the 1980s and who in the late 1990s was in charge of liaising with US solidarity [groups]; and others... all left the party and created the MRS.
>
> "In other words, the people who international solidarity activists and western media were most familiar with, most of whom spoke English, left the FSLN to form a new political party also rooted in *Sandinismo* and in the struggle against the Somoza dictatorship followed by the US-backed Contra War... Nicaragua Network approached the split as we would a family fight which pained us as outsiders to watch, but in which we felt we could play no positive role in resolving. We therefore maintained neutrality between what we viewed as the two parties of *Sandinismo* even through the 2006 election which returned the FSLN, led by Daniel Ortega, back into power. We even thought that it might not be a bad thing to have a party challenging the FSLN from the *Left*.

---

24. Kaufman, "Nicanotes: The MRS is not 'left' or democratic."

"Sergio Ramirez ran as the MRS presidential candidate in 1996 winning 1.3% of the vote and one seat in the National Assembly. The MRS has pretty much been stuck at that level of support ever since. It ran in coalition with the FSLN in national and municipal elections until 2006. . . .

"Our premise that the MRS was pushing the FSLN from the Left was proven false in the 2006 election. I led a delegation to investigate US interference in the election about five months before the vote. We met with representatives of all the parties, including Enrique Saenz, then president of the MRS. I asked him what the MRS was doing to politically educate voters and to build its base beyond Managua's educated class. His response troubled me deeply. He spoke nothing about a progressive agenda or of politically educating the base about neoliberalism's depredations against the majority poor. He espoused no party platform of poverty alleviation, education, healthcare, or reviving the rural economy. He only spoke about the MRS's progress in building alliances with right-wing parties and US-funded non-governmental organizations, what social scientists call civil society. All of these forces are intensely anti-Sandinista and have the same neoliberal/pro-US agenda that had caused such misery since the electoral defeat of 1990.

"Since 2006, the MRS has continued its drift to the Right, deepening its alliances with the Right-wing parties and anti-Sandinista civil society groups while taking no action to build a grassroots base or to take any actions or positions that could be defined as challenging the FSLN from the Left.

"In September 2017, the MRS publically violated the first of several now irreversible standards of legitimacy. MRS President Ana Margarita Vijil took active part in a delegation of Nicaraguan right-wing political leaders to meet with one of the most anti-Sandinista members of Congress, Iliana Ros-Lehtinen. The reason for the meeting? To call on the US Congress to pass the NICA Act, which, if it were to also pass the Senate and be signed by the president, would require the US to vote against loans to Nicaragua in the World Bank, IMF, and other international financial institutions (IFIs). While the US does not have veto power, I believe it is safe to say that the IFIs have never approved a loan opposed by the US . . .

"And then in 2009 the MRS officially supported a campaign led by their now political partner, US-favorite and failed 2006 presidential candidate banker Eduardo Montealegre, to convince the US and the EU to cut development aid to Nicaragua. The US cut US$60 million and the EU cut around US$45 million. Fortunately, Venezuelan oil aid more than made up the losses so the Sandinista government's poverty reduction programs continued to be fully funded. It is so sad that those who in their youth had fought for the rights of the poor against a real dictatorship today sabotage efforts to raise people out of poverty.

"And now, during the on-going violent coup attempt since April [2018], the MRS fully backs the violent forces and is among the faction that demands that President Ortega and Vice-President Murillo must step down before the roadblocks are removed and a dialogue can take place. There are credible reports of MRS leaders distributing money to opposition leaders. These are charges that must be investigated by credible independent investigators.

"In my opinion, the transformation of the MRS and its leadership has been so profound as to qualify as treasonous. Certainly no party using the name Sandino can legitimately use that name when it has publicly called on the United States to intervene in Nicaragua's sovereign affairs and openly calls for the overthrow of the democratically and legitimately elected government. U.S. and international solidarity activists should understand that they are being lied to and manipulated by people who long ago gave up any claim to our solidarity."

The MRS party has sent people around the world to criticize the Sandinista government under a left-wing guise, the guise of *Sandinismo*. They're a party that has participated in Nicaraguan politics since 1996 and typically polls around two percent. In mid-2018, the party was at its peak when it got six percent. But they poll well among the Western intelligentsia and the NGO world. They poll really well among USAID officials. They have played an important role in dividing the Western left on the question of Nicaragua and painting Daniel Ortega as a dictator with very little popular support.

Whatever glorious history the present members of UNAMOS (formerly MRS) had in the Sandinista revolution of 1979, they have changed drastically; they are no longer interested in government programs that actually help the poor, as does the FSLN party.

According to Nils McCune,[25] as interviewed by Max Blumenthal:[26]

"As soon as the Sandinista Front lost power in 1990, there was an exodus of these children of the oligarchy from the party, because they were used to being ministers. They didn't want to have to be opposition figures in an opposition party; they didn't want to have to defend the gains of the revolution out on the street, fighting cops. They didn't want to suffer with the Nicaraguan people. Many of them left and bought houses in Los Angeles or in Miami or in Spain. Many of them went on to write books.

"So these people have led their illustrious lives. They've maintained contact in many cases with the US solidarity activists who gave their time, their energy, their sweat, sometimes their lives, to support the Sandinista Revolution, and who were often able to make good friends with well-off Sandinistas who spoke English, people who had high-level positions in the Sandinista Front.

"The ex-Sandinistas have always had the ear of the US and European Left. And this party, the MRS, was formed out of a combination of legitimate grievances with the Sandinista Front at the 1994 congress, as well as a social democratic tendency which at the time wanted to reject . . . socialism . . . and wanted to form new alliances.

"So once that party was formed, they started to create their own idea for what they could do. They never had popular support, they never did neighborhood organizing like the Sandinista Front had, and they never went out to defend the gains of the revolution. So as soon as they went into an election, they were able to garner only this classic 2%.

"Meanwhile, the Sandinista Front, with all of its errors, stuck with and suffered with the large majority of the people and has never had less than 35% support here. So that's really a key to start to understand these two political forces that claim the Sandino tradition . . . So that's my take on the MRS. They're very strong outside of the country, they're very weak within the country."

---

25. When interviewed by Max Blumenthal in July 2018, Nils McCune had been living in Tipitapa, Nicaragua for several years working as a researcher with the rural campesino movement.

26. Nicaragua Notes, "Live from Nicaragua: Uprising or Coup?" 76–7.

One hero of the revolution who did not join the MRS is Omar Cabezas, a Sandinista commander in the fight to overthrow Anastasio Somoza in 1979. He is particularly well known because of his book *Fire from the Mountain*, a personal account of his days as a guerrilla fighting the Somoza dynasty. In the fall of 2021, Dan Kovalik set out to find Omar Cabezas near Managua and interview him. Dan teaches International Human Rights at the University of Pittsburgh School of Law. The resulting video[27] of the interview is a testimony to Cabezas's commitment to the Sandinista ideals including the policies of the present government. In the interview, Cabezas said: "We [the Sandinistas] continue to do the impossible for the oppressed, the poor ... There is a long way to go, but there has been a profound change ... Now people eat three meals a day."

Opposition in the U.S. to a "Socialist" Nicaragua

Despite all the achievements of the Nicaraguan government since 2006, the U.S. intelligence agencies and other makers and shakers of U.S. foreign policy reinforced their plans to effect the demise of the Sandinista government after the reelection of Daniel Ortega as President in 2016. They were anxious to prevent the reappearance of the support the Sandinistas enjoyed from many American liberals in the 1980s. They wanted to prevent any segment of the American electorate from backing a socialist-type government in Latin America, even one with a mixed economy. Latin American nations have always effectively served as economic, and hence political, colonies of the U.S., and our policy enforcers intended to do whatever was required for these nations to continue as our effective colonies.

To add to the fire, any indication or suspicion of U.S. efforts to intervene in the affairs of Nicaragua was often quite rightly met with angry denunciations of the United States by Daniel Ortega and other Sandinista commentators. This just gave the U.S. more ammunition in its anti-Nicaraguan rhetoric. "How can anyone accuse America of wrongdoing in any country in Latin America for the world knows how much we want to strengthen democracy and the welfare of all the people of the hemisphere?" Libya, Iran, and Venezuela also fell into that trap, for the U.S. was already plotting their demises, or in Iran's case had already overturned its democratically-elected government in 1953. In April of 2002, there was an attempted coup against the democratically-elected Chavez government in Venezuela, which was successfully thwarted by the citizens and loyal members of the military. Later

---

27. Kovalik, "Fire from the Mountain: In Search of Omar Cabezas."

it was revealed that the U.S. had prior knowledge of this coup attempt and that members of the U.S. government had ties to prominent participants in the coup (Wikipedia, "2002 Venezuelan coup d'état attempt").

The way the policymakers in Washington decided to soften U.S. liberals' support for leftist governments in Latin America was to: (1) eschew the now outmoded (hopefully) method of using proxy forces to fight messy wars; (2) strongly encourage internal protests against leftist governments and manipulate the media to show that when the government responds to the protests, it should be portrayed as violating the human rights of the protestors; (3) influence representatives of human-rights organizations so that they will pay attention to only the protestors' side of any conflict with leftist governments the former may have with the government/police; and (4) recruit authoritative people from academia who will speak against the ruling party (the FSLN in the case of Nicaragua), such as sociologists specializing in Latin America.

The power elite in the U.S. and Nicaragua realized they had to stay away from a repeat of the Contra war or any overtly violent attacks on the FSLN's government. But other than that, there were no holds barred. The U.S. made every effort to foster friendship with and among in-country political and social groups opposed to the Sandinistas. U.S. financial aid under innocuous-sounding names was distributed to these groups via the National Endowment for Democracy (NED) and the U.S. Agency for International Development (USAID).

Recently in June 2022, major media in the U.S. and elsewhere launched yet another attack on the Sandinista government, accusing it of "inching toward dictatorship." According to the Associated Press (6/2/22), Daniel Ortega's government in Nicaragua is "laying waste to civil society," The Guardian (6/2/22) called it a "sweeping purge of civil society," while according to the Washington Post's Spanish edition (5/19/22), the country is already "a dictatorship laid bare."

In an article by John Perry,[28] he asks, "What can possibly have provoked such widespread criticism? It turns out that the Nicaraguan National Assembly's "sweeping purge" was the withdrawal of the tax-free legal status of a small proportion of the country's nonprofit organizations: just 440 over a period of four years. In more than half the cases, these non-governmental organizations (NGOs) have simply ceased to function or no longer exist. In other cases, they have failed (or refused) to comply with legal requirements, such as producing annual accounts or declaring the sources of their funding.

28. Perry, "Nicaragua a 'Dictatorship' When It Follows US Lead on NGOs."

Modest legal steps that would go unnoticed in most countries are—in Nicaragua's case—clear evidence that it is 'inching toward dictatorship.'"

Perry points out that this type of closing non-profits is commonplace among many nations, including the U.S. For example, between 2006 and 2011, the IRS closed 279,000 nonprofits out of a US total of 1.7 million; it closed 28,000 more in 2020. These inferences against Nicaragua make it clear the major media are not looking for truth or fair comparisons when it comes to Nicaragua. The problem is that Nicaragua sticks up for itself and the U.S. State Department detests it, and so do its publicity outlets, the major media.

Spokespeople for U.S. policy against Nicaragua

I know of two academics who serve as spokesmen for U.S. policy: William I. Robinson of the Sociology Department of the University of California at Santa Barbara; and Benjamin Waddell, an Associate Professor of Sociology at Fort Lewis College in Colorado.

William Robinson is particularly interesting as he participates in debates with Sandinista supporters and has some leftist credentials. His research has been on global capitalism, particularly in Latin America. He espouses the theory that the world is trending increasingly toward a transnational economy wherein corporate entities are engineered to enhance and secure capital for a transnational capitalist class.

For Robinson, Nicaragua is a repressive capitalist regime. He thinks it operates to such a degree as a neoliberal society that there is no strand of socialism in it. He's also critical of Latin American governments that are part of the so-called "pink tide," such as Venezuela and Bolivia because he thinks they haven't gone far enough: they haven't yet nationalized their banks and major industries of their economy.

Robinson is at pains to demonstrate that the Sandinista government is not leftist *and* that the U.S. government is making no effort to overthrow it. He claims the U.S. is not now intervening and has not intervened in Nicaragua since 2006. However, this contradicts what he has said about any country that the U.S. views as too "pink." In an article on Venezuela,[29] Robinson states that U.S. interventionism in Latin America is currently intensifying. In two articles, one in a leftist website (theAnalysis.news)[30] and one not so

29. Robinson, "Venezuela: The epicenter of the 'pink tide.'"
30. theAnalysis.news, "Does Nicaragua under President Ortega Deserve Progressives' Support?"

left (therealnews.com),[31] he explains his belief that the U.S. did not play any role in the violent conflicts of 2018 nor did the protestors attack Sandinista supporters in any major way that year. He claims the protests were a "mass rebellion" against the Nicaraguan government.

Early in 2022, there was a debate moderated by Greg Wilpert: "Does Nicaragua under President Ortega Deserve Progressives' Support?" In the boxing ring were: William Robinson for the "Nay" side and the Nicaragua-based writer John Perry for the "Yea" side. Each of the two discussed the issues on the topic in some detail.

In his debate with John Perry,[32] Robinson made some of his arguments based on polling statistics. Robinson claimed that in polling by an organization called FIDEG, the number of families below the poverty line fell from 2007 to 2014 from 45 to 39 percent of the total population. Perry countered that FIDEG receives financial support from the U.S., and he quoted World Bank figures, which indicated that between 2006 and 2016, the poverty rate in Nicaragua fell from 48 to 25 percent. The World Bank got its figures from the Nicaraguan organizations *Instituto Nacional de Informacion de Desarrollo (INIDE)* and *Encuesta Nacional de Hogares sobre Medicion de Nivel de Vida* (EMNV).

Robinson mentioned that according to a CID Gallup poll[33] just before the November 2021 election, only 19 percent of the public favored Ortega. Perry countered that a poll[34] performed by the M&R organization a week or two before the election gave an accurate prediction of the results of the November 2021 election. The official election results were that the Sandinistas won 75 percent of the votes, and 66 percent of adults voted.

In another CID Gallup poll during December 5-13, 2021, sponsored by the right-wing media outlet *Confidencial* in Nicaragua,[35] the results revealed that President Daniel Ortega would have received 27% of the votes (the highest of any candidate from any party). To the question did you vote on November 7th, 58 percent said yes and 42 percent said they did not. Even these results are a little suspect because CID Gallup used a sample

---

31. Alvarez, "Nicaragua presents a challenge to the international left."

32. theAnalysis.news, "Does Nicaragua Under President Ortega Deserve Progressives' Support?"

33. Often paid by the opposition parties and not related to the International Gallup Organization.

34. A poll paid for by the government.

35. https://www.confidencial.com.ni/english/daniel-ortega-received-27-of-the-votes-not-75-reveals-cid-gallup-poll.

of 1000 persons nationwide who possessed an active cellphone line. How many poor Nicaraguans would have an active cellphone line?

During the debate, William Robinson was very reluctant to accept that Nicaraguans' lives, at least before 2018 were improved relative to their lives when neoliberal policies prevailed from 1990 to 2006. Also, he hardly mentioned anything about the MRS party and the fact that the party, so highly thought of by liberals in the U.S., had been active in urging right-wing representatives and senators in the U.S. Congress to support the U.S. government's intervention to overthrow the Sandinista government.

Robinson also blindly accepted the accusations against the Nicaraguan government in the 2018 Amnesty International reports that the preponderance of the approximate 300 deaths were protestors at the hands of the Sandinista police and supporters. This would imply that he was completely unaware of the several articles that dispute these claims or he preferred to pretend they didn't exist. He ignored any hint that more of the wounded and killed in 2018 were members of the national police and Sandinista supporters.

I first became aware of William Robinson on October 7, 2021, when I watched a webinar sponsored by the North American Congress in Latin America (NACLA). The topic was 'The Nicaraguan Crisis: A Left Perspective.' Robinson organized the webinar under the auspices of the "International Crisis Group" at https://www.crisisgroup.org/latin-america-caribbean/central-america.

The Crisis Group is a group of academics particularly concerned about the "crisis" in Nicaragua, among other countries. Although I doubt they have applied the word "crisis" to Honduras, which in 2009 had its democracy destroyed by a military coup with the tacit approval of the U.S.

The five speakers on the webinar spent a great deal of time criticizing the Ortega regime's human and civil rights record in Nicaragua. They spoke of the "overwhelming" violence meted out by the national police and the so-called Sandinista "shock forces" during the nationwide protests from April through September 2018. They claimed there was no freedom in the country and that political opponents were routinely jailed or worse. They said it was a foregone conclusion that Ortega would win in the November 2021 elections due to jailing and intimidating the opposition leaders.[36] They all pooh-poohed the idea that the U.S. sanctions by Trump on Nicaragua had negatively affected the country's ordinary people.

---

36. Most if not all the jailed opposition leaders had been involved in plans to overthrow the government.

There was hardly a word spoken by any of the speakers about how the Sandinistas may have abandoned their leftist principles. And yet the purported purpose of the webinar was "to address those claims from an explicitly leftist perspective."[37]

Robinson began the webinar by saying why he and a few colleagues had started the Crisis Group and began giving a hostile take on everything the Nicaraguan government has done and is doing. Near the end of the program, Robinson spoke again and was at pains to tell us that we, the audience, should understand that the government of Nicaragua has a very efficient propaganda machine. And in that connection, he mentioned articles written by Benjamin Waddell, a sociologist at Fort Lewis College in Colorado, who, like Robinson, had obtained his Ph.D. in Sociology at the University of New Mexico. Robinson called Waddell a "second-rate sociologist who is professor of sociology at Fort Lewis College." And by the tone of his voice he meant to demean that college. He claimed that Waddell, presumably as a tool of the Nicaraguan propaganda machine, had written at least one article in *Global Americans* in which he said that the National Endowment for Democracy (NED) had given money to the opposition, which helped them conduct the protests in 2018.

I found an article in the May 1, 2018, issue of *Global Americans* ("Laying the groundwork for insurrection: A closer look at the U.S. role in Nicaragua's social unrest"). In it, Waddell lays out in great detail how NED had spent its money in Nicaragua[38] and concludes with the statement:

> "And while the underlying causes of the turmoil are rooted in government mismanagement and corruption, it's becoming more and more clear that the U.S. support has helped play a role in nurturing the current uprisings."

Later I found another article by Waddell, "One year after Nicaraguan uprising, Ortega is back in control," on April 17, 2019, on www.theconservation.com.[39] It had the same theme as the previous article, which Robinson would approve of. Still, at the end, Waddell decided, as any honest academic would, to provide some details about likely U.S. funding of the opposition in Nicaragua. And indeed, there was a mention of the NED, which he said spent $4.1 million to "strengthen democratic institutions"

---

37. The claims by some sectors of the international Left that President Daniel Ortega and Vice President Rosario Murillo represent a leftist project for Nicaragua that should be defended.

38. Waddell, "Laying the groundwork for insurrection."

39. Waddell, "One year after the Nicaraguan uprising."

in Nicaragua since 2014. His article also mentioned that USAID had provided to Nicaraguan civil society groups between 2015 and 2018 $92 million "development" aid. I checked the references for these statements, and the quoted data appear factual.

So it seems that Robinson doesn't want a fair fight, especially with one of his own. He, as do most or all U.S. foreign-policy government officials and their mouthpieces, wants no fact to appear that might give the "other side" ammunition against their all-or-none philosophy about Nicaragua. This is an example of the "new" policy of the U.S. to assist opposition leaders in Latin America in organizing protests, often violently, and manipulating media so that the truth about the protests in terms of the complexity of civil society structures and the truth about human rights violations are ignored. Waddell, on the other hand, seems willing to play both sides of the street.

Part of this new war on the elected government of Nicaragua, I am convinced, also involved infiltrating peace and solidarity organizations with people, as spokespersons for the U.S. State Department who do little more than question Nicaragua's human-rights record and the democratic behavior of the government.

For example, two-left-leaning solidarity organizations, the North American Congress in Latin America (NACLA) and the Washington Office on Latin America (WOLA), were in the 1980s strongly opposed to the U.S.-sponsored Contra war on the country and were in some ways strong supporters of the Sandinista government. In the middle of the Contra war, these two, among others, were considered by the right to be hopelessly left-wing with respect to Latin America.[40] Not long after the FSLN regained power in 2006, these two organizations started to find fault with the Nicaraguan government, which reached a peak of fault-finding during the so-called uprising (coup attempt) during April to September 2018.

On December 13, 2022, NACLA presented an article on their website by William Robinson entitled "Oscar René Vargas is Nicaragua's Latest Prisoner of Conscience." According to the article: Vargas was "indicted by the government with 'conspiracy to undermine national integrity' and other trumped-up charges. Vargas is the latest high-profile prisoner of conscience in Nicaragua. He is being held at the notorious El Chipote prison outside of Managua, where he joins some 200 other political prisoners. The 77-year-old Vargas had been living in exile in Costa Rica since 2018, where he was forced to flee after the regime issued an arrest warrant because he had criticized the government's repression of mass protests that year."

40. Frawley, "Left's Latin American Lobby."

It turns out the charges were not trumped up and the charge against him was not that he had criticized the so-called government repression of protest in 2018. Reporter Ben Norton has captured a video of Vargas speaking on the *100% Noticias* TV station in Managua sometime in mid-2018, in which he openly called for the U.S. military to overthrow Nicaragua's elected government, while also inciting a massacre, insisting that people should storm the presidential neighborhood dying in the hundreds in order to murder the democratically elected President Daniel Ortega, and then calling to hang Ortega's body in public. ("How US govt-funded media fueled a violent coup in Nicaragua" by Max Blumenthal and Ben Norton, June 12, 2021)

Going on TV and publicly inciting murder and massacres like this is illegal in every country. I wrote to the editor of NACLA about the article by Robinson. I pointed out that much was omitted from the Robinson article about Vargas, and that Vargas's seditious statements on *100% Noticias* were completely omitted from the article. I have received no response from NACLA.

Witness for Peace itself may have been infiltrated by people desiring to put an end to the support many of its members gave to the Sandinista government. I know of one gentleman who was hired soon after 2015 as the Southeast region's Regional Organizer. I was told he did a good job for the region for the two years he was there. But my communication with him in 2018, in my attempt to understand the nature of the bloody conflicts in Nicaragua that year, indicated he was a strong enemy of the Sandinista government. Being well conversant with the political situation in the country, he would have known that the so-called peaceful protestors in 2018 may have been as violent, or more so, than the police.

I later looked at his entries on his Twitter account, which showed that when he wrote in English, he wanted to demonstrate what an avid liberal he is, even to the extent of being a devoted follower of Bernie Sanders. These were his liberal qualifications. But when he was messaging in Spanish, he would often express how much he opposed the Ortega government, blaming them entirely for the killings in 2018. And he would have known the extent to which U.S. government agencies funded the protest groups. And I learned via the internet that he himself had arranged speaking programs in the U.S. for MRS speakers who were urging some form of U.S. intervention in Nicaragua. So this gentleman failed the ultimate test of anyone associating himself/herself with Witness for Peace: complete opposition to U.S. intervention in the affairs of another country.

What did the FSLN government achieve since 2006?

In the Forward to Live from Nicaragua: Uprising or Coup?, Gabriela Luna summarizes the opinion of many of the contributors to that volume:[41]

> "Since 2007, hope and life have been redefined with the return of the Sandinista Front to government. The absolute number of undernourished people in the country has been reduced by half, access to free education and health care has been guaranteed to rural communities, maternal mortality has been reduced by 60% and infant mortality by 52%, while access to electricity has been increased from 54% to 96% of the population.
>
> "Nicaragua is the safest country in Central America, and is in sixth place globally for women's participation in public and civic spaces. Life in the countryside has recovered dignity, thanks to a policy that prioritizes and values the family economy, making it possible to reduce food imports and become 100% self-sufficient in beans, corn, eggs, milk, fruits, onions, peppers, tomatoes and beef.
>
> "These social advances have not been free of contradictions— such as alliances with the private sector and the Catholic Church that lasted until April 2018, when these traditional opponents of the Sandinista struggle began a violent coup attempt."

The Sandinista programs aimed at assisting the poor include: *Hambre Cero*, which offers plants and animals to women heads of household; *Usura Cero*, which provides micro-loans to women; *Plan Techo*, which provides roofing material for families in need; and *Agua Segura*, which provides clean water supplies to poor communities.

Following his electoral victory in 2006, Ortega and other Sandinista leaders recognized that for their government to survive in the face of proven U.S. animosity toward their party, they would have to moderate some of their leftist policies. They would have to demonstrate that they could, in some manner, make peace with the business community and the Catholic Church. The Sandinistas decided they would continue and enhance the neoliberal program started by Ortega's predecessor in 2006. President Bolaños had entered into the Central America–Dominican Republic Free Trade Agreement (CAFTA-DR) with the United States. So in 2007, the new government focused on leveraging this existing neoliberal policy to benefit workers.

---

41. Nicaragua Notes, "Live from Nicaragua," 6.

During the 1980s, the hierarchy of the Catholic Church in Nicaragua in the person of Cardinal (and Archbishop of Managua) Obando y Bravo had adamantly opposed the Sandinista government. But in 2004, Obando suddenly and unexpectedly reached an agreement with the FSLN. He announced his reconciliation with Daniel Ortega in a deal that offered support for the FSLN in return for Ortega's acquiescence to extending the complete ban on abortion, which the National Assembly had passed just before the national elections in November of 2006.[42] Soon after his inauguration as President in 2007, Daniel Ortega asked Obando to preside over the Peace and Reconciliation Commission, which was charged with ensuring the implementation of signed agreements with Nicaraguans, including former Contras, who were affected by the civil war of the 1980s. And Archbishop Obando accepted.

The Sandinista economy was successful at the macro level. In fact, before the uprising (or coup attempt) in 2018, Ortega's economy outpaced its neoliberal predecessors with an average GDP growth rate of 4.2%. Economic growth, alongside many social welfare programs, helped Ortega retain support among working-class Nicaraguans.

According to Sierakowski, in an article otherwise highly critical of the FSLN government:[43]

> "Until April 2018, Nicaragua was seen as an exceptional 'island of peace' in Central America, a region in which criminal violence carried out by street gangs and drug traffickers are an ever-present part of daily life ... its police force has consistently been recognised as a regional leader in the areas of public safety, human rights and community policing. Whereas the 'Northern Triangle' of Guatemala, El Salvador and Honduras registered homicide rates of 26.1, 60 and 42.8 murders per 100,000 people respectively in 2017, in Nicaragua, the figure dropped to a record-breaking low of 7 per 100,000. Even the far more economically developed Central American country of Costa Rica had a higher homicide rate at 12.1 per 100,000. While the Nicaraguan police force was considered the 'most efficient and least corrupt' in the region, that of Guatemala, El Salvador and Honduras competed for first place in hemispheric rankings of corruption. Opinion polls from 2014 suggest that crime was a distinctly secondary problem for the vast majority of Nicaraguans. Whereas 53.4 per cent of Salvadorans, 46.2 per cent of Hondurans, 37.6 per cent

42. Wikipedia, "Miguel Obando y Bravo."
43. Sierakowski, "'We didn't want to be like Somoza's Guardia': Policing, Crime and Nicaraguan Exceptionalism," 22.

of Guatemalans and 18.7 per cent of Costa Ricans chose 'crime' as their most pressing concern, an infinitesimal 3.5 percent of Nicaraguans did so. In 2015, The Economist went so far as to write that Nicaragua's police force, with its community policing and success against organised crime and gangs, was 'in danger of giving socialism a good name.'"

And according to Hilary Francis in an otherwise extremely critical article:[44]

> "In 2015 IMF executive director Otaviano Canuto described Nicaragua as 'a success story in the making' and by 2017, the country had the third highest growth rate in Latin America. The 'buoyant' economic growth was partly the result of aid from Venezuela, but it was also built upon the firm pact established between Ortega's government and the Nicaraguan private sector. This economic growth was closely linked to the central thread in the government's claims to exceptionalism: the idea that Nicaragua was the safest country in Central America. And while some have questioned the claim, the statistics certainly supported it: in 2017 murders in Nicaragua totalled 431, or 7 per 100,000 people, a fraction of the 60 per 100,000 reported in nearby El Salvador. Huge numbers of migrant children have arrived in the United States from Central America in recent years, but hardly any come from Nicaragua, even though it is the poorest country in the region."

Public support for the Sandinista government was high before the attempted coup in 2018. According to a *Latinobarometro* poll conducted in 2017, out of the Latin American countries, Nicaraguans were the first in thinking that their government ruled for the benefit of all the people (52 percent of respondents). To the question, "does the government rule for a small number of 'powerful groups,'" Nicaragua registered the lowest in Latin America (43 percent of respondents). When asked explicitly about their approval of Ortega's government, the approval rates were the highest in Latin America, with 67 percent of respondents.[45]

---

44. See Hilary Francis, "Introduction: Exceptionalism and agency in Nicaragua's revolutionary heritage," in Francis, ed. *A Nicaraguan Exceptionalism?*, 6.

45. Ripoll, "As good as it gets?" 5.

To Sum Up

Now is the time to sum up what I believe about post-2006 Nicaragua. In terms of a view from the other side, I give credit to Sociologist Benjamin Waddell who has otherwise written negatively about the FSLN government's role in the violence during 2018:[46] "Ortega and the Sandinista government may not be the ideal solution to neoliberal policies, but they're most certainly a symptom of its shortcomings." In that connection, he notes that researchers at King's College London recently found that neoliberal policies lead to higher income inequality while failing to cut unemployment rates.

I agree with John Perry that the protests of 2018 amounted to an attempted coup facilitated in part by the U.S. In the first two or three days in April 2018 when students were involved it appeared to be a peaceful protest, but then it quickly evolved into a unified attempt to overthrow the government.

I also believe that Perry's statement when Tom Ricker interviewed him in 2018 puts Nicaragua in the correct perspective:[47]

> "Nicaragua has a past history of conflict, but based on clearly conflicting ideologies—people fighting against the repressive Somoza dictatorship in the 1970s, and the revolutionary government against the US-funded Contras in the 1980s. This time the ideological divide is far from clear. On one side, we have a government which mixes a mildly neoliberal economic policy with social investment, but via a party machine which stifles dissent and fails to bring on a new generation of leaders. It supports LGBT rights and promotes the role of women in politics, yet imposes strict abortion laws. But whatever its deficiencies, it stands in contrast to the governments between Nicaragua and the Texas border, which all have far greater problems of democratic failure, corruption and violence, whether led by the state or by criminal gangs."

Meanwhile, the U.S. response in opposing the existence of this small "socialist" country to our south is to impose sanctions after sanctions. This bully-like activity is despicable.

As John Perry has noted in an article on the NACLA website,[48] sanctions, called "unilateral coercive measures" by the United Nations, are illegal

46. Waddell, "Nicaragua: Better the Devil you know."
47. Ricker, "Update on Nicaragua: Interview about Situation in Masaya."
48. Perry, "Sanctions may impoverish Nicaraguans."

in international law, yet are deployed by the United States against 39 countries. Several resolutions of the UN General Assembly are violated by imposing sanctions of this type, for instance, Resolution 2625 regarding friendly relations between states (24 October 1970), in the preamble of which the states agree "not to interfere with internal matters of another state." This was perceived to be "a crucial condition for the peaceful co-existence of nations." Moreover, the signatories agreed "to abstain from any military, political, economic or other coercion directed against political independence or territorial integrity of another state in their international relations."

In the case of Nicaragua, such sanctions are explicitly aimed at putting pressure on the poorest sectors of Nicaraguan society to undermine the Sandinista government's most reliable base of support. When the Sandinistas lost power in 1990, U.S. sanctions ceased. But when Daniel Ortega won reelection in 2006 and again in 2011, his opponents began to lobby the United States to reimpose them. For example, Ana Margarita Vijil, then leader of the Movimiento de Renovación Sandinista (MRS) came to Washington and met with Representative Ileana Ros-Lehtinen (R-FL) several times from 2015 onwards to push for the U.S. to impose sanctions on Nicaragua. In 2016, Ros-Lehtinen introduced the Nicaraguan Investment Conditionality Act, known as the NICA Act, in response to alleged fraud in the 2016 election process and the ending of presidential term limits, which had enabled Ortega to seek reelection. The NICA bill was finally passed in December 2018 as the Nicaragua Human Rights and Anticorruption Act. By then, the violent attempt to overthrow the Nicaraguan government between April and September 2018 had failed, spurring on the Act's proponents.

John Perry has noted[49] sanctions are only part of the US regime-change agenda for Nicaragua. One of several other measures has included "democracy promotion," in which the U.S.-funded National Endowment for Democracy (NED) provided training for up to 8,000 young Nicaraguans leading up to the uprising in 2018 with the ultimate goal of displacing the Ortega government.

The NICA Act allowed targeted sanctions against Nicaraguan officials. It required U.S. officials to oppose loans to Nicaragua from international financial institutions (IFIs), excluding those to address "human needs" or "promote democracy." Sanctions apply until Nicaragua is "certified" as meeting various requirements, including having "free and fair" elections.

Another major sanctions bill (The RENACER Act) [Reinforcing Nicaragua's Adherence to Conditions for Electoral Reform Act of 2021] was

---

49. theAnalysis.news, "Does Nicaragua Under President Ortega Deserve Progressives' Support?"

signed by President Biden in November 2021. It includes the power to exclude Nicaragua from the Dominican Republic-Central America Free Trade Agreement (CAFTA-DR) and to obstruct multilateral loans to the country. It monitors IFIs even more strictly than under the NICA Act, expands the targets of personal sanctions to tens of thousands of Sandinista party members, requires closer collaboration with U.S. partners to implement the act, and adds Nicaragua to the list of countries deemed to be "corrupt."

While the sanctions have hit specific projects that benefitted poor communities, they have also begun to impact mainstream services such as healthcare, where replacing defective equipment or obtaining supplies during the pandemic has proven problematic.

Perry asks:[50] What will the U.S. do if Nicaragua—one of the safest countries in Latin America—loses its traditional security because the economy collapses and poorer Nicaraguans travel north to look for jobs, as they do from Honduras, Guatemala, and El Salvador? What would be the response if U.S. action caused a humanitarian crisis? Sanctions, he says, are clearly not in Nicaragua's interest, but they may not be in the United States' interest either.

In another article,[51] Perry points out using statistics for 2021: " . . . not only is Nicaragua well below all of the Northern Triangle countries in terms of numbers seeking asylum or claiming refugee status, there is basically no internal displacement and few 'other' categories of concern to the UN Refugee Agency." He notes that some of the major news outlets ignore the fact that, while numbers of Nicaraguan migrants have risen in the last year or two, so have those from almost everywhere else in Central America. Perry argues effectively against the major media's attributing increased migration from Nicaragua to repression by the government. He concludes:

> "The myth that Nicaragua is a major source of migrants heading to the Mexico/US border, and that this is primarily due to repression at home, is a very dangerous one, for at least two reasons. First, it diverts attention from the much more significant drivers of migration from the countries to its north, where, in addition to natural (and human-augmented) disasters, people are fleeing severe problems of increased poverty, violence, repressive government, often poor public services and systemic corruption. Pretending such problems are worse in Nicaragua than in the Northern Triangle countries is not only absurd, but produces a

50. Perry, "Sanctions may impoverish Nicaraguans."
51. Perry, "Are Nicaraguan Migrants Escaping 'Repression'—or Economic Sanctions?"

perverse political focus on Nicaragua that allows the US to evade responsibility for the conditions that have developed in those three countries [to the north]—at least in part as a consequence of its policy of supporting corrupt, neoliberal governments. Second, the media's exaggeration of the scale of Nicaraguan migration and its message that repression is the main driver for it helps justify the US government's hostility towards the Sandinista government, enabling it to claim that sanctions and other forms of political pressure will help keep migration down."

In My Older Years

El Salvador And Guatemala

IT WAS 1994 AND I was 63. Two years earlier, I had left my wife Jane in Iowa and started a new single life in Newtown, Pennsylvania. I had chosen eastern Pennsylvania to be near three of my four children who lived in neighboring New Jersey. I got a job as a groundwater hydrologist with a nearby environmental engineering firm.

I was still in contact with Witness for Peace and learned they were going to sponsor a one-week delegation to El Salvador to help monitor the national elections there. These were the first national elections since the UN-sponsored Truth Commission issued their report in March 1993 on the leftist FMLN[1] guerillas' actions opposing the political party in power, ARENA, who effectively supported death squads against the populace. I decided to sign up for the delegation and requested vacation time off from work at Vincent Uhl Associates. This was granted but only after I would complete a few weeks assignment they had for me in Africa.

In February of that year, Uhl Associates sent me to Botswana in Southern Africa for three weeks to work with a local hydrogeological firm, Water Resources Consultants, in preparing a proposal to the government of Botswana to install deep water-supply wells in the Kalahari Desert. During that time, I stayed in the capital, Gaborone, with the owner of the firm, Tej Bakaya, and his family. They hailed from India and so every day I enjoyed the most delicious Indian food one can imagine. I was in Tej's office daily, worked on the proposal, and gave introductory training to his staff of ten Indian and Botswanan geologists in groundwater modeling.

As the proposal was nearing completion, it came time to specify to the government proposal reviewers who we were proposing to direct the work in the field as project manager. Both Tej and Vincent Uhl, back home, suggested that I should be listed as the project manager. But my emotional reaction was completely negative. It seemed that even though two years had passed since my divorce, I still felt shaken by it, and the prospect of directing such a large operation for at least several months out in the wilds of the Kalahari Desert was deeply unsettling. I called Vince from Gaborone and told him my decision. He accepted it, but it turned out

---

1. Farabundo Martí National Liberation Front

that within two weeks of my returning home, he told me he was laying me off, nominally because he said work was scarce.

In any case, I started my vacation within a few days of coming home. I flew to San Salvador, El Salvador to join the Witness for Peace delegation for election monitoring. By way of the recent history of El Salvador I offer the following summary:

In 1981, leftist guerrillas and left political groups joined forces, forming the FMLN. They fought for a fairer society, one in which the poor had a chance to raise themselves up. Throughout the 1980s, civil war raged between the FMLN and the U.S.-backed Salvadoran military forces. Eventually, upon request of the two warring parties, the United Nations intervened to help mediate a resolution. On January 16, 1992, the UN brokered a peace agreement that ended the war, and in July of that year, the Commission on the Truth for El Salvador was created and began its work.

The commission was mandated to investigate serious acts of violence occurring since 1980 and the nature and effects of the violence. They were also to recommend methods of achieving national reconciliation. In March 1993, the Commission presented its report, *From Madness to Hope: The 12-Year War in El Salvador: Report of the Commission on the Truth for El Salvador.*

Among over 22,000 documented complaints, 60 percent involved extrajudicial killings, 25 percent involved disappearances, 20 percent involved torture, and some alleging more than one form of violence. Based on the collected testimony, the commission attributed 85 percent of the acts of violence to agents of the government of El Salvador, which took place predominantly in rural areas. Approximately 5 percent of the acts of violence were attributed to the FMLN.[2] The civilian government and the armed forces of El Salvador largely rejected the commission's report, including the commission's recommendations, and no follow-up organization was established.

* * *

This was the situation when the national elections were held in March 1994. Despite the government's largely rejecting the findings and recommendations of the truth commission, there was a genuine sense of hope for the country in the minds of many Salvadorans at the time of the elections.

My WFP delegation of 18 people arrived in San Salvador, the capital, on March 18th, and we stayed overnight in a convent in the middle of the

---

2. United States Institute of Peace, "Truth Commission: El Salvador."

city. That afternoon we and many other election monitoring groups from the U.S. gathered in a large auditorium in the convent to receive orientation and training on how the election would be run and how we would perform our job. The next morning we were assigned to a town west of San Salvador, Sonsonate, where we were to do the monitoring. Three passenger vans drove us to the city, about 35 miles west of the capital. During the afternoon of our arrival in town, we listened to the local supporters and representatives of the two major parties, ARENA and FMLN. I was particularly impressed by a few of the FMLN spokesmen, as they were smart and understood U.S. politics better than most of our citizens. We ate supper there and bedded down in a local school building.

Three of my fellow WFP delegates to El Salvador in March 1994

After breakfast the next day, March 20th, we were taken to our different polling stations. We observed no abnormalities, including no stuffing of the ballot boxes. Each voting "booth" provided the barest privacy for the voter, but it seemed to suffice in a rudimentary way. This was the first round of elections.

It turned out that a second round was necessary because no one presidential candidate obtained at least 50 percent of the vote. The ARENA candidate got 49 percent of the vote and the FMLN candidate, the runner-up, got only 25 percent. So they scheduled the second-round election between just the ARENA and FMLN candidates for April 24th.

I returned home on March 22nd. When I went to work the next day, Vince confirmed I would be laid off from Uhl Associates by the end of the month. The next day I applied for unemployment compensation.

Witness for Peace was sponsoring another election monitoring delegation to cover the next month's second-round of elections in El Salvador. I decided I had nothing to lose if I went on this delegation also, and I immediately applied to go and was accepted. It turned out that Gail Phares from Raleigh, North Carolina, was leading the delegation. Gail was one of the founders of Witness for Peace in 1983, so I was very much looking forward to being with her on the delegation. My Friends Meeting in Trenton kindly gave me a donation of $500 to help cover part of the cost of the airfare and in-country delegation expenses. So I booked myself on a flight to San Salvador from Philly, leaving Friday April 22nd. I flew out of Philly late that morning, and in the late afternoon I met up with Gail Phares and the other delegation members in San Salvador. The duration of this delegation was only five days, and there were only eight of us.

Our delegation was assigned to monitor the election in the town of San Miguel, about 70 miles east of the capital. We traveled there the next day by a rented mini-van. After an orientation meeting that evening, we spent the night in a small motel having the tiniest rooms you can imagine. The next day we oversaw three polling stations, which were busy throughout the day. At the end of the day we submitted our report, which disclosed no abnormalities in the election process for those stations.

As it turned out, in the second round of the elections, the ARENA candidate Armando Calderon Sol won 68 percent of the votes while the FMLN party's candidate, Ruben Zamora, won only 32 percent. The FMLN candidates did win 21 out of the 84 seats in the legislative assembly to ARENA's 39.

The next day we returned to San Salvador, from which most of the delegation members headed directly home to the States. But I already had made plans to travel to Guatemala for a month of some intensive Spanish language training.

Quetzaltenango was a city in the mountains of Guatemala famous for its Spanish language schools. For a few to several weeks, Gringos or people of other nationalities could study Spanish during the day while living with families who spoke only Spanish. I traveled by bus from San Salvador to Guatemala City, the capital of Guatemala. After an overnight in a local hotel, I boarded a bus to *Quetzaltenango* up in the mountains. It seemed an endless journey filled with many stops and local people bringing onboard large bundles and sometimes chickens.

When we finally arrived, I searched for a hotel and luckily found one. That night I went to bed early as I did not feel well. In the morning, I realized that I had come down with the worst cold or flu I had experienced in many years. Before I could even think about getting up to have some breakfast, a slight, well-dressed Guatemalan gentleman knocked on my door. I roused myself and got out of bed to greet him.

He was the director of the SISAI Spanish School located near the center of Quetzaltenango. His spies had informed him that I was in town to study Spanish. I quickly got dressed and, despite my feeling sick, went with him to see the school building while he explained the features of the language program. At the end of his presentation, I agreed to enroll in the program at his school for four weeks.

Suddenly, my sickness did not seem terribly important, as I was so excited to start improving my Spanish. He took me to the home of the family, the Gomezes, where I was to stay over the next four weeks. They were to be my kind and generous hosts. I settled in with them that very morning. There was the husband and wife, a 21-year-old son, and a teenage daughter. The son wanted to talk to me often about the soccer World Cup. They were a poor family, but by Guatemalan standards were middle class. They showed me my bedroom and their clever but simple shower and bathing system. They provided all my meals which were simple and good, and I usually sat at their table with the four of them for the evening meal.

The next morning was my first day at the school, and I met my Spanish tutor, Alicia Morales. Her husband was an engineer, and they had two small children. She knew only a little English, so I was forced to do my exercises with her only in Spanish. Each weekday she would devote five hours of conversation with me. Sometimes she would decide what we would talk about and sometimes she would ask me to pick a topic. I was her only student during those five hours. And I must say that over the days I did improve my ability and my confidence to speak in Spanish. It's such a lovely language.

On weekday afternoons, the school often showed videos/movies for all the students about Guatemalan life and history. Many of the movies were documentaries, a few showing how the U.S. had grievously taken advantage of the Guatemalan people during the 20th century. One marked example was the 1954 coup arranged by the CIA and as requested by the United Fruit Company to depose the then democratically-elected President of Guatemala, Jacobo Árbenz, thus ending what Guatemalans have called the "Guatemalan Spring," the ten years of representative democracy in Guatemalan history.

The reforms Árbenz enacted included an expanded right to vote, the ability of workers to organize, legitimizing political parties, and allowing public debate. The centerpiece of his policy was an agrarian reform law under which uncultivated portions of extensive land holdings were expropriated in return for compensation and redistributed to poverty-stricken agricultural laborers. Most of Guatemalan history after the coup has been marked by oppressive dictators who take actions to keep the poor down while supporting the interests of the wealthy and the large corporations.

During the weekends, particularly on Saturdays, the school arranged for day trips to Mayan ruins, local hot mineral springs, and nearby markets of note. The cost I paid for my time at the school was just $100 per week, including my room, board, tuition, and weekend side trips. I made several friends during the month I was in *Quetzaltenango* but have not kept up with them. I felt a mixture of sadness and contentment when it was time to leave the city and the teachers and director of the school the third week of May.

Witness for Peace Mid-Atlantic

In June of 1994, I got a call from a friend who was part of my delegation for the first-round election monitoring in El Salvador in March. She had heard there was to be a Witness for Peace (WFP) organizing meeting in the Boston area coming up in a couple of weeks and wondered if I might like to accompany her to it. I agreed, and we drove up together on the appointed Saturday.

We joined several other people, some from as far away as Maryland, who were interested in strengthening the WFP presence in the Northeast. Carol Richardson, on the national staff of Witness for Peace, led the meeting, which involved a lot of brainstorming. She was the national outreach coordinator, and she had called the meeting to see if we could organize at least one WFP region in the Northeast. Since 1990, the WFP regions supported Witness for Peace-National in its goals of defending human rights in Guatemala and Colombia and speaking the truth about Nicaragua's new neoliberal government.

We discussed what an active WFP region might look like. Other currently active regions, such as Witness for Peace Southeast, headed by Gail Phares, one of the founders of Witness for Peace, had a broad program to publicize WFP and share its principles with communities in its region. It became clear that any new WFP region should, at a minimum, include: annual or semi-annual speaking tours; annual or semi-annual sponsorship of a short-term delegation to the countries where WFP had international teams; an annual retreat; participation in rallies or political events that reflected WFP principles; seasonal newsletters, and fundraising for all the above. As we talked, we also realized that setting up a region for the entire northeast would be too cumbersome; the distances were just too great. So we narrowed our focus to setting up separate regions for New England and for the Mid-Atlantic states.

It was a challenge and one not to be taken lightly. On the principle of "fools rush in where angels fear to tread," I volunteered to serve as the Coordinator of the new Mid-Atlantic region. I had nothing to lose. I was the only one present who was completely available as I had recently been laid off from my job and had decided I would not be immediately looking for a job.[1] I was ready and willing to start at least a few of the activities desired of a WFP region.

After questioning my background for the work (I had none), the group decided that I displayed enough enthusiasm for the work that I would be worth a try. At the same time, a small group of people from the region, including John Mateyko, an architect from Delaware, volunteered to be part of an embryonic steering committee for the region. The steering committee would make suggestions to me and guide my work, in addition to fulfilling certain needed functions for the region. The new Mid-Atlantic region included the states of New York, Pennsylvania, New Jersey, Delaware, and Maryland, as well as DC. By the end of the meeting, the status of the New England region was sort of left up in the air, although a few months later they did find a Coordinator for the region and started their work.

After returning home, I lost little time starting the work out of my small apartment in Newtown, Pennsylvania. Thus began my association with Witness for Peace Mid-Atlantic (WFPMA) for the next 18 years. The first thing I did was to reach out to contacts to fill out the steering committee (SC). People volunteered and others suggested names. We decided the committee would meet once a quarter. And before long, we had eight people, most of whom came faithfully to every meeting, which took place at different venues in the region.

In July 1994, I received from WFP-National a starting electronic list of contacts living in the Mid-Atlantic region. I spent many hours on the phone and on the computer reaching out to people who could help me in my job as Coordinator. Almost immediately, I sent out a fundraising letter to a few hundred people. We started receiving donations, and our new region was off and running!

I was always responsible for keeping the contact and donor list up to date. I also organized the fund-raising mailings to potential donors. We would send out fund-raising letters two or three times a year to our expanding list. Four or five of us would join in to make an envelope-stuffing party, which we would often have at my house. My wife Helen would always provide lunch for us and join us in envelope stuffing!

---

1. In the fall, I was able to get a part-time job doing groundwater modeling for two environmental engineering firms.

IN MY OLDER YEARS

From right to left: John Mateko, Julia Graff and me preparing a mailing

With help from my steering committee, I arranged a speaking tour for October of the first year. We invited a woman from Managua, Nicaragua, Ileana Zuniga, to speak in several cities around the region. She would talk about the effects of her neoliberal government's arbitrary cuts in social spending on the poor working-class people. After she came, I drove her to a few speaking locations in southeastern Pennsylvania. Other steering committee members did the same in other parts of the region. We usually had decent turnouts for all the venues she spoke at, mainly because the local steering committee member had effectively promoted advance publicity for her.

Our Nicaraguan speaker, Ileana Zuniga, and SC member Joyce Penfield

That first year we were unable to sponsor a short-term delegation to Nicaragua or Guatemala, but during later years we sponsored several.

I produced my first newsletter in January 1995, in which I announced that we were having a planned retreat for June and included other news about the region and the upcoming in-country delegations sponsored by WFP-National. Then in April, I sent out a flyer with a tear-off form inviting people to come to the retreat, giving the retreat schedule and cost, and describing the theme of the retreat and the keynote speaker. The retreat in June turned out to be great, and it was wonderful to meet the folks I had been addressing in my mailings for the last 11 months.

One of the most important aspects of this retreat and others in the following years was meal preparation. For so many years, Linda Manzo from Langhorne, Pennsylvania, came to our rescue and prepared excellent meals. All she asked was that we didn't make her attend any committee meetings! All the retreat participants took part in the cleaning up.

Our Speaker from Guatemala and me in Fall 1995

WFPMA steering committee and Guatemalan speaker in 1995

I was always very involved in planning and organizing the annual retreat when from 25 to 50 people would attend. John Mateyko would often arrange for very interesting keynote speakers, including on different years: Edward Herman, Rabbi Arthur Waskow, and Ray McGovern. Before his death in 2017, Ed Herman was Professor Emeritus of finance at the Wharton School of Business of the University of Pennsylvania and a media critic opposing media propaganda that supports U.S. wars. Rabbi Arthur Waskow is an American author and political activist. He founded the Shalom Center in 1983 and serves as its director; the center opposed the US war in Iraq as well as attacks on American Muslims. Ray McGovern was a CIA analyst from 1963 to 1990, and in the 1980s, chaired National Intelligence Estimates and prepared the President's Daily Brief. But after his retirement, together with other former CIA employees, he founded in 2003 the Veteran Intelligence Professionals for Sanity (VIPS). His organization is dedicated to analyzing and criticizing the use of intelligence, at first concerning the Iraq War, and opposing torture committed by U.S. soldiers and CIA agents.

Advertising our group at a retreat, from left to right: Gil Ortiz, John Mateyko, Robin Hoy and Ray Torres

John Mateyko introducing the featured speaker,
Edward Herman, at 2003 retreat

I spent a lot of my time responding to donors and maintaining the regional contact list. I also took part in actions representing the region, including a demonstration in April 1995 on the Capitol steps in DC opposing our country's operating the so-called "School of Americas" (SOA) in Fort Benning, Georgia. After they returned home, many of the Latin American graduates from that school have taken part in repressive and violent actions against the poor's leaders in their own countries. Graduates of the SOA, on behalf of the right-wing government of El Salvador, directed the assassination of Bishop Oscar Romero in March of 1980.

Maryknoll Father Roy Bourgeois addressing protest group
on steps of U.S. Capitol April 1995

The WFPMA region lasted from June 1994 to February 2013, when we laid it down because fund-raising results were low, and the steering committee members had grown older and lacked the energy to continue the work. I served as Coordinator of the region (or Organizer) for the first two years, after which John Mateyko took over from me; Ray Torres served for a year or two and then Ben Beachy took over for a couple of years followed by Julia Graff. I served as treasurer for a couple of years, which Gil Ortiz took over until the very end. Over the 18-plus years, steering committee members naturally came and went. But some of the most faithful ones over the years were: John Mateyko, Barry Stoner, Ray Torres, Robin Hoy, Gil Ortiz, Eleanor Oakley, Lynn Biddle, Tom Driver, Paula Bronstein, Doug Burkholder, Joyce Penfield, Serafina Youngdahl Lombardi, Nancy Gwen, Lorenzo McCarty, and Lenore McGarry.

It was sad to give up the region. And no one has come forward so far to restart this region for Witness for Peace. But I was so happy to have had the opportunity to help advance the name and principles of Witness for Peace over the 18 years. I am indebted to the tireless assistance of steering committee members and those others who volunteered to help the region's programs over these years. Most of all, I enjoyed my friendship with the steering committee members and with some of the many members of WFPMA from all over the region. I was blessed and inspired by them.

Letters to the Editor

In my 80s and 90s, I have necessarily limited my activism mostly to writing op-eds and letters to the editor, although four or five years ago I did some lobbying of my Congressional representative to vote for peace initiatives affecting several parts of the world. But as I grew older, about the only thing I could manage physically was writing, a remnant of my former activism.

Appendix B contains a few examples of the letters and commentaries I've had published from 2004 to the present. The entries appear in reverse chronological order. I was unable to include any of the many letters to the editor I wrote earlier because I didn't keep copies then. In the 1960s and 1970s, I wrote many letters in opposition to the Vietnam War and in the 1980s in opposition to U.S. interventions in Nicaragua, El Salvador, and Haiti.

In the spring of 2019, one of my letters to the editor resulted in an auspicious surprise. I had a short letter published in the *Bucks County Herald*, a weekly newspaper for an adjoining county to mine. The letter concerned the rights of Palestinians to be treated respectfully and humanely by Israel. Within a couple of days of the publication of the letter, the editor of the paper, Bridget Wingert, emailed me that a well-known Palestinian-American graphic artist, Rajie Cook, wanted to contact me. She gave me his number and I called him. He told me how much he appreciated my letter to the *Bucks County Herald*. He then invited Helen and me to come to his house the next Sunday afternoon. He and his wife lived in nearby Washington Crossing, Pennsylvania. We had a delightful time with Rajie and his wife, and he kindly gave me a copy of his book, *A Vision for My Father: The Life and Work of Palestinian-American Artist and Designer Rajie Cook*. This wonderful book illustrates some of his graphic art and tells as well the story of the Palestinian people and pleads for an understanding of their rights.

Knowing Rajie, led to my meeting Susan Abulhawa, a Palestinian-American writer, who also lived in Bucks County. I read her gripping and beautiful novel, *Mornings in Jenin*. Rajie gave me her telephone number, and I called Susan about the possibility of her and me lobbying my Congresswoman Madeleine Dean about the need for the U.S. to pressure Israel to protect the rights of Palestinian children. Rajie was not well and so could not come to meet with the Congresswoman. One day in October 2019, Linda Hanna, another Palestinian-American woman, and Susan and

I met with Congresswoman Dean. I think we made our case cogently, but her response in the end was that she was not going to abandon the people in her district who supported Israel's policies; she would not support a bill that would limit the degree to which U.S. funds could be used to arrest and detain Palestinian children.

Back in 2015, I organized a small peace group to lobby U.S. Senator Bob Casey from Pennsylvania, encouraging him to vote in favor of the Iran Nuclear Agreement. We met with his Aide, Joe Hill, in Casey's office in Philadelphia. Casey had been undecided on the agreement but wound up voting in favor of it.

My lobbying group August 28, 2015 with Joe Hill in Senator Casey's Philadelphia office. Joe Hill is the third person from the right.

* * *

The thrust of most of my submissions has been to set the record straight. Often outright fabrications have been used to justify the wars the U.S. has entered into. As we have often heard, truth is the first casualty in a war or an impending war. Good examples of this are the gas attacks in Syria, which occurred in 2017 and 2018. There is evidence to believe that these apparent gas attacks were not carried out by the Syrian government as our government claims, but that U.S.-supported rebel groups in Syria staged them for the purpose of inciting the U.S. to pursue the war against Syria more vigorously. The goal was, and is, to overthrow Assad's Syrian government. Then there was the falsehood we were told by the George W.

Bush administration about weapons of mass destruction supposedly in the hands of Saddam Hussein, which "allowed" us to invade Iraq, with all the horrors and mass murders accompanying that action.

Very recently I sent a comment online to the NPR Public Editor questioning the veracity of their statements about the reason why the U.S. invaded Afghanistan. In the first part of a series of reports on Afghanistan, NPR host Steve Inskeep (Morning Edition on 8/5/22) interviewed the son of the former head of the Taliban, Mullah Muhammad Omar. Inskeep stated to the son: "He was the leader who refused to turn over Osama bin Laden in 2001, a refusal that led to the US attack."

The line that the Taliban "refused to turn over Osama bin Laden" and that this "led to the U.S. attack," though part of the commonly accepted chronology of the war, is a gross distortion of history. The series of events leading up to the U.S. Afghanistan invasion were laid out recently in a *Current Affairs* essay by Nathan Robinson and Noam Chomsky[1] titled "What Do We Owe Afghanistan?" After the 9/11 attacks, the Bush administration demanded that the Taliban immediately hand Osama bin Laden over to the United States. The Taliban, in response, offered to put bin Laden on trial if the United States provided evidence of his guilt. Bush refused. Nor did he consider the Taliban's offer to give up bin Laden to a neutral third country. He would not provide the requested evidence. Even after our bombs began to fall on Afghanistan, the Taliban repeated their offers to give up Bin Laden—even dropping the requirement for actual evidence. Still, the U.S. continued its onslaught, initiating the 20-year occupation.

Often my submissions have tried to bring to light U.S. actions relating to civil and human rights that were poorly covered by the leading news media. One example of this was the 2009 coup in Honduras that unseated democratically-elected President Manuel Zelaya. The coup, covertly approved by the U.S., brought to power a cruel autocratic government (the National Party) that began to violate the human rights of its populace. This is the government the U.S. has been supporting with our police training programs.[2] Other examples are the U.S. military hardware support of Israeli attacks on Palestinians and the U.S. military support of Saudi Arabia's attacks on Yemen.

1. Robinson and Chomsky, "What do we owe Afghanistan?"
2. In the general elections held in Honduras on November 28, 2021, Xiomara Castro of the leftist Libre party won handily. She is the wife of ex-President Manuel Zelaya and was inaugurated as president on January 27th. But it doesn't look as if the U.S. is going to support anything like progressive reforms in Honduras. On October 25, 2022, U.S. Ambassador to Honduras Laura Dogu attacked reforms the new President is proposing to eliminate corruption in the pricing of electrical energy.

At other times, I would summit commentaries when the whole truth about an issue was missing, in cases where the omitted portion could bring a change in U.S. policy: from war-making to peacemaking. An example showing the power of the federal government and the media to sway public opinion by failing to tell the whole truth is the current war in Ukraine. The following paragraphs illustrate what we have not been told about this war:

To avoid a war, Russia asked that the U.S., and therefore NATO, in January 2022, promise not to extend NATO any farther east than the western boundary of Ukraine. This came after two decades of anti-Russian and anti-Putin propaganda by the State Department and by four of our major media; the *New York Times*, the *Washington Post*, CNN, and MSNBC.

In 1990, President George H. W. Bush promised Mikhail Gorbachev, then head of state of the Soviet Union, that the U.S. would never push for NATO to encompass any of the Eastern European countries. Bush's Secretary of State James Baker famously stated "not one inch eastward" in his assurances about NATO expansion in his meeting with Soviet leader Mikhail Gorbachev on February 9, 1990. This was just one part of a cascade of assurances about Soviet security given by Western leaders to Gorbachev and other Soviet officials throughout the process of German unification in 1990 and on into 1991, according to declassified U.S., Soviet, German, British, and French documents posted on December 12, 2017, by the National Security Archive at George Washington University.[3]

The agreement involved the Soviet Union's agreeing to the reunification of Germany (Russia's worst enemy) and allowing the reunified Germany to join NATO. The stipulation was that the U.S. would agree not to extend NATO any farther east than it was at that time, which would be up to the eastern border of East Germany.

However, soon after he took office, Bill Clinton began listening to the Pentagon generals' advice and the defense industries' lobbyists. So during his administration and subsequently during the George W. Bush administration, at least ten Eastern European countries, formerly under Soviet influence, were courted by the U.S. and were admitted into NATO in contravention of the agreement. These included Poland, Romania, Bulgaria, Croatia, Estonia, Latvia, Lithuania, Slovenia, the Czech Republic, and Slovakia.

So the U.S. and the western European members of NATO broke their promise, badly. Russia, as embodied by their leader Putin, was determined to stop any further encroachment of NATO into its sphere of influence by insisting that Ukraine never be admitted into NATO. It seemed to be

---

3. National Security Archive, "NATO Expansion: What Gorbachev Heard."

a reasonable request. Particularly considering that Russia no longer represents a communist bulwark feverishly trying to impose its will on the western world, which was why NATO was set up in the first place.

One of the main reasons the U.S. has been interested in enlarging the membership of NATO eastward was the opportunity for our defense industries to sell more F-16s and other military hardware to the new members. The only rationality for not guaranteeing that Ukraine would not become a member of NATO was that a lot of money would be made. By a few people.

For the best elaboration of the recent state of U.S.-Russia relations, see Stephen Cohen's *War with Russia?* published in 2019.[4] Before his death in 2020, Stephen was Professor of Politics, Emeritus at Princeton University and taught Russian and Slavic studies at New York University. His academic work concentrated on modern Russian history since the Bolshevik Revolution and Russia's relationship with the United States. In the book, he lays out painstakingly the recent history of the U.S. throwing away shining opportunities to cooperate with Russia to both countries' benefit. There was a hope in several quarters that with the rise of Putin to President of Russia in 2000, and the end of Boris Yeltsin's problematic terms there, there would be every reason for the two superpowers to cooperate in several ways. Instead, the U.S., aided by the major media, set out to demonize Putin and bad-mouth Russia at every opportunity. One of the major problems inherent in this approach was a complete refusal by the U.S. and its European allies to recognize Russia's legitimate security needs.

The war in Ukraine didn't have to happen. The Minsk agreement, if implemented, could have averted the war. On February 12, 2015, the Minsk II agreement was signed between Ukraine and Russia as brokered by France and Germany. It would have stopped the fighting in the Donbas region of eastern Ukraine between Russian Separatists and the Ukrainian military and granted a degree of autonomy to the Donetsk and Lugansk regions of the Donbas that had voted for independence from Ukraine after the 2014 coup in Ukraine. The problem with Minsk II was that the Ukrainians either refused to let the Donbas republics become independent or to pass the laws on autonomy necessary to implement the Minsk agreement.

Volodymyr Zelenskyy defeated Petro Poroshenko in the 2019 election in Ukraine on a platform that included making peace with Russia and implementing the Minsk II Agreement. Unfortunately, Zelenskyy came under intense pressure not to implement Minsk II, to which he succumbed—pressure from far-right ultra-nationalists. Zelenskyy

---

4. Cohen, *War with Russia?*

abandoned his campaign peace promise and refused to talk to the leaders of the Donbas and implement the Minsk Agreement.

The United States and the UN both endorsed the Minsk II agreement. But the West did nothing to push the Ukrainians into implementing it. And Ukraine also refused to offer a treaty of neutrality. Nothing can excuse the Russian invasion of Ukraine. But the U.S. and the Ukrainians tragically and inexcusably missed numerous diplomatic chances of averting this war.

* * *

I hope that the included sample of my letters and op-eds might encourage others to research the reasons given by the government and media to justify our going to war. And having researched them to speak out via the print world.

In my favorite daily newspaper, *The Intelligencer,* out of Doylestown, Pennsylvania, an op-ed appeared on May 12, 2022, written by one of the paper's Editorial Board members.[5] It was entitled "Keep those cards and letters coming." Dick Sakulich, the author of the piece, mentioned that in the 1960s, he had written the CEO of a well-known national company that he thought one of their TV ads was in very poor taste. The company never responded to him, but several weeks later, a news story indicated that the company had withdrawn the ad because there was an "off-the-charts negative response to the ad." Dick learned that the number of negative letters the company received about the ad was about 80. That's just 80 letters from a nation of hundreds of millions. Eighty letters were all it took to change a large company's advertising decisions!

So take heart, dear reader. It can often be surprisingly effective to raise your voice through letters. But you must realize that not all newspapers may be willing to publish your commentary depending on its content and the sensitivities of readers in the local area. For example, I have found it impossible to get a letter published in the *Philadelphia Inquirer* about the rights of Palestinians in Israel and the occupied territories.

Of course, the editor may decide to edit your commentary before publishing which could affect the point you are trying to make. As given in Appendix B, my op-ed about the cause of Black Lives Matter published in the Intelligencer on 9/21/2016 appeared with a different headline than I proposed. My proposed headline said simply, "Black Lives *Do* Matter." But the editorial page editor changed it to the much weaker "Black lives don't

5. Sikulich, "Keep those cards and letters coming."

matter more; they matter equally." He didn't change the text of the op-ed, but in modifying the headline, the whole commentary lost its punch.

In preparing the letters and commentaries in Appendix B, I relied upon several news and commentary sources, including Paul Jay's theAnalysisNews.com, Fairness & Accuracy in Reporting (FAIR), The Nation magazine, Jewish Voice for Peace, American Friends Service Committee, and Witness for Peace among others. I have also referenced articles on Syria by Pulitzer Prize winner Seymour Hersh.

Epilogue

VIEWING MY SENSE OF urgency for justice and peace, a few of my friends and relatives have come close to dismissing my actions by saying that I'm trying to "Save the World." But what I'm trying to do is just my job: reporting for duty to do my understanding of God's will to challenge racist slurs and stop racist actions, and to oppose and shine a light on, elements in the government and the media that promote wars.

Jesus said: Blessed are the peacemakers. Those who make peace among nations and harmony among different races and those of differing wealth. This does not mean we have to be "goody-two-shoes" or perfectly righteous people to work for peace and justice, as that's not going to happen. The Apostle Paul reminded us that none of us is righteous. No, not one. But God wants us to live under his grace and work for his kingdom, imperfect though we are.

Let's remember Smedley Darlington Butler,[1] a Quaker from West Chester, Pennsylvania, who joined the Marine corps at age 17 against his father's wishes. He made the Marines his career until 1931, when he retired from the military. He rose to the rank of Major General, and at the time of his death, he was the most decorated U.S. Marine in U.S. history. Four years after his retirement, Smedley wrote a popular but short book entitled *War is a Racket*.[2] On the first page of the book, we read: "War is racket. It always has been. It is possibly the oldest, easily the most profitable, surely the most vicious.... Only a small 'inside' group knows what it is about. It is conducted for the benefit of the very few, at the expense of the very many."

In 1931, in a speech Smedley delivered before the American Legion, he said:

"I spent thirty-three years and four months in active military service, and during that period I spent most of my time being a high-class muscle man for Big Business, for Wall Street and the bankers."

1. Smedley's mother was a Darlington, as was my mother's mother, also a Quaker and from the West Chester area. So he and I could be not-too-distant relatives!
2. Butler, *War is a Racket*.

Let's also remember Dwight D. Eisenhower, the 34th President of the United States, for his warning to monitor and control the power of the military-industrial complex given in his farewell address to the nation: "In the councils of government, we must guard against the acquisition of unwarranted influence, whether sought or unsought, by the military-industrial complex. The potential for the disastrous rise of misplaced power exists and will persist. We must never let the weight of this combination endanger our liberties or democratic processes."

There has been little effort expended since Eisenhower in high places of power to control the military-industrial complex, more accurately rendered now as the military-industrial-media complex.

In an earlier speech by Eisenhower upon the death of Joseph Stalin in March 1953, he said among other peaceful statements: "Every gun that is made, every warship launched, every rocket fired signifies, in the final sense, a theft from those who hunger and are not fed, those who are cold and are not clothed."

The major media like to tell us that everything is fine, that everything our country does is for our good and the good of other countries in the world. But racism abounds and our non-democratic intervention into other countries' affairs continues, often resulting in devastating wars. The result is more and more money squandered on foreign wars usually for enhancing the profits of a few. This money could have been spent on bolstering school facilities all over the country, child-care subsidies, or researching carbon-free energy sources.

I dedicate this book to my broader family, both past and present. You have helped my emerging understanding and appreciation for the black experience in our country and for the ways we as a country have fostered wars.

Being devoted to peace and justice comes with a price, however, depending on the level of devotion. The highest cost by far involves time taken away from our families. The best approach is to discuss it with your partner early in the relationship to determine how committed she or he is to the cause(s). Perhaps she/he will want to volunteer alongside you, or at minimum, may be willing to support your being the activist. Ideally, every person in the family should, in one way or another, "sign off" on whatever activism you undertake.

I hope this book might encourage you to choose one cause to take up in your life: working against racism in our society, working against war policies, or both, for we are all children of our God. We belong to each other.

Appendix A

Voices of Ex-Slaves

Stories told by Former Slaves
in the United States
to WPA Interviewers in the 1930s

Excerpts from the Writings on Slavery by John Woolman
in the 18th century
A Quaker from Mount Holly, New Jersey[1]

"These are a people by whose labour the other inhabitants are in a great measure supported, and many of them in the luxuries of life. These are a people who have made no agreement to serve us and who have not forfeited their liberty that we know of. These are souls for whom Christ died, and for our conduct toward them we must answer before that Almighty Being who is no respecter of persons."

Journal of John Woolman, 1757

"We may further consider that they are now amongst us, and those of our nation the cause of their being here, that whatsoever difficulty accrues thereon we are justly chargeable with, and to bear all inconveniences attending it with a serious and weighty concern of mind to do our duty by them is the best we can do. To seek a remedy by continuing the oppression because we have power to do it and see others do will, I apprehend, not be doing as we would be done by."

---

1. Moulton, *Journal and Major Essays of John Woolman.* (Included by permission of the editor, Phillips Moulton.)

APPENDIX A: VOICES OF EX-SLAVES

John Woolman, "On Keeping Negroes," 1754

"I have been informed that there are a large number of Friends in your parts who have no slaves, and in tender and most affectionate love I now beseech you to keep clear from purchasing any. Look, my dear Friends, to divine providence, and follow in simplicity that exercise of body, that plainness and frugality, which true wisdom leads to; so may you be preserved from those dangers which attend such who are aiming at outward ease and greatness.

"Treasures, though small, attained on a true principle of virtue are sweet in the possession, and while we walk the light of the Lord there is true comfort and satisfaction. Here neither the murmurs of an oppressed people, nor throbbing, uneasy conscience, nor anxious thoughts about the event of things hinder the enjoyment of it."

Letter by John Woolman in 1757 to Quakers at their Monthly Meetings at New Garden and Cane Creek, North Carolina Journal of John Woolman, 1757

APPENDIX A: VOICES OF EX-SLAVES

Contents

Mrs. Hannah Davidson | 148
Frankie Goole | 152
Mrs. Georgina Giwbs | 156
"Uncle Joe" Clinton | 157
Carrie Bradley Logan Bennet | 159
An Ex-Slave | 161
Viney Baker | 162
Charlie Crump | 163
Charles Coles | 163
Reverend Williams | 164
An Ex-Slave | 167
Reverend Squire Dowd | 168
Clay Bobbit | 168
Mary Barbour | 169
Andrew Moss | 169
Mrs. Minnie Fulkes | 171
Belle Williams | 172
John Beckwith | 174
Belle Buntin | 175
Frank Fikes | 176
Lillie Baccus | 177
Tom Douglas | 178
Candis Goodwin | 179
Martha Allen | 182
Millie Simpkins | 183
Albert Jones | 184

Mrs. Hannah Davidson
Toledo, Ohio
(Interviewed by K. Osthimer on August 12, 1937)

It is with regret that Hannah Davidson recalls the shadows and sufferings of the past. She says, "It is best not to talk about them. The things that my sister May and I suffered were so terrible that people would not believe them. It is best not to have such things in our memory.

"My father and mother were Isaac and Nancy Meriwether. All the slaves went under the name of my master and mistress, Emmett and Susan Meriwether. I had four sisters and two brothers. There was Adeline, Dora, Alice, and Lizzie. My brothers were Major and George Meriwether. We lived in a log cabin made of sticks and dirt, you know, logs and dirt stuck in the cracks. We slept on beds made of boards nailed up.

"I don't remember anything about my grandparents. My folks were sold around and I couldn't keep track of them.

"The first work I did out from home was with my mistress's brother, Dr Jim Taylor, in Kentucky, taking care of his children. I was an awful tiny little somethin' about eight or nine years old. I used to turn the reel for the old folks who was spinning. That's all I've ever known—work.

"I never got a penny. My master kept me and my sister Mary twenty-two long years after we were supposed to be free. Work, work, work. I don't think my sister and I ever went to bed before twelve o'clock at night. We never got a penny. They could have spared it, too; they had enough.

"We ate corn bread and fat meat. Meat and bread, we kids called it. We all had a pint tin cup of buttermilk. No slaves had their own gardens.

"The men just wore jeans. The slaves all made their own clothes. They just wove all the time; the old women wove all the time. I wasn't old enough to go in the field like the oldest children. The oldest children, they worked. After slavery ended, my sister Mary and me worked as ex-slaves, and we worked. Most of the slaves had shoes, but us kids used to run barefoot most of the time.

"My folks, my master and mistress, lived in a great white frame house, just the same as a hotel. I grew up with the youngest child, Mayo. The other white children grew up and worked as overseers. Mayo always wanted me to call him "Master Mayo." I fought him all the time. I never would call him "Master Mayo." My mistress wouldn't let anyone harm me and she made Mayo behave.

"My master wouldn't let the poor white neighbors, no one, tell us we was free. The plantation was many, many acres, hundreds and hundreds of acres, honey. There were about 25 or 30 families of slaves. They got up and stood until daylight, waiting to plow. Yes'm child, they was up early. Our folks don't know how we had to work. I don't like to tell you how we were treated, how we had to work. It's best to brush those things out of our memory.

"If you wanted to go to another plantation, you had to have a pass. If my folks was going to somebody's house, they'd have to have a pass. Otherwise they'd be whipped. They'd take a big man and tie his hands behind a tree, just like that big tree outside, and whip him with a rawhide and draw blood every whip. I know I was scared every time I'd hear the slave say, 'Pray, Master.'

"Once, when I was milking a cow, I asked Master Ousley, 'Master Ousley, will you do me a favor?' He said in his drawl, 'Of course I will.' 'Take me to McCracken County,' I said. I didn't even know where McCracken County was, but my sister was there. I wanted to find my sister. When I reached the house where my sister stayed, I went through the gate. I asked if this was the house where Mary Meriwether lived. Her mistress said, 'Yes, she's in the back. Are you the girl Mr. Meriwether's looking for?' My heart was in my mouth. It just seemed I couldn't go through the gate. I never saw my sister that time. I hid for a while and then went back.

"We didn't have any churches. My master would come down Sunday morning with just enough flour to make bread. Coffee, too. Their coffee was parts of meal, corn and so on. Work all week and that's what they had for coffee.

"We used to sing, 'Swing low, sweet chariot.' When our folks sang that, we could really see the chariot.

"Once, Jim Ferguson, a colored man, came to teach school. The white folks beat and whipped him and drove him away in his underwear. I wanted so hard to learn to read, but I didn't even know I was free, even when slavery was ended.

"I been so exhausted working. I was like an inch-worm crawling along a roof. I worked till I thought another lick would kill me. If you had something to do you did it, or got whipped. Once I was so tired I couldn't work any more. I crawled in a hole under the house and stayed there till I was rested. I didn't get whipped, either.

"I never will forget it; how my master always used to say, 'Keep a nigger down!' I never will forget it. I used to wait on table and I heard 'em talk.

"The only fun we had was on Sunday evening, after work. That was the only chance we got. We used to go away off from the house and play in the haystack.

"Our folks was so cruel, the slaves used to whisper 'round. Some of them knew they was free, even if the white folks didn't want 'em to find out they was free. They went off in the woods sometimes. But I was just a little kid and I wasn't allowed to go around the big folks.

"I seen enough what the old folks went through. My sister and I went through enough after slavery was over. For 21 long years we were enslaved, even after we were supposed to be free. We didn't even know we were free. We had to wash the white people's feet when they took their shoes off at night, the man and woman.

"Sundays the slaves would wash out their clothes. It was the only time they had to themselves. Some of the old men worked in their tobacco patches. We never observed Christmas. We never had no holidays, son, no sir! We didn't know what the word was.

"I never saw any slave funerals. Some slaves died, but I never saw any of them buried. I didn't see any funerals at all.

"The white folks would come down to the cabins to marry the slaves. The master or mistress would read a little out of a book. That's all there was to it.

"We used to play a game called 'Hulgul.' We'd play it in the cabins and sometimes with the white children. We'd hold hazelnuts in our hands. I'd say 'Hulgul! How many?' You'd guess. If you hit it right, you'd get them all and it would be your turn to say 'Hulgul.' If you'd say 'Three!' and I only had two, you'd have to give me another to make three.

"The kids nowadays can go right to the store and buy a ball to play with. We'd have to make a ball out of yarn and put a sock around it for a cover. Six of us would stay on one side of a house and six on the other side. Then we'd throw the ball over the roof and say, 'Catch!' If you'd catch it you'd run around to the other side and hit somebody, then start over. We worked so hard, we couldn't play long on Sunday evenings.

"School? We never seen the inside of a schoolhouse. Mistress used to read the Bible to us every Sunday morning. We say two songs I still remember:

> I think when I read that sweet story of old,
> When Jesus was here among men,
> How he called little children like lambs to his fold,
> I should like to have been with them then.

> I wish that his hands had been placed on my head,

That his arms had been thrown around me,
That I might have seen his kind face when he said
Let the little ones come onto me.

Yet still to his footstool in prayer I may go
And ask for a share of his love,
And that I might earnestly seek him below
And see him and hear him above.

"Then there was another:

I want to be an angel
And with the angels stand
With a crown upon my forehead

And a harp within my hand.
And there before my Saviour,
So glorious and so bright,
I'd make the sweetest music
And praise him day and night.

"And as soon as we got through singing those songs, we had to get right out to work. I was always glad when they called us in the house to Sunday School. It was the only chance we'd get to rest.

"When the slaves got sick, they'd take and look after themselves. My master had a whole wall of his house for medicine, just like a store. They made their own medicines and pills. My mistress's brother, Dr. Jim Taylor, was a doctor. They done their own doctoring. I still have the mark where I was vaccinated by my master.

"People was lousy in them days. I always had to pick louses from the heads of the white children. You don't find children like that nowadays.

"My mistress had a little roan horse. She went all through the war on that horse. Us little kids never went around the big folks. We didn't watch folks' faces to learn, like children do now. They wouldn't let us. All I know about the Civil War was that it was goin' on. I heard talk about killin' and so on, but I didn't know nothin' about it.

"My mother was the last slave to get off the plantation. She traveled across the plantation all night with us children. It was pouring rain. The white folks surrounded her and took away us children, and gave her so many minutes to get off the plantation. We never saw her again. She died away from us.

"My brother came to see us once when slavery was over. He was grown up. My master wasn't going to let him see us and he took up his gun. My mistress said he should let him see us. My brother gave me a little coral ring. I thought it was the prettiest thing I ever saw.

"I made my sister leave. I took a rolling pin to make her go and she finally left. They didn't have any more business with us than you have right now.

"I remember when Yankee soldiers came riding through the yard. I was scared and ran away crying. I can see them now. Their swords hung at their sides and their horses walked proud, as if they walked on their hind legs. The master was in the field trying to hide his money and guns and things. The soldiers said, 'We won't hurt you, child.' It made me feel wonderful.

"What I call the Ku Klux were those people who met at night and if they heard anybody saying you was fece [fresh?], they would take you out at night and whip you. They were the plantation owners. I never saw them ride, but I heard about them and what they did. My master used to tell us he wished he knew who the Ku Kluxers were. But he knew, all right, I used to wait on table and I heard them talking. 'Gonna lynch another nigger tonight!'

"The slaves tried to get schools, but they didn't get any. Finally they started a few schools in little log cabins. But we children, my sister and I, never went to school.

"I married William L. Davidson, when I was 32 years old. That was after I left the plantation. I never had company there. I had to work. I have only one grandchild still living, Willa May Reynolds. She taught school in City Grove, Tennessee. She's married now.

"I thought Abe Lincoln was a great man. What little I know about him, I always thought he was a great man. He did a lot of good.

"Us kids always used to sing a song, 'Gonna hang Jeff Davis to a sour apple tree as we go marchin' home.' I didn't know what it meant at the time."

Frankie Goole
Nashville, Tennessee

"I was bawn in Smith County on other side ob Lebanon. I'll be 85 years ol' Christmas Day.

APPENDIX A: VOICES OF EX-SLAVES

"Mah ol' Missis was named Sallie, an' mah Marster was George Waters. Mah mammy's name was Lucindia. She was sold fum me when I was six weeks ol', an' mah missis raised me. I allus slept wid her. Mah missis was good ter me, but (her son) mah Marster whupped me.

"Dunno ob any ex-slaves votin' er holdin' office ob any kind.

"I 'member de Ku Klux Klan an' Pat-a-rollers [Patrollers]. Dey would come 'rounan' whup de niggers wid a bull whip. If'n dey met a niggah on de road dey'd say, 'Whar is you gwin dis time ob mawnin'?' De slaves would say, 'We is gwin ovuh yer ter stay awhile.' An' den dey would start beatin' dem. I'se stood in our door an' heard de hahd licks an' screams ob de ones dat was bein' whupped. An' I'd tell mah missis, 'Listen ter dat!' She would say, 'See dat is what will happen ter you if'n you try ter leave.' I 'member one night a Ku Klux Klan rode up ter our door. I tole mah Missis somebody was at de door wantin' ter know whar mah Marster was. She tole 'im he was dead an' her son had gone 'way dat mawnin'. He hunted all through de house, an' up in de loft, an' said, 'Whar is de niggers?' Mah missis tole 'im dey was down in de little house. He went down dere, woke 'em up, axed dem 'bout dere Marster an' den whupped all ob dem. If dey had de Ku Klux Klan now, dere wouldn't be so many people on de county road or in de open.

"I use ter drive up de cows, an' mah feet would be so col' an' mah toes cracked open an' bleedin', an' I'd be cryin' 'til I got almos' ter de house. Den I'd wipe mah eyes on de bottom ob mah dress, so de Marster wouldn' know dat I had been cryin'. He'd say, 'Frankie, ain't you cryin'?' I'd say, 'No, suh.' 'Is you col'?' 'Yes, suh.' He would say, 'Come in an' warm.'

"When de Niggers was freed, all ob mah Missis' slaves slipped 'way, 'cept me. One mawnin' she tol me ter go down an' wake dem up, I went an' knocked, nobody said nothin' . I pushed on de door, it come open, an' I fell in de room an' hurt mah chin. I went back ter Missis, an' she says, 'What is de matter wid you?' I says, 'Uncle John an' all ob dem is gone. I pushed on de door an' it fell in.' She says you know dey is not gone, go back an' git dem up. I had ter go back, but dey wer'ent dere.

"No, I don't 'member de stars fallin'.

"Mah Missis didn't gib me nothin', 'cept mah clothes, an' she put dem in a carpet bag. After freedom, mah mammy come frim Lebanon an' got me. I'll neber fergit dat day, Oh, Lawdy! I can see her now. Mah ol' Missis' daughter-in-law had got a bunch ob switches ter whup me. I was standin' in de door shakin' all ovuh, an' de young Missis was tellin' me ter git mah clothes off. I says, 'I see'd a 'oman comin' through de gate.' Mah Missis says, 'Dat is Lucindia.' An' de young Missis hid de switches. Mah mammy says, 'I'se come ter git mah chile.' Mah Missis tole her ter let me spend de night wid her, den she'd send me ter de Court House at 9 o'clock next mawnin'. So I stayed wid de Missis dat night, an' she tole me ter allus be a good girl, an' don't let a man er boy wip me. I didunt know what she mean but I allus 'members what she said. I guess I was 'bout 12 years or when l lef' mah Missis, an' mah mammy brought me ter Nashville an' put me ter wuk. De mawnin' I lef' mah Missis, I went ter de Court House an' met mah mammy. De Court room was jammed wid people. De Jedge tol' me ter hold my right hand up. I was so skeered I stuck both hands up. Jedge says, 'Frankie, is dat yo mammy?' I says, 'I dunno, she says she is.' (What did I know ob a mammy dat was tuk fum me at six weeks ol'.) He says, 'Was yo Marster good ter you?' I says, 'Mah Missis was, but mah Marster wasn't; he whupped me.' De Jedge said, 'Whar de he whup you?' I tole him on mah back. He says, 'Frankie, is you laughin'?' I says, 'No, sir.' He said ter mah mammy, 'Lucindia tek dis chile an' be good ter her fer she has been mistreated. Some day she can make a livin' for you.' (An' thank de Lawd I did keep her in her ol' days an' was able ter bury her.) At dat time money was called 'chin plaster.' An' when I lef' out ob de court room, diff'ent people gib me money, an' I had mah hat almos' full. Dat was de only money I had gib ter me.

"I nussed Miss Sadie Pope Fall. She married Mat Gardner. I also nussed Miss Sue Porter Houston. I den wuk'd at de Bline School.

"De fust pair oh shoes I eber had was after I come ter Nashville. Dey had high tops an' was called bootees. I had some red striped socks wid dem.

"De ol' songs I 'member: 'De Ole Time 'Ligion. I'm goin' ter join de ban.' When dey would sing dese songs, hit would almos' mek yo hair stand up on yo haid, de way dem peoples would jump an' shout!

"I 'member when some ob de slaves run 'way durin' slavery.

"I dunno any tales; mah mammy wasn't a 'oman ter talk much. Maybe if she had been, I would hab had an easier time. As far as I know, de exslaves hab had diff'ent kinds ob wuk since dere freedom. No, I ain't neber see'd any ghos'. I'se bin in de woods an' dark places, but didn't see nothin', an' I'se not goin' ter say I did, cause I might git par'lized.

"I went ter school one year at Fisk, in de year 1869.

"De last man I wuk'd fer was at de Link Hotel. Den I started keepin' boarders. Hab fed all dese Nashville police. De police is de ones dat hep'd git dese relief orders fer me. I hab lived on dis street fer 60 years. I lived 22 years whar de Hermitage laundry is. Dat is whar I got de name, 'Mammie.' Whiles livin' dere I raised 18 chilluns, white an' black, an' some ob dem is good ter me now.

"I had some papahs 'bout mah age an' diff'ent things, but w'en de back waters got up, dey got lost. I didn't hab ter move but I kep prayin' an' talkin' ter de Lawd an' I b'lieve he 'yeard me fer de water didn't git in mah house

"I 'member w'en de yellow fever an' de cholera was here, in 1870 an' 1873. Dey didn't hab coffins nuff ter put dem in, so dey used boxes an' piled de boxes in wagons lak haulin' wood.

"I'se ain't worth a dime now w'en hit comes ter wukin' fer I'se ain't able ter do nothin, though I can't complain ob mah livin' since de relief has bin takin' keer ob me.

"Dis young peoples, Oh, mah Lawd! Dey ain' worth talkin' 'bout. I tries ter shame dese 'omen; dey drink (I call hit ol' bust-haid whiskey), an' do such mean things. I'se disgusted at mah own color. Dey try ter know ter much, an' dunno nothin', an' dey don' do 'nuff wuk.

"I nebber voted an' dunno nothin' 'bout hit. Hab nebber had any frens in office. Cain' 'member nothin' 'bout re'struction. I hab been sick an' still don' feel right. Sometimes I feels crazy.

"Hab bin tol' dat black cat crossin' road in front ob you was bad luck. I nebber did b'lieve in any signs. If I is ter hab bad luck, ah'll hab hit.

"I b'long ter de Baptist Church. De colored peoples use ter hab camp meetin's, an' dey'd last fer two weeks. Lawd hab mercy, did we hab a time at dem meetin's—preachin', singin', an' shoutin'. An' ovuh some whar neah dey would be cookin' mutton an' diff'ent good things ter eat. Some ob dem would shout 'til dere throats would be sore, an' hit seemed dat some ob dem niggahs didn't keer if dey got home ter wuk er not.

"I sometimes wish fer de good ol' days. Dese days folks don't hab time fer 'ligion. De dog-gone ol' radio an' udder things is taking' hits place.

"Oh Lawdie, how dey did baptize down at de wharf! De Baptist people would gather at de wha'f on de fust Sunday in May. Dey would come fum all de Baptist chu'ches. Would leave de chu'ch singin' an' shoutin' an' keep dat up 'til dey got ter de river. Hab seen dem wid new clothes on git down on de groun' an' roll an' git covered wid dirt. Some ob dem would almos' lose dere clothes, an' dey'd fall down lak dey was dying.

"Dese last few y'ars dey hab got ter stylish ter shout."

Mrs. Georgina Giwbs
707 Lindsey Avenue, Portsmouth, Virginia
(Interviewed by Thelma Dunston on January 15, 1937)

"All of de cloth during slavery time was made on de loom. My mastah had three slaves who worked in de house. After de cloth was made, mastah sent hit over town to a white woman who made hit into clothes. We had to knit all our stockings and gloves. We'd plait blades of wheat to make us bonnets. We had to wear wooden bottom shoes. Der weren't no stores, so we growed everything we et, an' we'd make everything we'd wear.

"We had a washing house. Der was five women who done de washing an' ironing. Dey had to make de soap. Dat was done by letting water drip over oak ashes. Dis made oak ash lye, and dis was used in making soap. After de clothes had soaked in dis lye-soap and water, dey put de clothes on tables and beat 'em 'till dey was white.

"Mastah give us huts to live in. De beds was made of long boards dat was nailed to de wall. De mattress was stuffed wif straw and pine tages. De only light we had was from de fireplace. We didn't use no matches, 'stead we'd strick a rock on a piece of steel. We'd let the sparks fall on some cotton.

"My mastah had 'bout 500 slaves. He'd never sell none of his slaves, but he'd always buy more. Dat keeps de slaves from marrying in dere famblies. When yer married, yer had to jump over a broom three times. Dat was de license. If mastah seen two slaves together too much he would marry them. Hit didn't make no difference if yer won't but 14 years old.

"Work began at sunrise and last 'till sundown. When I was eight years old, I started working in de field wif two paddles to keep de crows from eatin' de crops. We had a half day off on Sunday, but you won't 'lowed to visit. Sometimes de men slaves would put logs in de beds, and dey'd cover 'em up, den dey go out. Mastah would see de logs and think dey was de slaves.

"My father told me dere was once a mastah who sold a slave woman and her son. Many years after dis, de woman married. One day when she was washing her husband's back she seen a scar on his back. De woman 'membered de scar. It was de scar her mastah had put on her son. 'Course dey didn't stay married, but de woman wouldn't ever let her son leave her."

"Uncle Joe" Clinton
Marvell, Arkansas [1]

"Uncle Joe" Clinton, an ex-Mississippi slave, lives on a small farm that he owns a few miles north of Marvell, Arkansas. His wife has been dead for a number of years. He has only one living child, if indeed his boy, Joe, who left home 15 years ago for Chicago and from whom no word has been received since, is still alive. Due to the infirmities of age, "Uncle Joe" is unable to work and obtains his support from the income received off the small acreage he rents each year to the Negro family with whom he lives. Seated in an old cane-bottomed chair "Uncle Joe" was dozing in the warm sunshine of an afternoon in early October as I passed through the gate leading into the small yard enclosing his cabin. Arousing himself on my approach, the old Negro offered me a chair. I explained the purpose of my visit and this old man told me the following story:

"I'se now past 86 year ol', an' was borned in Panola County, Mississippi, 'bout three miles from Saris. My ol' mars was Mark Childress, an' he sure owned a heap of peoples, womens an' men bofe, an' jus' gangs of chillun. I was real small when us lived in Panola County; how-same-ever I riccolect it well when us all lef' dar and ol' mars sold out his land and took us all to de delta where he had bought a big plantation 'bout two or three miles wide in Coahoma County not far from Friar Point. De very place dat my mars bought and dat us moved to is what dey call now, de 'Clover Hill Plantation'. The fust year dat us lived in de delta, us stayed on de place what dey called de 'Swan Lake Place'. Dat place is over dere close to Jonestown and de very place dat Mr. Billy Jones and his son John bought, an' dat's zackly how come dat town git its name. It was named for Mr. John Jones.

"My mars, Mark Childress, he never was married. He was a bachelor, an' I'se tellin' you dis, boss, he was a good, fair man, and no fault was to be found wid him. But dem overseers dat he had, dey was real mean. Dey was cruel, least one of them was 'bout de cruelest white man dat I is ever seen. Dat was Harvey Brown. Mars had a nephew what lived with him names Mark Sillers. He was mars' sister's son and was named for mars. Mr. Mark Sillers, he helped with de runnin' of the place, an' sich time dat mars 'way from home, Mr. Mark he the real boss den.

"Mr. Harvey Brown, the overseer, he mean sure 'nough, I tell you, and de onliest thing that keep him from beatin' de niggers up all de time would be old mars or Mr. Mark Sillers. Bofe of dem was good and kind most all de time. One time dat I remembers, ol' mars, he gone back to Panola County for somepin', an' Mr. Mark Sillers, he attend in' de camp meeting. That was de day dat Mr. Harvey Brown come mighty nigh killin' Henry. I'll tell you how dat was, boss. It was on Monday morning that it happened. De Friday before dat Monday morning, all of de hands had been pickin' cotton and Mr. Harvey Brown didn't think dat Henry had picked enough cotton dat day an' so he give Henry er lashin' out in de field. Dat night, Henry he git mad and burn up his sack and runned off and hid in de canebreak 'long de bayou all of de nex' day. Mr. Harvey, he missed Henry from de field an' sent Jeff an' Randall to find him and bring him in. Dey found Henry real soon an' tell him iffen he don't come on back to de field dat Mr. Harvey gwine to set de hounds on him. So Henry he comed on back den 'cause de niggers was skeered of dem wild bloodhounds what they would set on 'em when dey try to run off. . .

"My mars, he didn't go to de War, but he sure sent er lot er corn, an' he sent erbout 300 head er big, fat hogs one time dat I 'members. Den too, he sent somepin' like 20 or 30 niggers to de Confedrites in Georgia. I 'members it well de time dat he sent dem niggers. They was all younguns, 'bout grown, an' dey was skeered to death to be leavin' an' goin' to de War. Dey didn't know but what dey gwine make 'em fight. But mars tol' 'em dat dey just gwine to work diggin' trenches an' sich. But dey didn't want to go nohow, an' Jeff an' Randall, they runned off an' come back home all de way from Georgia an' mars let 'em stay.

"Boss, you has heered me tellin' dat my mars was er good, kine man an' dat his overseer, Mr. Harvey Brown, was terrible cruel, an' mean, an' would beat de niggers up every chance he git, an' you ask me how come it was dat de mars would have sich a mean man er working for him. Now I'se gwine to tell you de reason. You know de truth is de light, boss, an' dis is de truth that I'se gwine to say. Mars, he in love with Mr. Harvey Brown's wife, Miss Mary, and Miss Mary's young daughter, she was mars' chile. Yas, suh, she was dat. She wasn't no kin er tall to Mr. Harvey Brown. Her name was Miss Markis, dat's what it was. Mars had done willed dat chile er big part of his property and a whole gang of niggers. He was gwine give her Tolliver, Beckey, Aunt Mary, Austin, an' Savannah, an' er heap more 'sides dat. But de War, it come on an' broke Mars up , an' all de darkies set free, an' atter dat, I heered Mr. Harvey Brown an' Miss Mary, and de young lady Miss Markis, dey moved up North some place, an' I ain't never heared no more from dem.

"Mr. Clarke and Mrs. Clarke what de town of Clarksdale is named for, dey lived not far from our place. I knowed dem well. Albert, one of mars' darkies, married Cindy, one of Mr. Clarke's women. General Forrest, I know, you is heered of him. I speck he 'bout de bes' general in de War. He sure was a fine-looking man, an' he wore a beard on he face. De general, he had a big plantation down dere in Coahoma County where he would come ever so offen. A lot of times he would come to our place an' take dinner wid ol' Mars, an' I would be er waitin' on de table er takin' dem de toddies on de front gallery where dey talkin' 'bout dey business."

Carrie Bradley Logan Bennet
Helena, Arkansas
(Interviewed by Miss Irene Robertson)

"I was born not a great piece from Mobile but it was in Mississippi in the country. My mother b'long to Massa Tom Logan. He was a horse trader. He got drowned in 1863, durin' the War, the old war. His wife was Miss Liza Jane. They had several children, and some gone from home I jus' seed when they be on visits home. The ones at home I can recollect was Tiney, John, Bill, and Alex. I played wid Tiney and nursed Bill, and Alex was a baby when Massa Tom got drowned.

"We never knowed how Massa Tom got drowned. They brought him home and buried him. His horse come home. He had been in the water—water was froze on the saddle. They said it was water soaked. They thought he swum the branch. Massa Tom drunk some. We never did know what did happen. I didn't know much 'bout 'em.

"We had two or three families of slaves. Ma cooked, washed and. ironed for all on the place. She went to the field in busy times. Three of the men drove horses, tended to 'em. They fed 'em and curried and sheared 'em. Ma said Massa Tom sure thought a heap of his niggers and fine stock. They'd bring in three or four droves of horses and mules, care for 'em, take 'em out, sell 'em. They go out and get droves, feed 'em up till they looked like different from what you see come there. He'd sell 'em in the early part of the year. He did make money. I know he must er. My pa was the head blacksmith on Massa Tom's place; them other men helped him along.

"I heard ma say no better-hearted man ever live than Massa Tom if you catch him sober. He give his men a drink whiskey 'round every once in a while. I don't know what Miss Liza Jane could do 'bout it. She never said nothin' as ever I knowed. They sent apples off to the press and all of us drunk much cider when it come home as we could hold, and had some long as it lasts. It turn to vinegar. I heard my pa laughing 'bout the time Massa had the Blue Devils. He was p'isoned well as I understood it. It had er been on whiskey and something else. I never knowed it. His men had to take keer of 'im. He acted so much like he be crazy they laughed 'bout whats he do. He got over it.

"Old mistress—we all called her Miss Liza Jane—whooped us when she wanted to. She brush us all wid the broom, tell us go build a play house. Children made the prettiest kinds of play houses them days. We made the walls out er bark sometimes. We jus' marked it off on the ground back of the smokehouse. We'd ride and bring up the cows. We'd take them to a mill. It was the best hoecake bread can be made . . .

"We had plenty to eat, jus' common eatin'. We had good cane molasses at the time. The clothes was thin 'bout all time 'ceptin' when they be new. We got new clothes in the fall of the year. They last till the next year.

"I never seed Massa Tom whoop nobody. I seen Miss Liza Jane turn up little children's dresses and whoop 'em with a little switch, and her hand. She 'most blister you wid her bare hand. Plenty things we done to get whuppin's. We leave the gates open, we'd run the cows and try to ride 'em, we'd chunk at the geese. One thing that make her mad was for us to climb up in her fruit trees and break off a limb. She wouldn't let us be eating the green fruit mostly 'cause it would make us sick. They had plenty trees. We had plenty fruit to eat when it was ripe. Massa Tom's little colored boys have big ears. He'd pull 'em every time he pass one of 'em. He didn't hurt 'em, but it might have made their ears stick out. They all had big ears. He never slapped nobody, as ever I heard 'bout.

"I don't know how my parents was sold. I'm sure they was sold. Pa's name was Jim Bradley. He come from one of the Carolinas. Ma was brought to Mississippi from Georgia. All the name I heard for her was Ella Logan. When freedom come on, I heard pa say he thought he stand a chance to find his folks and them to find him if he be called Bradley. He did find some of his brothers, and ma had some of her folks out in Mississippi. They come out here hunting places to do better. They wasn't no Bradleys. I was little and I don't recollect their names. Seem lack one family we called Aunt Mandy Thornton. One was Aunt Tillie and Uncle Mack. They wasn't Thorntons. I knows that.

"My folks was black, black as I is. Pa was stocky, guinea man. Ma was heap the biggest. She was raw bony and tall. I love to see her wash. She could bend 'round the easier ever I seed anybody. She could beat the clothes in a hurry. She put out big washings, on the bushes and a cord they wove, and on the fences. They had paling fence 'round the garden.

"Massa Tom didn't have a big farm. He had a lot of mules and horses at times. They raised some cotton, but mostly corn and oats. Miss Liza Jane left b'fore us. We all cried when she left. She shut up the house and give the wornen folks all the keys. We lived on what she left there and went on raising more hogs and tending to the cows. We left everything. We come to Hernando, Mississippi. Pa farmed up there and run his blacksmith shop on the side. My parents died close to Horn Lake. Mama was the mother of ten and I am the mother of eight. I got two living, one here and one in Memphis. I lives wid 'em, and one niece in Natchez I live with some.

"I was scared to death of the Ku Klux Klan. They come to our house one night and I took my little brother and we crawled under the house and got up in the fireplace. It was big 'nough fer us to sit. We went to sleep. We crawled out next day. We seen 'em coming, run behind the house and crawled under there. They knocked about there a pretty good while. We told the folks about it. I don't know where they could er been. I forgot, it been so long. I was 'fraider of the Ku Klux Klan den I ever been 'bout snakes. No snakes 'bout our house—too many of us.

"I tried to get some aid when it first come 'bout, but I quit. My children and my niece take keer er me. I ain't wantin' fer nothin' but good health. I never do feel good. I done wore out. I worked in the field all my life.

"A heap of dis young generation is triflin' as they can be. They don't half work. Some do work hard, and no 'pendence to be put in some 'em. Course they steal fo' dey work. I say some of 'em work. Times done got so fer 'head of me I never 'speck to ketch up. I never was scared of horses. I sure is of dese automobiles. I ain't plannin' no rides on them airplanes. Sure you born, I ain't! Folks ain't acting lack they used to. They say, so I got all I can get, you can no dout. It didn't used to be no sich way. Times is heap better, but heap of folks is worse an' ever folks been before."

An Ex-Slave
(Name not known)

"Mama said she was sold once, away from her mother, but they let her have her four children. She grieved for her old mama, 'fraid she would have a hard time. She sold for one thousand dollars. She said that was half price, but freedom was coming on. She never laid eyes on her mama ag'in.

"After freedom, they had gone to another place and the man owned the place run the Ku Klux off. They come there and he told them to go away. If he need them he would call them back out there. They never come back, she said. They was scared to death of the Ku Klux. At the place where they was freed, all the farm bells rung slow for freedom. That was for miles about. Their master told them up at his house. He said it was sad thing, no time for happiness—they hadn't 'sperienced it—but for them to come back he would divide long as what he had lasted. They didn't go off right at first. They was several years getting broke up. Some went, some stayed, some actually moved back. Like bees trying to find a setting place. Seem like they couldn't get to be satisfied even being free.

"I had eleven children my own self. I let the plough fly back and hit me once and now I got a tumor there. I love to plough. I got two children living. She comes to see me. She lives across over here. I don't hear from my boy. I reckon he living. I gets help from the relief on account I can't work much with this tumor."

Viney Baker
South Harrington Street, Raleigh, North Carolina
(Interviewed by Mary A. Hicks)

"My mammy was Hannah Murray, an' so fur as I know I ain't got no father, tho I reckon dat he was de plantation stock nigger. I was borned in Virginia, as yo' might say ter my marster Mr. S. L. Allen.

"We moved when I was little ter Durham County whar we fared bad. We ain't had nothin' much ter eat aftr' ter war. He had a hundert slaves, an' I reckon five hundert acres o' lan', He made us wuck hard, de little ones included.

"One night I lay down on de straw mattress wid my mammy, an' de nex' mo'nin I woked up an' she was gone. When I axed 'bout her I fin's dat a speculator comed dar de night before an' wanted ter buy a 'oman. Dey had come an' got my mammy widout wakin' me up. I had always been glad somehow dat I was asleep.

"Dey uster tie me ter a tree an' beat me till de blood run down my back. I don' 'member nothin' dat I done. I jist 'members de whuppin's. Some of de rest was beat wuser dan I was too, an' I uster scream dat I was sho' dyin'.

"Yes'm, I seed de Yankees go by, but dey ain't bodder us none. 'Case dey knows dat 'hind ever bush jist about, a Confederate soldier pints a gun.

"I warn't glad at de surrender, 'case I don' understand hit. An' de [Master] Allen's keeps me right on, an' whups me wuser dan eber.

"I reckon I was twelve years old when my mammy come ter de house an' axes Mis' Allen ter let me go spen' de weeken' wid her. Mis' Allen can't say no, 'case mammy might go ter de carpet baggers so she lets me go fer de weeken'. Mammy laughs Sunday when I says somethin' 'bout goin' back. Naw, I stayed on wid my mammy, an' I ain't seed Mis' Allen no mo'."

Charlie Crump
near Cary, North Carolina

"I was borned at Evans Ferry in Lee or Chatham County, an' I belonged ter Mr. Davis Abernathy an' his wife Mis' Vick. My pappy was named Ridge, an' my mammy was named Marthy. My brothers was Stokes an' Tucker, an' my sisters was Lula an' Liddy Ann. Dar was nine o' us in all, but some o' dem was sold, an' some o' dem was dead.

"De Abernathys wasn't good ter us. We got very little ter eat, nothin' ter wear, an' a whole lot of whuppin's. Dey ain't had no slaves 'cept seben or eight. In fact, dey was poor white trash tryin' ter git rich. So dey make us wuck.

"Dey wucks us from daylight till dark, an' sometimes we jist gits one meal a day. De Marster says dat empty niggers am good niggers, an' dat full niggers has got de debil in dem.

"An' we ain't 'lowed ter go nowhar at night, dat is, if dey knowed it. I'se seed de time dat niggers from all ober de neighborhood gang up an' have fun anyhow, but if dey hyard de patterollers comin' gallop in' on a hoss, dey'd fly. Crap shootin' was de style den, but a heap of times dey can't find nothin' ter bet."

Charles Coles
1106 Sterling Street, Baltimore, Maryland

"I was born near Pisgah, a small village in the western part of Charles County, about 1851. I do not know who my parents were, nor my relatives. I was reared on a large farm owned by a man by the name of Silas Dorsey, a fine Christian gentleman, and a member of the Catholic Church.

"Mr. Dorsey was a man of excellent reputation and character, was loved by all who knew him, black and white, especially his slaves. He was never known to be harsh or cruel to any of his slaves, of which he had more than 75.

"The slaves were Mr. Dorsey's family group. He and his wife were very considerate in all their dealings. In the winter, the slaves wore good heavy clothes and shoes, and in summer they were dressed in fine clothes.

"I have been told that the Dorseys' farm contained about 3,500 acres, on which were 75 slaves. We had no overseers. Mr. and Mrs. Dorsey managed the farm. They required the farm hands to work from 7 AM to 6 PM. After that, their time was their own.

"There were no jails nor was any whipping done on the farm. No one was bought or sold. Mr. and Mrs. Dorsey conducted regular religious services of the Catholic church on the farm in a chapel erected for that purpose, and in which the slaves were taught the catechism. And some learned how to read and write, and were assisted by some Catholic priests who came to the farm on church holidays and on Sundays for that purpose.

"When a child was born, it was baptized by the priest, and given names, and they were recorded in the Bible. We were taught the rituals of the Catholic church, and when anyone died, the funeral was conducted by a priest. The corpse was buried in the Dorseys' graveyard, a lot of about 1-1/2 acres, surrounded by cedar trees and well cared for. The only difference in the graves was that the Dorsey people had marble markers and the slaves had plain stones.

"I have never heard of any of the Dorseys' slaves running away. We did not have any trouble with the white people.

"The slaves lived in good quarters, each house was weather-boarded and stripped to keep out the cold. I do not remember whether the slaves worked or not on Saturdays, but I know the holidays were their own. Mr. Dorsey did not have dances and other kinds of antics that you expected to find on other plantations.

"We had many marbles and toys that poor children had. In that day, my favorite game was marbles. When we took sick, Mr. and Mrs. Dorsey had a doctor who administered to the slaves, giving medical care that they needed. I am still a Catholic, and will always be a member of St. Peter Clavier Church."

Reverend Williams
Lebanon, Ohio
(Interviewed by Miriam Logan)

"I was born on the estate of Miss Frances Cree, my mother's mistress. She had set my grandmother Delilah free with her sixteen children, so my mother was free when I was born, but my father was not.

"My father was butler to General Davis, nephew of Jefferson Davis. My father, Allen Williams, was not free until the Emancipation.

"Grandmother Delilah belonged to Dr. Cree. Upon his death and the division of his estate, his maiden daughter came into possession of my grandmother, you understand. Miss Frances nor her brother Mr. Cam never married. Miss Frances was very religious, a Methodist; and she believed Grandmother Delilah should be free, and that we colored children should have schooling.

"Yes, ma'am, we colored people had a church down there in West Virginia, and grandmother Delilah had a family Bible of her own. She had fourteen boys and two girls. My mother had sixteen children, two boys, and fourteen girls. Of them—mother's children, you understand-there were seven teachers and two ministers. All were educated, thanks to Miss Frances and to Miss Sands of Gallipolis [Ohio]. Mother lived to be 97 years old. No, she was not a cook.

"In the south, you understand, there is the Colored M. E. Church and the African M. E.-Church, and the Southern Methodist and Methodist Episcopal Churches of the white people. They say there will be a Union Methodist of both white and colored people, but I don't believe there will be, for there is a great difference in beliefs, even today. Southern Methodist do believe in slavery, while the Methodist to which Miss Frances Cree belonged did not believe in slavery. The Davis family (one of the finest) did believe in slavery and they were good Southern Methodists. Mr. Cam, Miss Frances' brother, was not so opposed to slavery as was Miss Frances. Miss Frances willed us to the care of her good Methodist friend Miss Eliza Sands of Ohio.

"Culture loosens prejudice. I do not believe in social equality at all myself; it cannot be. But we all must learn to keep to our own road, and bear Christian good will towards each other.

"I do not know of any colored people who are any more superstitious than are white people. They have the advantages of education now, equally, and are about on the same level. Of course, illiterate whites and the illiterate colored man are apt to believe in charms. I do not remember of hearing of any particular superstitions among my church people that I could tell you about. No, ma'am, I do not.

"In church music, I hold that the good old hymns of John and of Charles Wesley are the best to be had. I don' like shouting Spirituals, show-off, and carrying on-never did encourage it! Inward Grace will come out in your singing more than anything else you do, and the impression we carry away from your song and from the singer are what I count. Read well, sing correctly; but first, last, remember real inward Grace is what shows forth the most in a song.

"In New Orleans where I went to school (graduated in 1887 from the Freedman's Aid College), there were 14 or 15 colored churches (Methodist) in my youth. New Orleans is one-third colored in population, you understand. Some places in the south, the colored out-number the whites 30 to 1.

"I pastored St. Paul's church in Louisville, a church of close to 3,000 members. No, ma'am, can't say just how old a church it is.

"To live a consecrated life, you'd better leave off dancing, drinking, smoking, and the movies. I've never been to a movie in my life. When I hear some of the programs colored folks put on the radio, sometimes I feel just like going out to the woodshed and getting my axe and chopping up the radio, I do! It's natural and graceful to dance, but it is not natural or good to mill around in a low-minded smoky dance hall.

"I don't hold it right to put anybody out of church, no, ma'am. No matter what they do, I don't believe in putting anybody out of church.

"My mother and her children were sent to Miss Eliza Sands at Gallipolis, Ohio after Miss Frances Cree's death, at Miss Frances' request. Father did not go, no, ma'am. He came later and finished his days with us. We went first to Point Pleasant, then up the river to Gallipolis.

"After we got there we went to school. A man got me a place in Cincinnati when I was twelve years old. I blacked boots and ran errands of the hotel office until I was thirteen. Then I went to the Freedman's Aid College in New Orleans; remained until I graduated.

"Shoemaking and carpentering were given to me for trades, but as a young fellow I shipped on a freighter plying between New Orleans and Liverpool, thinking I would like to be a seaman. I was a mean tempered boy. As cook's helper one day, I got mad at the boatswain—threw a pan of hot grease on him. The crew wanted to put me into irons, but the captain said 'no, leave him in Liverpool soon as we land, in about a day or two.' When I landed there, they left me to be deported back to the States according to law.

"Yes, I had an aunt live to be 112 years old. She died at Granville, Ohio, some thirty years ago. We know her age from a paper on Dr. Cree's estate where she was listed as a child of twelve, and that had been one hundred years before.

"About the music now, you see, I'm used to thinking of religion as the working out of life in good deeds, not just a singing-show-off kind. Some of the Spirituals are fine, but still I think Wesley hymns are best. I tell my folks that the good Lord isn't a deaf old gentleman that has to be shouted up to, or amused. I do think we colored people are a little too apt to want to show off in our singing sometimes.

"I was very small when we went away from Greenbriar County to Point Pleasant, and from there to Gallipolis by wagon. I do remember Mr. Cam Cree. I was tearing around the front lawn where he didn't want me; he was cross. I remember somebody taking me around the house, and that's all—all that I can remember of the old Virginia home where my folks had belonged for several generations.

"I've pastored large churches in Louisville and St. Louis. In Ohio, I have been at Glendale, and at Oxford, other places. This old place was for sale on the court house steps one day when I happened to be in Lebanon. Five acres, yes, ma'am.

"There's the cornerstone with 1822, age of the house. My sight is poor, can't read, so I do not try to preach anymore. But I help in church in any way that I am needed; keep busy and happy always.

"I am able to garden and enjoy life every day. Certainly, my life has been a fortunate one in my mother's belonging to Miss Frances Cree. I have been a minister some forty years. I graduated from Wilberforce College."

An Ex-Slave

"Niggers had to go through thick an' thin in slavery time, with rough rations most of de time, wid jes' enough clothin' to make out wid. Our houses were built of logs an' covered wid slabs. Dey was 'rived out of blocks of trees, about 3 x 6 and 8 feet in length. De chimleys was built of sticks and mud, den a coat of clay mud daubed over 'em. De cracks in de slave houses was daubed wid mud too.

"We worked from sun to sun. If we had a fire in cold weather where we was workin', marster or de overseer would come an' put it out. We et frozen meat an' bread many times in cold weather. After de day's work in de fields was over, we had a task of pickin' de seed from cotton till we had two ounces of lint, or spin two ounces of cotton on a spinnin' wheel. I spun cotton on a spinnin' wheel. Dats de way people got clothes in slavery time.

"I can't read an' write, but dey learned us to count. Dey learned us to count dis way. 'Ought is an ought, an' a figger is a figger; all for de white man an' nothin' fer de nigger.' Hain't you heard people count dat way?

"Dey sold slaves jes' like people sell hosses now. I saw a lot of slaves sold on de auction block. Dey would strip 'em stark naked. A nigger scarred up or whaled an' welted up was considered a bad nigger an' did not bring much . . ."

Reverend Squire Dowd
202 Battle Street, Raleigh, N.C.

"My name is Squire Dowd, and I was born April 3, 1855. My mother's name was Jennie Dowd. My father's name was Elias Kennedy. My mother died in Georgia at the age of 70, and my father died in Moore County at the age of 82. I attended his funeral. My sister and her husband had carried my mother to Georgia, when my sister's husband went there to work in turpentine. My mother's husband was dead. She had married a man named Stewart. You could hardly keep up with your father during slavery time. It was a hard thing to do. There were few legal marriages. When a young man from one plantation courted a young girl on the plantation, the master married them, sometimes hardly knowing what he was saying.

"My master was General W. D. Dowd. He lived three miles from Carthage, in Moore County, North Carolina. He owned fifty slaves. The conditions were good. I had only ten years experience, but it was a good experience. No man is fool enough to buy slaves to kill. I have never known a real slave owner to abuse his slaves. The abuse was done by patterrollers [patrollers] and overseers.

"Negro women having children by the masters was common. My relatives on my mother's side, who were Kellys are mixed blooded. They are partly white. We, the darkies and many of the whites, hate that a situation like this exists. It is enough to say that seeing is believing. There were many that are now mixed blooded people among the race."

Clay Bobbit
Harrington Street, Raleigh, N.C.
(Interviewed on May 27,1937)

"I was borned May 2, 1837 in Warren County to Washington an' Delisia Bobbit. Our Marster was named Richard Bobbit, but we all calls him Massa Dick.

"Massa Dick ain't good ter us, an' on my arm hyar, jist above de elbow am a big scar dis day whar he whupped me wid a cowhide. He ain't whupped me fer nothin' 'cept dat I is a nigger. I had a whole heap of dem whuppins, mostly case I won't obey his orders an' I'se seed slaves beat 'most ter deth.

"I was married onct 'fore de war by de broom stick ceremony, lak all de rest of de slaves was but, shucks, dey sold away my wife 'fore we'd been married a year, an' den de war come on.

"Massa Dick owned a powerful big plantation an' ober a hundert slaves, an' we wucked on short rations an' went nigh naked.

"We ain't gone swimmin' ner huntin' ner nothin' an' we ain't had no pleasures less we runs away ter hab 'em. Eben when we sings we had ter turn down a pot in front of de do' ter ketch de noise.

"I knowed some poor white trash. Our oberseer was one, an' de 'shim shams' [free issues or Negroes of mixed blood] was nigh 'bout also. We ain't had no use fer none of 'em an' we shorely ain't carin' whether dey has no use fer us er not."

Mary Barbour
801 S. Bloodworth Street, Raleigh, N.C.

"I reckon dat I was borned in McDowell County, case dat's whar my mammy, Edith, lived. She 'longed ter Mr. Jefferson Mitchell dar, an' my pappy 'longed ter Mr. Jordan in Avery County, so he said.

"'Fore de war, I don' know nothin' much 'cept dat we lived on a big plantation an' dat my mammy wucked hard, but was treated pretty good.

"We had our little log cabin off ter one side, an' my mammy had sixteen chilluns. Fas' as dey got three years old de marster sol' 'em till de las' four dat she had wid her durin' de war. I was de oldes' o' dese four; den dar was Henry an' den de twins, Liza an' Charlie."

Andrew Moss
88 Auburn Street, Knoxville, Tennessee

"One ting dat's all wrong wid dis world today," according to Andrew Moss, aged Negro, as he sits through the winter days before an open grate fire in his cabin, with his long, lean fingers clasped over his crossed knees, "is dat dey ain' no 'prayer grounds.' Down in Georgia what I was born, dat was way back in 1852, us colored folks had prayer grounds. My Mammy's was a ol' twisted thick-rooted imscadine bush. She'd go in dar and pray for deliverance of de slaves. Some colored folks cleaned out knee-spots in de cane brakes. Cane, you know, grows high and thick, and colored folks could hide de seves in dar, an' nobody could see an' pester 'em.

"You see it was jes like dis. Durin' de war, an befo' de war too, white folks make a heap o' fun of de colored folks for all time prayin'. Sometime, say, you was a slave 'an you git down to pray in de field or by de side of de road. White marster come 'long and see a slave on his knees. He say, 'What you prayin' 'bout?' An' you say, 'Oh, Marster, I'se jes prayin' to Jesus 'cause I wants to go to Heaven when I dies.' An' Marster say, 'Youse my negro. I git ye to Heaven. Git up off'n your knees.'

"De white folks what owned slaves thought that when dey go to Heaven de colored folks would be dar to wait on 'em. An ef'n it was a Yank come 'long, he say too, 'What you prayin' 'bout?' You gives de same 'sponse. An' he say, ' We'se gwine save you. We goin' to set you free. You wants to be free, don't you?' 'Yes sir, boss!' 'Well den,' Yank say, 'come go 'long wid me. Ain' no use keep sayin' please sir, Boss. I'll have to arsk my Marster.' Yank say, 'What you mean, 'Marster '? You ain't got no Marster. We're settin' you free!'

"Sometimes dey takes a tie a rope 'round you, and they starts ridin' off but dey don't go too fas' so you walks behind. Sometimes 'long comes another Yank on a horse an' he arsk, 'Boy, ain' you tired?' 'Yes sir, Boss!' 'Well den, you git up here behind me and ride some.' Den he wrop de rope 'round de saddle horn, but leaves some slack. But he keeps you tied, so's you won't jump down and run away. An many's de time a prayin' negro got took off like dat, and want never seen no more.

"Course, ef'n you goes wid 'em, you 'member your trainin' and 'fore you leaves de field, you stacks your hoe nice, like you was quittin' de days work. Dey learned the little'uns to do dat, soon's dey begins to work in de fields. Dey had little hoes, handles 'bout de size of my arm for de little fellers. I've walked many a mile, when I was, a little feller, up and down de rows, follow in' de grown folks, an' choppin' wid de hoe 'round de corner whar de earth was soft so de little uns could hoe easy. Whoopee! Let dat dinner horn blow, and evybody stacks dey hoes, nice, neat stacks standin' up, and starts to run. Some eats in dey own cabins, but dem what eats at de big house, sets down at a long table, and gets good grub too! Evy night, our Marster give us evyone a glass o ' whiskey. Dat's to keep off disease. Mornin's we had to all drink tar water for de same purpose. Dat wernt so tasty.

"My Marster's name was George Hopper. Dat man paid taxes on more'n two-thousand acres of land in two counties. I lived in them two counties. Was born in Wilkes and raised in Lincoln County, Georgia. We called it de middle-south. My Marster he never did marry. Lots of folks didn't. Dey jes took up wid one another. Marster Hopper had five children by my grandmother. She was his house woman; dat's what he call 'er. An' when he died he willed her an' all dem chillun a house, some land, and a little money. He'd of left 'em a heap more money and wud been one the richest men in the county, ef'n de war hadn't broke out. When it was over he had a barrel full of 'Federate greenbacks. But t'wernt no count. He done broke den. One day my uncle, he was the colored overseer, he went to Danbury, six miles from whar we lived at, and he paid $5 for a pound of coffee. Dat was befo' de North whopped de South, and dey had'n killed-down de money value for de South.

"Talk about hard times! We see'd 'em in dem days, durin' de war and most specially after de Surrender. Folks dese days don't know what trouble looks like. We was glad to eat ash-cakes and drink parched corn and rye 'stead o' coffee. I've seed my grandmother go to de smoke house, and scrape up de dirt whar de meat had dropped, and take it to de house fer seasonin'. You see, both armies fed off'n de white folks, and dey cleaned out de barrel and cellars and smoke houses when dey come. One time, when de Yanks was on de way to Augusta, I was picking up chips to make the supper fire, when I seed 'em comin'. I hit it out from dar and hide behind two little hills down by de big spring. After a while my brother find me and he tell me to come on back to the house and see dem white men's dance. De Yanks kep' comin' and dey eat all night. By daylight they was through, marchin' past.

"An' den come de Rebels. When dey come we had five-thousand bushel of corn, one-hundred head o' hogs, three-hundred and fifty gallons of syrup 'an sech. When dey left, dey took an' set fire to evything, to keep it away from the Yanks, aimin' to starve 'em out 'o dat country. Dat's what dey done. Some of dem Rebs was mean as the Yanks. And dat was bein' mean. Some called de Yanks, 'de Hornets', 'cause dey fight so. Take a Yank an' he'd fight acrost a buzz saw and it circlin' fifty mile a minute.

"Dat time when the Yanks was goin' to Augusta, an' I went to black my Marster's boot, he'd give us a two-cent piece, big as a quarter, for boot blackin' . I say, 'Marster, who is dem soldiers?' An' he say to me, 'Dey's de Yankees, come to try to take you away from me.' An' I say, 'Looks like to me, Marster, if'n dey wants to take us dey'd arsk you fer us.' Marster laughed and say, 'Boy, dem fellers don't axes wid words. Dey does all dey talkin' wid cannons.'"

Mrs. Minnie Fulkes
459 Byrne Street, Petersburg, Virginia
(Interviewed by Susan Byrd on March 5, 1937)

"I was born the twenty-fifth of December and I am 77 years old. My mother was a slave and she belonged to Dick Belcher in Chesterfield County. Old Dick sold us again to Gillespie Graves. 'Member now fifteen of mother's chillun went with her having de same master.

"Honey, I don't like to talk 'bout dem times, 'cause my mother did suffer misert. You know dar was an overseer who use to tie mother up in the barn with a rope aroun' her arms up over her head, while she stood on a block. Soon as dey got her tied, dis block was moved an' her feet dangled, you know, couldn't tech de flo'.

"Dis ol' man, now, would start beatin' her naked 'til the blood run down her back to her heels. I took an' seed the whelps an' scars for my own self wid dese here two eyes. (Was a whip like they use to use on horses.) It was a piece of leather 'bout as wide as my han' from little finger to thumb. After dey had beat my mama all dey wanted, another overseer [came]. Lord, Lord, I hate white people and do flood waters gwine drown some. Well, honey, dis man would bathe her in salt and water. Don't you know dem places was a hurtin'? Um, um!

"I asked mother what she done for 'em to beat and do her so. She said, 'nothin', tother than she refused to be wife to dis man. An' mama say, if he didn't treat her dis way a dozen times, it wasn't nary one. Mind you, now mama's marster didn't know dis was gain' on. You know, if slaves would tell, why dem overseers would kill 'em.

"And she said dat dey use to have meetings an' sing and pray an' the ol' paddy rollers [patrollers] would hear dem, so to keep the sound from goin' out, slaves would . . ."

Belle Williams
Hutchinson, Kansas
(Interviewed by E. Jean Foote)

"Yes, I was a slave. I was born a slave on a plantation in Carroll County, Arkansas and lived there 'till after the war. Law sakes, honey, I can see them 'Feds' yet, just as plain as if it was yesterday. We had a long lane—you know what a lane is—well, here they come! I run for mah mammy, and I'll never forget how she grabbed me and let out a yell, 'It's them Feds, them blue coats.'

"You see my massa was a good massa. He didn't believe in whipping niggers and he didn't believe in selling niggers, and so my mammy and me, we didn't want to leave our mistress and massa. We called them 'Mother Hulsie' and 'Massa Sid.' One officer told my mammy that she could take along with her, anything out of the cabin that she wanted. Mammy looked around and said, 'I don't want to take nothin' but my chillun,' so we all told Mother Hulsie 'goodbye,' and when my mammy told her 'goodbye,' why Mother Hulsie cried and cried, and said, 'I just can't let you go, Elizabeth, but go on peacefully, and maybe some day you can come back and see me.'"

"Oh, honey, it was awful! You see I never been nowhere and I was scairt so I hung onto my mammy. The soldiers took us to camp that night, and after staying there several days, we went on to Springfield, Missouri, and it was right at fifty-two years ago that I came here. I was married to Fuller, my first husband and had seven chilluns. He helped me raise them that lived and after he died, I married Williams and had two chilluns, but he didn't help me raise my chilluns. Why, honey, I raised my chilluns and my chilluns' chilluns, and even one great-grandchild now. Why, I always been a slave. I worked for all the early white families in this here town that needed help.

I asked 'Auntie' if she were ever sold on the block, and she answered, "Law sakes, honey, I must tell you. No, I never was sold, but nothin' but the Dear Blessed Lawd saved me. You see Massa Sid had gone away for a few days, and his boys was takin' care of things, when some nigger traders came and wanted to buy some 10 niggers, and they picked on my grandmammy and me. How old was I? Well, I reckon I was about fourteen. You see, honey, I never could read or write, but I can count, and I can remember—Lawdy! how I can remember. Well, there I was on the block, just scairt and shivering—I was just cold all over—and them nigger traders was jest a talkin', when down that long lane came Massa Sid, and I'm tell in' you, it was the Dear Lawd that sent him. He was ridin' on his hoss, and he stopped right in front of me, standing there on the block. He looked at his boys, then he turned to them nigger traders and yelled out, 'What you all doin' here?' The boys told him there was just so many niggers on the place, and they wanted some money and when the nigger traders come along they thought they would sell a few niggers. Honey, I'm tellin' you, Massa Sid turned to them nigger traders and said, 'you nigger traders get out of here. These are my niggers and I don't sell niggers. I can feed them all, I don't want any help.' He grabbed me right off of the block and put me on the hoss in front of him and set me down in front of my cabin. Sceered, oh Lawdy, I was sceered! No, suh, Massa never sold no niggers.

"I must tell you about what happened one night while we were all there in the camp. One of the massa's boys that loved my uncle, came crawling on all fours, just like a pig, into camp. He passed the pickets, and when he found my uncle he laid there on the ground in my uncle's arms and cried like a baby, My uncle was old but he cried too and after a while he told the boy that he must go back—he was 'fraid that the pickets would see him and he would be shot, so he went with him crawling on all fours just like a pig, till he got him past the pickets, and our young master never saw my uncle any more. Oh, honey, them was heart-breakin' times.

"The first night we was in camp, my mammy got to thinking about Mother Hulsie and how she was left all alone with all the work, and not a soul to help her. The blue coats had gone through the house and upset everything, so in the morning she asked the captain if she could ask just one thing of him, and that was that she and my uncle go back to Mother Hulsie just for the day, and help put everything away and do the washing. The captain said they could go, but they must be back by five o'clock, and not one nigger child could go along, so they went back for the day and mammy did all the washing, every rag that she could find, and my uncle chopped and stacked outside the house, all the wood that he could chop that day, and then they came back to camp. My mammy said she'd never forget Mother Hulsie wringing her hands and crying, 'Oh, Lawd, what will I do,' as they went down the land."

John Beckwith
Cary, North Carolina

"I reckon dat I was 'bout nine years old at de surrender, but we warn't happy an' we stayed on dar till my parents died. My pappy was named Green an' my mammy was named Molly, an' we belonged ter Mr. Joe Edwards, Mr. Marion Gully, an' Mr. Hilliard Beckwith, as de missus married all of 'em. Dar was twenty-one other slaves, an' we got beat ever' onct in a while.

"When dey told us dat de Yankees was comin' we was also told dat iffen we didn't behave dat we'd be shot; an' we believed it. We would'uv behaved anyhow, case we had good plank houses, good food, an' shoes. We had Saturday an' Sunday off an' we was happy.

"De missus, she raised de nigger babies so's de mammies could wuck. I 'members de times when she rock me ter sleep an' put me ter bed in her own bed. I was happy den as I thinks back of it, until dem Yankees come.

"Dey come on a Chuesday; an' dey started by burnin' de cotton house an' killin' most of de chickens an' pigs. Way after awhile dey fin's de cellar an' dey drinks brandy tell dey gits woobly in de legs. After dat dey comes up on de front porch an' calls my missus. When she comes ter de do' dey tells her dat dey am goin' in de house ter look things over. My missus dejects, case ol' marster am away at de war, but dat don' do no good. Dey cusses her scan'lous an' dey dares her ter speak. Dey robs de house, takin' dere knives an' splittin' mattresses, pillows an' ever' thing open lookin' for valerables, an' ol' missus dasen't open her mouth.

"Dey camped dar in de grove fer two days, de officers takin' de house an' missus leavin' home an' goin' ter de neighbor's house. Dey make me stay dar in de house wid 'em ter tote dere brandy from de cellar, an' ter make 'em some mint Julep. Well, on de secon' night dar come de wust storm I'se eber seed. De lightnin' flash, de thunder roll, an' de house shook an' rattle lak a earthquake had struck it.

"Dem Yankees warn't supposed tar be superstitious, but lemmie tell yo', dey was some skeered dat night; an' I hyard a Captain say dat de witches was abroad. Atter awhile lightin' struck de Catawba tree dar de side of de house an' de soldiers camped round about dat way marched off ter de barns, slave cabins an' other places whar dey was safter dan at dat place. De next mornin' dem Yankees moved from dar an' dey ain't come back fer nothin'.

"We wasn't happy at de surrender an' we cussed ol' Abraham Lincoln all ober de place. We was told de disadvantages of not havin' no edercation, but shucks, we don' need no book larnin' wid ol' marster ter look atter us'.

"My mammy an' pappy stayed on dar de rest of dere lives, 'an I stayed till I was sixteen. De Ku Klux Klan got after me den 'bout fightin' wid a white boy. Dat night I slipped in de woods an' de nex' day I went ter Raleigh. I got a job dar an eber' since den I'se wucked fer myself, but now I can't wuck an' I wish dat yo' would apply fer my ol' aged pension fer me.

"I went back ter de ol' plantation long as my pappy, mammy, an' de marster an' missus lived. Sometimes, when I gits de chanct I goes back now. Course now de slave cabins am gone, ever 'body am dead, an' dar ain't nothin' familiar 'cept de bent Catawba tree; but it 'minds me of de happy days."

Belle Buntin
Mariana, Arkansas
(Interviewed by Miss Irene Robertson)

"I never was sold. I was born in Oakland, Mississippi. My master said he wanted all he raised. He never sold one. He bought my mother in Lexington County. She was a field hand. Our owners was Master Johnson Buntin and Mistress Sue Buntin. They had two children—Bob and Fannie.

"I have seen colored folks sold at Oakland. They had a block and nigger traders come. One trader would go and see a fine baby. He keep on till he got it. I've seen them take babies from the mother's arm and if the mother dare cry, they would git a beatin'. They look like they bust over their grief.

"That selling was awful and crowds come to see how they sell. They acted like it was a picnic. Some women was always there, come with their husbands. Some women sold slaves and some bought them.

"I never did see none well naked. I seen men took from their wives and mothers and children. Let me tell you they didn't have no squalling around or they would get took off and a beating.

"It was my job to brush the flies off the table. I had a fly brush. I would eat out of Bob's and Fannie's plates. Miss Sue say, 'Bell, I'm going to whoop you.' I say, 'Miss Sue, please don't, I'm hungry too.' She say, 'You stop playing and eat first next time.' Then she'd put some more on their plates. We sat on a bench at the table. We et the same the white folks did all cooked up together."

Frank Fikes
El Dorado, Arkansas
(Interviewed by Pernella M. Anderson)

"My name is Frank Fikes. I live between El Dorado and Strong and I am 79 years old if I make no mistake. I know my mama told me years ago that I was born in watermelon time.

"My work was very easy when I was a slave. Something got wrong with my foot when I first started to walking and I was crippled. I could not get around like the other children, so my work was to nurse all of the time. Sometimes, as fast as I got one baby to sleep I would have to nurse another one to sleep. We belonged to Mars Colonel Williams and he had, I guess, a hundred families on his place and nearly every family had a baby, so I had a big job after all. The rest of the children carried water, pine, drove up cows and held the calves off and made fires at old mars' house.

"And old miss fed all of us children in a large trough. She fed us on what we called the 'licker' from the greens and peas with bread mashed in it. We children did not use spoons. We picked the bread out with our fingers and got down on our all fours and sipped the licker with our mouth. We all had a very easy time we thought because we did not know any better then.

"I never went to church until after surrender. Neither did we go to school but the white children taught me to read and count.

"I went in my shirt tail until I was eleven or twelve years old. Back in slavery time boys did not wear britches. They wore shirts and our hair was long. The slaves say if you cut a child's hair before he or she was ten or twelve years old, they won't talk plain until they are old."

Lillie Baccus
Madison, Arkansas
(Interviewed by Miss Irene Robertson)

"I'll tell you what I heard. I was too little to remember the Civil War. Mama's owner was _____ Dillard. She called him 'Master' Dillard. Papa's owner was _____ Smith. He called him 'Master' Smith. Mama was named Ann and Pap Arthur Smith. I was born at West Point, Mississippi. I heard Ma say she was sold. She said Pattick sold her. She had to leave her two children Cherry and Ann. Mama was a field hand. So was grandma, yet she worked in the house some she said. After freedom, Cherry and Ann come to mama. She was going to be sold agin but was freed before sold.

"Mama didn't live only till I was about three years old, so I don't know enough to tell you about her. Grandma raised us. She was sold twice. She said she run out of the house to pick up a star when the stars fell. They showered down and disappeared.

"The Yankees camped close to where they lived, close to West Point, Mississippi, but in the country close to an artesian well. The well was on their place. The Yankees stole grandma and kept her at their tent. They meant to take her on to wait on them and use, but when they started to move old master 'spicioned they had her hid down there. He watched out and seen her when they was going to load her up. He went and got the head man to make them give her up. She was so glad to come home. Glad to see him 'cause she wanted to see him. They watched her so close she was afraid they would shoot her leaving. She lived to be 101 years old. She raised me. She used to tell how the overseer would whip her in the field. They wasn't good to her in that way.

"I have three living children and eleven dead. I married twice. My first husband is living. My second husband is dead. I married in daytime in the church the last time. All else ever took place in my life was hard work. I worked in the field till I was too old to hit a tap. I live wid my children. I get $8 and commodities.

"I come to Arkansas because they said money was easy to get—growed on bushes. I had four little children to make a living for and they said it was easier.

"I think people is better than they was long time ago. Times is harder. People have to buy everything they have as high as they is, makes money scarce nearly bout a place as hen's teeth. Hens ain't got no teeth. We don't have much money I tell you. The welfare gives me $8."

Tom Douglas
Route 2, Box 19A, El Dorado, Arkansas
(Interviewed by Pernella M. Anderson)

"I was born in Marion, Louisiana, September 15, 1847 at 8 o'clock in the morning. I was eighteen years of age at surrender. My master and missus was B. B. Thomas and Miss Susan Thomas. Old master had a gang of slaves and we all worked like we were putting out fire. Lord child, wasn't near like it is now. We went to bed early and got up early. There was a gang of plow hands, hoe hands, hands to clear new ground, a bunch of cooks, a washwoman. We worked too and din't mind it. If we acted like we didn't want to work, our hands was crossed and tied and we was tied to a tree or bush and whipped until we bled. They had a whipping post that they tied us to to whip us.

"We was sold just like hogs and cows and stock is sold today. They built nigger pens like you see cow pens and hog pens. They drove niggers in there by the hundred and auctioned them off to the highest bidder. The white folks kept up with our age so when they got ready to sell us they could tell how old we were. They had a 'penetenture' for the white folks when they did wrong. When we done wrong, we was tied to that whipping post and our hide busted open with that cow hide.

"We stayed out in the field in a log house and old master would allowance our week's rations out to us and Sunday morning we got one biscuit each. If our week's allowance give out before the week we did not get any more . . .

"Cooked on fireplaces, wasn't no stoves. We did not have to worry about our clothes. Old missus looked after everything. We wore brogan shoes and homespun clothes. There was a bunch of women that did the spinning and weaving just like these sewing-room women are now. I was a shoemaker. I made all the shoes during the time we wasn't farming. We had to go nice and clean. If old missus caught us dirty, our hide was busted. I got slavery-time scars on my back now. You ought to see my back. Scars on my back for 75 years.

"I never went to school a day in my life. I learned my ABC's after I was 19 years old. I went to night school, then to a teacher by the name of Nelse Otom. I was the first nigger to join the church on this side of the Mason and Dixie line. During slavery in 1866, they met in conference and motioned to turn all of the black sheep out then. There was four or five they turned out here and four or five there, so we called our preacher, and I was the first one to join. Old master asked our preacher what we paid him to preach to us. We told him 'old shoes and clothes.' Old master say, 'Well, that's damn poor pay.' Our preacher says, 'And they got a damn poor preacher.'

"I did not know anything about war. Only I know it began in 1861, closed in 1865, and I know they fought at Vicksburg. That was two or three hundred miles from us but we could not keep our dishes upon the table whenever they shot a bomb. Those bombs would jar the house so hard and we could see the smoke that far.

"We was allowed to visit Saturday night and Sunday. If you had a wife you could go to see her Wednesday night and Saturday night, and stay with her until Monday morning. If you were caught any other time the patrollers would catch you. That is where the song come from, 'Run, Nigger, run, don't the padarolls will catch you.' Sometimes a nigger would run off and the nigger dogs would track them. In slavery, white folks put you together. Just tell you to go to bed with her or him. You had to stay with them whether you wanted them or not.

"After freedom, old master called all us slaves and told us we was free; opened a big gate and drove us all out. We didn't know what to do~-not a penny, nowhere to go—so we went out there and set down. In about 30 minutes master came back and told us if we wanted to finish the crop for food and clothes we could. So we all went back and finished the crop, and the next year they gave us half. So ever since then we people been working for half."

Candis Goodwin
Cape Charles, Virginia

"Ah ain't knowd, 'xactly, how ol' ah is, but ah bawn 'fo de war. Bawn ovuh yonder at Seaview, on ol' Masser Scott's plantation. Tain't fur f'om here. Yes, reckon ah 'bout six yeah ol' when de Yankees come, jes' a lil' thin', you know.

"My white people dey good tuh me. Cose dey gits mad wid you but dey don' beat none o' us; jes' ack lak it. Why, ah was jes lak dey's chillun; ah played wid 'em, et wid 'em, an' eb'n slep' wid 'em. Ah kinder chilish, ah reckon. Had muh own way. Muh mommer, she wuck in de quater kitchen. She ain't haftuh wuck hawd lak some. Had it kinder easy, too. Jes' lak ah tells yuh, ah al'ys had my way. Ah gits what ah wants an' ef'n dey don't gi' tuh me, ah jes' teks it.

"No neber had no wuck to do in dem days 'ceptin' nursin' de babies. 'Twas jes' lak play; twan' no wuck. Uster go ober to Nottingham's tuh play, go long wid Missus' chillun, yuh know. Ah laks tuh go ober there cause dey has good jam an' biscuits. Er'n dey don' gi' me none, ah jes' teks some.

Dey don' do nuttin'; jes' say, 'Tek yuh han' out dat plate.' But ah got what ah wants den. Whew! We chillun user hab a time 'round ol' Missus' place. All us chillun uster git togeder an' go in de woods tuh play. Yes, de white and blackuns, too. De grea' big whi' boys uster go 'long wid us, too, Know how we play? We tek de brown pine shadows an' mek houses outer 'em an' den mek grass outer de green uns. Den we go ober Missus' dairy and steal inything we want an' tek it to our houses in de woods. Dem was good ol' times, ah tel yuh, honey.

"Tel yuh what ah uster do. Ah uster play pranks on ol' Masser Scott. Ah's regular lil' devil, ah was. Come night, ev'ybody sit 'round big fire place in libing room. Soon it git kinder late, Massa git up outer his cheer tuh win' up de clock. Ah gits 'hin' his cheer ret easy, an' quick sneak his cheer f'om un'er him; an' when he finish he set smack on de flow! Den he say, 'Dogone yuh lil' cattin', ah gwan switch yuh!' Ah jes fly out de room. Won' scared though cause am yet livin' in die same house, dat she an' us all labored an' worked fo' by de sweat of our brow, an wid dese hands. Lordl Lord! Child, dem days. was some days. Let me finish, baby, tellin' you 'bout die house. De groun' was bought from a lady (colored) name Sis Jackey, an' she was sometimes called in dem days de Mother of Harrison Street Baptis' Church. I reckon dis church is de ol'est one in Petersburg.

"O, yes, honey I can 'member when de Yankees came into dis town; dey broke in stores an' told all de niggers to go in an' git anything dey wanted.

"When slaves ran away they were brought back to their Master and Mistress; when dey couldn't catch 'em they didn't bother, but let 'em go. Sometimes de slaves would go an' take up at tother places; some of 'em lived in de woods off of takin' things, sech as hogs, corn, an' vegetables from other folks farm. Well, if dese slaves was caught, dey were sold by their new masters to go down South. Dey tell me dem masters down South was so mean to slaves dey would let 'em work dem cotton fields 'til dey fall dead wid hoes in der hands, an' would beat dem. I'm glad to say we had good owners.

"There was a auction block, I saw right here in Petersburg on the corner of Sycamore Street and Bank Street. Slaves were auctioned off to de highest bidder. Some refused to be sold. By dat, I mean, 'cried.' Lord, Lord, I done seen dem young'uns fought and kick like crazy folks. Child, it was pitiful to see 'em. Den dey would handcuff an' beat 'em unmerciful. I don' like to talk 'bout back dar. it brun' a sad feelin' up me. If slaves 'belled, I done seed dem whip 'em wid a strop cal' 'cat nine tails.' Honey, dis strop was 'bout broad as yo' hand, from thumb to little finger, an' 'twas cut in strips up. Yo' done seen dese whips dat they whip horses wid? Well dey was used too.

"You said some thin' 'bout how we served God. Um, um, child, I tell you jest how we used to do. We used to worship at different houses. You see you would get a remit to go to dese places. You would have to show your remit. If de Paddyrollers [patrollers] caught you dey would whip yo'. Dats de way dey done in dem days. Paddyrollers is a gang of white men gitting together goin' through de country catching slaves, an' whipping an' beatin' 'em up if dey had no remit. Marster Allen wouldn't 'llow no one to whip an' beat his slaves, an' he would handle anybody if dey did. So, Marster's slaves met an' worshiped from house to house, an honey, we talked to my God all us wanted.

"You know, we use to call Marster Allen, Colonel Allen. His name was Robert. He was a home general, an' a lawyer, too. When he went to court any slave he said to free, was freed an' turned loose. De white folks as well as slaves obeyed Marster Allen.

"Did you know that poor whites like slaves had to get a pass? I mean, a remit like as slaves, to sell anythin' an' to go places, or do anythin'. Jest as we colored people, dey had to go to some big white man like Colonel Allen, dey did. If Marster wanted to, he would give dem a remit 'Or pass an' if he didn't feel like it, he wouldn't do it. It was jes' as he felt 'bout hit. Dats what made all feared him. Ol' Marster was more hard on dem poor white folks den he was on us niggers.

"I don't know but two sets of white folks were like slaves up my way. One was name Chatman, an' de tother one Nellovies. Dese two families worked on Allen's farm as we did, off from us on a plot called Morgan's lot. There dey lived as slaves jes like us colored folks. Yes, de poor white man had dark an' tough days, like us poor niggers; I mean were lashed an' treated some of 'em, jes as pitiful an' unmerciful. Lord, Lord, baby, I hope yo' young folks will never know what slavery is, an' will never suffer as yo' foreparents. O God, God, I'm livin' to tell de tale to yo', honey. Yes, Jesus, yo've spared me.

"For clothin' we were 'llowed two suits a year—one fer spring an' one fer winter, was all yo' had. De underclothes were made at home. Yo' also got two pairs of shoes an' homemade hats an' caps. The white folks or your slave owners would teach dem who could catch on easy, an' dey would teach de other slaves, an' dat's how dey kept all slaves clothed. Our summer hats were made out of platted straw, underclothes made out of sacks an' bags.

"We had plenty of food sech as twas—cornbread, butter milk, an' sweet potatoes in wuck days. Ha, Ha, honey, guess dat's why niggers don't like cornbread today. Dey got a dislike for dat bread from back folks. On Sunday we had biscuits, and sometimes a little extra food, which ol' Mistress would send out to Mother for us.

"Fer as I think, if slavery had lasted, it would have been pretty tough. As it was, some fared good, while others fared common. You know, slaves who were beat and treated bad, some of dem had started gittin' together an' killin' de white folks when dey carried dem out to de fields to work. God is punishin' some of dem ol' suckers an' their chillun right now fer de way dey use to treat us poor Colored folks.

"I think by Negro gittin' educated he has profited, an' dis here younger generation is gwine to take nothin' off dese here poor white folks when dey don't treat dem right, cause now dis country is a free country. No slavery now.

Martha Allen
aged 78 years
1318 South Person Street, Raleigh, North Carolina

"I was borned in Craven County seventy eight years ago. My pappa was named Andrew Bryant an' my mammy was named Harriet. My brothers was John Franklin, Alfred, an' Andrew. I ain't had no sisters. I reckon dat we is what yo' call a general mixture case: I am part Injun, part white, an' part nigger.

"My mammy belonged ter Tom Edward Gaskin, an' she wasn't half fed. De cook nussed de babies while she cooked, so dat de mammies could wuck in de fiel's, an' all de mammies done was stick de babies in at de kitchen on dere way ter de fiel's. I'se hyard mammy say dat dey went ter wuck widout breakfast, an' dat when she put her baby in de kitchen she'd go by de slop bucket an' drink de slops from a long handled gourd.

"De slave driver was bad as he could be, an' de slaves got awful beatin's.

"De young marster sorta wanted my mammy, but she tells him 'no,' so he chunks a lightwood knot an' hits her on de haid wid it. Dese white men's what had babies by nigger wimmens was called 'Carpet Gitters.' My father's father was one o' dem.

"Yes, ma'm, I'se mixed plenty, 'case my mammy's grandmaw was Cherokee Injun.

"I don' know nothin' 'bout no war, case marster carried us ter Cedar Falls, near Durham an' dar's whar we come free.

"I 'members dat de Ku Klux uster go ter de Free Issues houses, strip all de family an' whup de ol' folkses. Den dey dances wid de pretty yaller gals an' goes ter bed wid dem. Dat's what de Ku Klux was, a bunch of mean mens tryin' ter hab a good time.

"I'se wucked purty hard durin'my life an' I done my courtin on a steer an' cart haulin' wood ter town ter sell. He was haulin' wood too on his wagin, an' he'd beat me ter town so's dat he could help me off'n de wagon. I reckon dat was as good a way as any.

"I tries ter be a good Christian but I'se got disgusted wid dese young upstart niggers what dances in de chu'ch. Dey says dat dey am truckin' an' dat de Bible ain't forbid hit, but I reckin dat I knows dancin' whar I sees hit."

Millie Simpkins
aged 109 years
1004 10th Avenue, North, Nashville, Tennessee

"I claims I'se 109 years ol' an' was bawn neah Winchester, Tennessee. Mah marster was Boyd Sims an' mah missis was Sarah Ann Ewing Sims. Mah mammy was named Judy Ewing an' mah daddy was Moses Stephen an' he was 'free bawn.' He was de marster's stable boy an' followed de races. He run 'way an' nebber come back. '

"Mah fust missis was very rich. She had two slave 'omen ter dress her eve'y mawnin' an' I brought her breakfast ter her on a silvah waitah. She was married three times, her second husband was Joe Carter an' de third was Judge Gork.

"Mah fust missis sold me 'cause I was stubborn. She sent me ter de 'slave yard' at Nashville. De yard was full ob slaves. I stayed dere two weeks 'fore marster Simpson bought me. I was sold 'way fum mah husband an' I nebber see'd 'im 'gin. I had one chile which I tuk wid me.

"De slave yard was on Cedar Street. A Mr. Chandler would bid de slaves off, but 'fore dey started biddin' you had ter tek all ob yo clothes off an' roll down de hill so dey could see dat you didn't hab no bones broken, or sores on yer. (I wouldin' tek mine off.) Ef nobody bid on you, you was tuk ter de slave mart an' sold. I was sold der. A bunch ob dem was sent ter Mississippi an' dey had der ankles fastened tergedder an' dey had ter walk w'iles de tradahs rid [traders rode].

"When I was sold ter marster Simpson, mah second mistress made me a house slave an' I wuked only at de big house an' mah wuk was ter nuss an' dress de chilluns an' he'ps mah missis in her dressin'.

"De young slaves was hired out ter nuss de white chilluns. I was hired as nuss girl at seven ye'ars ol' an' started cookin' at ten. I nebber had a chance ter go ter school.

"I'm de mammy ob 14 chilluns, seven boys an' seven girls. I was next ter de ol'est ob four chillun. Mah missis use ter hire me out ter hotels an' taverns.

"Some marsters fed dere slaves meat an' some wouldin' let dem hab a bite. One marster we useter 'yer 'bout would grease his slaves mouth on Sunday mawnin', an' tell dem ef anybody axed ef dey had meat terday, 'yes, lots ob hit.'

"When dey got ready ter whup dem, dey'd put dem down a pit widout any clothes, stand back wid a bullwhip an' cut de blood out. I 'member de niggers would run 'way an' hide out.

"De only fun de young folks had was when de ol' folks had a quiltin'. W'ile de ol' folks was wukin' on de quilt, de young ones would git in 'nother room, dance an' hab a good time. Dey'd hab a pot turned down at de do'er ter keep de white folks fum 'yearin' dem. De white folks didn't want us ter larn nothin', an' ef a slave picked up a little piece ob papah, dey would yell 'put dat down, you; you want ter git in our business.'

"De white folks wouldin' let de slaves pray. Ef dey got ter pray, hit was w'iles walkin' 'hind de plow. White folks would whup de slaves ef dey 'yeard dem sing er pray."

Albert Jones
726 Lindsey Avenue, Portsmouth, Virginia
(Interviewed by Thelma Dunston on January 8, 1937)

On entering a scanty room. in the small house, Mr. Jones was nodding in a chair near the stove. When asked about his early life, he straightened up, crossed his legs, and said, "I'se perty old, ninety six. I was born a slave in Souf' Hampton County, but my mastah was mighty good to me. He won't ruff—dat is, if yer done right."

The aged man cleared his throat and chuckled. Then he said, "But you better never let mastah catch yer wif a book or paper, and yet couldn't praise God so he could hear yer. If yer done dem things, he sho' would beat yer. 'Course he was good to me, 'cause I never done none of 'em. My work won't hard never. I had to wait on my mastah, open de gates fer him, drive de wagon and tend de horses. I was sort of a house boy.

"For twenty years I stayed wif mastah, and I didn't try to run away. When I was twenty one, me and one of my brothers run away to fight wif the Yankees. Us left Souf' Hampton County and went to Petersburg. Der we got some food. Den us went to Fort Hatton where we met some more slaves who had run away. When we got in Fort Hatton, us had to cross a bridge to git to de Yankees. De rebels had torn de bridge down. We all got together and builded back de bridge, and we went on to de Yankees. Dey give us food and clothes."

The old man then got up and emptied his mouth of the tobacco juice, scratched his bald head and continued. "Yer know, I was one of de first colored cavalry soldiers, and I fought in Company 'K'. I fought for three years and a half. Sometimes I slept outdoors, and sometimes I slept in a tent. De Yankees always give us plenty of blankets."

"During the war some o' us had to always stay up nights and watch fer de rebels. Plenty of nights I has watched, but de rebels never 'tacked us when I was on.

"Not only was dere men slaves dat run to de Yankees, but some o' de women slaves followed dere husbands. Dey use to help by washing and cooking. One day when I was fighting, de rebels shot at me, and dey sent a bullet through my hand. I was lucky not to be kilt. Look! See how my hand is?"

The old man held up his right hand, and it was half closed. Due to the wound he received in the war, that was as far as he could open his hand. Still looking at his hand, Mr. Jones said, "But dat didn't stop me. I had it bandaged and kept on fighting. The uniform dat I wore was blue wif brass buttons, a blue cape, lined wif red flannel, black leather boots and a blue cap. I rode on a bay color horse; 'fact, everybody in Company 'K' had bay color horses. I tooked my knapsack and blankets on de horse back. In my knapsack I had water, hard tacks and other food.

"When de war ended, I goes back to my mastah and he treated me like his brother. Guess he was scared of me 'cause I had so much ammunition on me. My brother, who went wif me to de Yankees, caught rheumatism duing de war. He died after de war ended."

Appendix B

My Letters and Op-Eds to Newspapers

Philadelphia Inquirer 4/20/2022

War in Ukraine Didn't Have to Happen

Since the beginning of the war in Ukraine on February 24th, thousands of Ukrainian soldiers and civilians have died and millions have fled the country or been internally displaced. This didn't have to happen.

Our U.S. policy makers failed to understand that despite Russia's history as a communist state, it still had a legitimate need for national security, just as we do. The prospect of Ukraine's becoming a member of NATO and its accepting missiles systems to be directed toward Russia, would be very much like if Canada decided to belong to the Russian Federation and Russia was threatening to place missiles near Montreal or Toronto directed toward New York City or Cleveland. What would be the response of the United States? We might also want to head off that possibility by invading Canada.

The Minsk agreement, if implemented, could also have averted the war.

Volodymyr Zelenskyy defeated Petro Poroshenko in the 2019 election on a platform that included making peace with Russia and signing the Minsk II Agreement. Unfortunately, he came under intense pressure and abandoned his campaign peace promise.

The United States and the UN both endorsed the Minsk agreement in 2015. But the West did nothing to push the Ukrainians into implementing it. Nothing can excuse the Russian invasion of Ukraine. But the U.S. and the Ukrainians tragically and inexcusably missed numerous diplomatic chances of averting this war.

Andrew Mills, Lower Gwynedd

The Intelligencer 1/16/2022

Stop Extending NATO Farther East

War in Ukraine could be almost inevitable. According to americanmilitarynews.com, on December 22nd Russia had about 265,000 troops stationed within 250 miles of its border with Ukraine. To avoid the possibility of a war, Russia is asking that the U.S., and therefore NATO, promise not to extend NATO any farther east than the western boundary of Ukraine.

Let's explore why the U.S. is not likely to agree to promise that, and what it could mean in terms of the lives of the people of Ukraine.

President George H. W. Bush in 1990 promised Mikhail Gorbachev, then head of state of the Soviet Union, that the U.S. would never push for NATO to encompass any of the East European countries.

Bush's Secretary of State James Baker's famously stated "not one inch eastward" in his assurances about NATO expansion in his meeting with Soviet leader Mikhail Gorbachev on February 9, 1990. This was just one part of a cascade of assurances about Soviet security given by Western leaders to Gorbachev and other Soviet officials throughout the process of German unification in 1990 and on into 1991 according to declassified U.S., Soviet, German, British and French documents posted on December 12, 2017, by the National Security Archive at George Washington University (http://nsarchive.gwu.edu).

Some people downplay this agreement because it was only verbal and not written on paper. Although there was no paper treaty, the validity of the agreement is demonstrated in that it appears in multiple memoranda of conversation between the Soviets and the highest-level Western interlocutors offering assurances throughout 1990 and into 1991 about protecting Soviet security interests.

The agreement involved the Soviet Union's agreeing to the reunification of Germany (Russia's worst enemy) and allowing the reunified Germany to join NATO provided the U.S. would agree not to extend NATO any farther east than it was at that time, which was up to the eastern border of East Germany.

However, soon after he took office, Bill Clinton began listening to the advice of the Pentagon generals and the lobbyists for the armaments industries. So during his administration and subsequently during the George W. Bush administration, at least ten Eastern European countries, formerly under Soviet influence were courted by the U.S. and were admitted into NATO in contravention of the agreement. These included Poland, Romania, Bulgaria, Croatia, Estonia, Latvia, Lithuania, Slovenia, Czech Republic, and Slovakia.

So the U.S. and the western European members of NATO broke their promise, badly. Russia, as embodied by their leader Putin, is determined now to stop any further encroachment of NATO into its sphere of influence by insisting that Ukraine never be admitted into NATO. It seems to be a reasonable request. Particularly considering that Russia no longer represents a communist bulwark feverishly trying to impose its will on the western world, which was why NATO was set up in the first place.

One of the main reasons the U.S. has been interested in enlarging the membership of NATO eastward was the opportunity for our armaments industries to sell more F-16s and other military hardware to the new members. Not only that, but the American taxpayers are paying for a portion of these weapon sales, because they are just so expensive many of these countries, for example, Poland, Hungary, Czech Republic, and Slovakia, can't afford full price. Lockheed Martin doesn't care whether they get paid through Polish auspices or directly by the taxpayer.

It's just plain dangerous and idiotic if the United States doesn't accept the Russian request. The only rationality for not doing so is that there would be a lot of money to be made. By a few people.

Since we've already been assured that a war in Ukraine will not be fought using U.S. or U.K. troops or any other western-nation forces, we would be asking Ukrainian young men and women to die or be maimed for the sake of our hang-up about having to expand NATO to Russia's borders.

Andrew Mills lives in Lower Gwynedd

Philadelphia Inquirer 8/17/2021

What the U.S. Must Do to Aid Afghanistan

The unexpectedly rapid fall of Afghanistan to the Taliban means that the U.S. should take extraordinary steps to ensure that the U.S. embassy in Kabul remains open until all the Afghans who assisted Allied troops in any way and all the major leaders in the Afghan government have been provided with US visas and have been brought to the United States.

The sudden fall of Afghanistan is the fault of neither the Biden administration nor the Trump administration. It is because the government we had in 2001 set up an artificial government in Afghanistan not based on the wishes or the culture of the Afghans. The total inability or unwillingness of the Afghan army to now defend this artificial government only means that the U.S. and our NATO friends should have completely left Afghanistan years and years ago.

Andrew Mills, Lower Gwynedd

The Intelligencer 3/23/2020

War with Iran Has Been Going On for Years

Depending on their bent, our politicians are either fearful of a war with Iran or eager for the U.S. to find an excuse to attack Iran in an all-out war. Few acknowledge that America is already at war with Iran. I'm talking about the sanctions the U.S. has imposed on Iran because of its presumed bad behavior. Sanctions are presented as, "Oh, OK. Well, you know, it's only sanctions, right?" The media coverage presents sanctions as though they're somehow an alternative to war. The sanctions against Iran are actually killing people and significantly lowering the average Iranian's level of living. They're causing cancer patients to die from not being able to access medicine, and they're interfering with the food supply in Iran. This is already, in many respects, a hot war that the United States is prosecuting against Iran. We must be clear that the sanctions significantly predate Trump, but he has intensified them and made them more stringent.

Iran's bad behavior boils down to: (1) the Iranian revolution in 1979 when 52 American diplomats were held hostage for 444 days; (2) Iran's support of the Palestinian cause by sending arms to Hezbollah and Hamas, enemies of Israel; by this Iran has been helping the Palestinians level that playing field just a little, but nothing compared to Israel's military prowess and actions; (3) Iran's having the audacity of taking steps to become another nuclear power—largely for fear of being subject to a nuclear attack from either Israel or the U.S.; and (4) Iran's support for the Houthi rebels in Yemen, though Saudi Arabia is even more strongly supporting their side in that cruel and horrible war.

Regarding the diplomatic hostage taking the U.S. suffered during the Iranian revolution, our columnists and media foreign-policy 'experts' conveniently forget the recent history of U.S. relations with Iran that produced such an outburst of anger against America during their revolution. A study of recent history reveals that the U.S. has *made* Iran our enemy through many actions we have taken. in 1953 the CIA and MI6 in a coup d'état removed the popular prime minister, Mohammad Mosaddegh, and gave the total power of the government over to the Shah, Mohammad Reza Shah. For many Iranians, this was the moment that the U.S. went from friend to foe. Originally thought to be a supporter of Iran's movement towards democracy, the U.S. had instead orchestrated a coup. This resentment would be one of the major driving forces, 26 years later, when a popular protest movement ultimately overthrew the U.S.-backed Shah. It also lies at the very foundation of the current government's anti-Americanism.

The American people don't have to buy into who our politicians and Pentagon brass claim are our enemies, particularly when they tell lies about them just to get us into another war. Remember these words as you hear our politicians giving the reasons why we should get into a shooting war with Iran. But in resisting another war like this, we the public must realize that being on a war footing is extremely necessary for the munition factory owners and the military brass. They will try to make us feel unpatriotic if we don't support their effort to keep the military-industrial complex humming along.

See how stock prices for weapons manufacturers began to rise as soon as Iranian General Soleimani was assassinated last month. Defense contractors spent $84 million lobbying Congress last year and it certainly wasn't to promote diplomacy and restraint. We need to petition our Senators and Representatives to stop the war of sanctions and prevent a shooting war with Iran.

Andrew Mills, who lives in Lower Gwynedd, is a retired engineer and programmer

---

The Intelligencer 9/22/2019

Facts Are Important

A guest opinion writer in the August 30-31st edition of the Intelligencer says "Liberals are rewriting history" and states that he just wants the facts. However, at least two of his assertions in that piece failed to meet his own test.

First he claims that one or more members of the Democratic caucus made "anti-Semitic rants." In fact, no Democratic representative in Congress has issued anything approaching anti-Semitic statements of any kind. A few have questioned whether or not the U.S. should be supporting Israel because of its treatment of Palestinians. It is not anti-Semitic to question our support for Israel.

Further down in his piece, he makes the erroneous statement that "much of Central America is controlled by socialist governments . . . " It turns out that the only Central American country that comes even close to being socialist is Nicaragua. Importantly, we don't hear of very many Nicaraguans seeking refuge at our southern border with Mexico. Perhaps they take care of their poor citizens better.

But we know that many, many of those coming to our borders are from Honduras. In 2009 Honduras endured a coup d'état against a democratically-elected president, Manuel Zelaya, and he was replaced by an army general.

Apparently Zelaya was too eager to help the country's poor. Real democracy has not yet returned to the country and the government has been involved in several cases of human-rights abuses. The U.S. overlooked the coup at the time and has continued to give aid to Honduras, which apparently has not helped its poor people very much.

Guest writers need to be careful of their facts also.

Andrew Mills, Lower Gwynedd

The Intelligencer 6/12/2019

Bill HR2407 Deserves Our Support

More than 10,000 Palestinian children aged 12 to 17 have been arrested, detained, abused, and prosecuted by Israeli security forces in the Israeli military court system since 2000. Independent monitors such as Human Rights Watch and the B'Tselem organization in Israel have repeatedly documented that these children are subject to abuse and, in some cases, torture—specifically citing the use of chokeholds, beatings, and coercive interrogation.

Congresswoman Betty McCollum (DFL-Minn.) has recently introduced bill H.R. 2407—the *Promoting Human Rights for Palestinian Children Living Under Israeli Military Occupation Act*. This legislation amends the provision of the *Foreign Assistance Act* known as the "Leahy Law" to prohibit funding for the military detention of children in any country, including Israel.

The bill also establishes the "Human Rights Monitoring and Palestinian Child Victims of Israeli Military Detention Fund," authorizing $19 million annually for non-governmental organizations to monitor human rights abuses associated with Israel's military detention of children.

The bill deserves our support and the support of our Congressional Representatives.

Andrew Mills, Lower Gwynedd Township

Philadelphia Inquirer 5/16/2019

Attempted Coup

On April 30th, the US-supported coup in Venezuela failed. It failed because the vast majority of the military supported the government, which is consistent with the results of the May 20, 2018 elections in which Maduro won 68 per cent of the vote. The election was observed by more than 150 members of the International Electoral Accompaniment Mission.

U.S. officials and our major media justify their support of the coup because they allege Maduro is a "dictator." This despite the fact that he heads a country with a legislative branch controlled by the opposition and where in October 2017 the opposition won five governorships. These salient facts are not covered by the AP which the Inquirer relies upon for news on Venezuela. Would the U.S. show such prolonged support for the opposition if Venezuela didn't have vast reserves of oil?

Andrew Mills, Lower Gwynedd

Bucks County Herald 2/28/2019

U.S. Sanctions Are Making Matters Worse

The majority of Venezuelans want a new government and for good reason. The economy has shrunk by a record 50 percent in the last five years, and inflation is over a million percent annually.

But the harsh sanctions the U.S. imposed on the country in 2015 and 2017 have combined to make that depression and hyperinflation worse. These sanctions have resulted in the death of many Venezuelans, because they've made it almost impossible to afford life-saving medicines. The new sanctions announced by the Administration last week will take more billions of dollars of revenue from the government, severely worsening the depression.

In this country our electorate is really upset because of what we believe was another nation's (Russia) buying political ads with our elections in 2016. What we're doing now by recognizing Juan Guaido as Venezuela's interim president is far worse.

For the sake of the Venezuelan people and for the principle of national sovereignty, the U.S. and its allies should instead support negotiations between the Venezuelan government and its opponents that will allow the country to finally emerge from its political and economic crisis.

The US should have learned something from its regime-change ventures in Iraq, Syria, Libya, and its long, violent history of sponsoring regime change in Latin America.

Andrew Mills, Lower Gwynedd

The Intelligencer 11/16/2018

Thumbs Up for the International Criminal Court

The International Criminal Court (ICC) is an intergovernmental organization and international tribunal that has been set up in The Hague in the Netherlands. It is the court of last resort for the prosecution of serious international crimes, including genocide, war crimes, and crimes against humanity.

The ICC was set up to complement existing national judicial systems and it may therefore only exercise its jurisdiction when certain conditions are met. Investigations can be requested by states who are a party to the court. States that are not a party to the court that have had a crime committed in their territory can also request an investigation if they accept the court's jurisdiction.

The court was modeled after the Nuremberg trials and the ad hoc tribunals for the Yugoslavia conflicts of the 1990s and the Rwandan genocide. Hundreds of nongovernmental organizations joined together as the Coalition for the International Criminal Court. Among the 25 founders of the coalition were Amnesty International, Human Rights First, and Human Rights Watch. The court began its work on July 1, 2002, the date the Rome Statute became effective.

The Rome Statute is a multilateral treaty adopted in 1998 which serves as the ICC's governing document. In 2000, President Clinton signed the Rome treaty but never submitted it to the Senate for ratification. When the statute came into force in 2002, then-President George W. Bush effectively withdrew the U.S. signature, notifying the U.N. secretary-general that the United States no longer intended to ratify the treaty and did not recognize any obligation it had under the Rome Statute.

The Office of the Prosecutor of the ICC has opened ten official investigations and is also conducting an additional eleven preliminary examinations. Thus far, 39 individuals have been indicted in the ICC, including Ugandan, Sudanese, Kenyan, Libyan, Ivorian and Congolese leaders. However, the court has faced setbacks, and as human rights crises marked by international crimes continue to proliferate, its mandate has proven to be both needed and more daunting than its founders envisioned.

National security adviser John Bolton clearly has the International Criminal Court (ICC) in his crosshairs. In a speech to the conservative Federalist Society in September, Bolton pledged the United States would never cooperate with what he called an "illegitimate" court. Bolton warned: If the ICC proceeds with launching an investigation into alleged war crimes committed by US military and intelligence staff during the war in Afghanistan or pursues any investigation into Israel or other US allies, the US would impose sanctions against the court and, where possible, prosecute its officials.

Amnesty International USA's deputy director for advocacy and government relations said in a statement the day after Bolton's speech: "The United States' attack on the International Criminal Court is an attack on millions of victims and survivors who have experienced the most serious crimes under international law and undermines decades of groundbreaking work by the international community to advance justice."

If the Catholic Church is not above the law in the case of sexual misconduct of its clergy, neither is the U.S. military or intelligence personnel for potential crimes they may commit. No one would say that the Nuremberg trials were unnecessary.

As the most powerful country in the world, some abuse of power may very well come with the territory. We cannot apply American exceptionalism to avoid just prosecution if crimes are committed by our personnel or those of our allies. We need to support and build up the ICC, not tear it down.

Andrew Mills is a resident of Lower Gwynedd

Philadelphia Inquirer 10/31/2018

Thumbs Up, Solomon

I couldn't agree more with Solomon Jones in his column 'A protest role that has cost him nothing' in Sunday's Inquirer. Colin Kaepernick and Eric Reid have indeed paid the price. Racism including the killing of unarmed Black people is truly a stain on our country. Kaepernick and Reid had every right to bring that to the public's attention the way they did without being forced to give up their careers. They were simply bringing to light a major flaw in our society consistent with the prayer in America the Beautiful: "God mend thy every flaw."

Andrew Mills, Lower Gwynedd

The Intelligencer 9/13/2018

World Trade Center Buildings' Collapse Subject of Research

As we approach the 17th anniversary of the 9/11 attacks, it is important to note that even at this late date there is academic research underway probing the precise causes of the collapse of the World Trade Center (WTC) buildings on that day. A team of researchers at the University of Alaska at Fairbanks (UAF) has begun a finite-element structural engineering study of the collapse of WTC Building 7. One preliminary conclusion of the study is that the official narrative by NIST in 2008 that fire caused the building's collapse is false. NIST (National Institute of Standards and Technology) was the main federal agency that evaluated the collapse of the WTC towers. The conclusion by the UAF researchers makes sense considering that the devastating fire which consumed the 24-story Grenfell Tower in London in June of last year still left the steel frame standing. Watch a video about the WTC buildings that fell in New York on 9/11 at https://www.facebook.com/ae911truth/videos/10155079274151269/

Andrew Mills, Lower Gwynedd

The Intelligencer 6/12/2018

Blaming Palestinians for Their Own Slaughter

The Great Return March in Gaza was a six-week-long protest action. Thousands of unarmed Palestinian protestors from every walk of life and political alignment gathered at the Israel-Gaza border every Friday from March 30th to May 15th. The protest gathering at the border on Monday May 14th commemorated the 70th anniversary of the Nakba, the Palestinian word for the 1948 ethnic cleansing of Palestine by Zionist forces in the process of creating Israel.

The main goal of the protest action was to bring attention to the Palestinians' Right of Return as enshrined in United Nations Resolution 194, which states in part: "refugees wishing to return to their homes and live at peace with their neighbours should be permitted to do so at the earliest practicable date." The protestors were also demanding an end to Israel's blockade of Gaza that has made Gaza little more an open-air prison.

Between March 30th and May 15th, 101 of the unarmed Palestinian protestors were killed by the Israel Defense Forces snipers, including 60 on May 14th alone. And more than 3,000 Palestinians were injured from live fire. No Israeli was killed and only one is reported to have been injured as a result of the protests. The major media commonly referred to these bloody events as "*clashes*" between Israeli troops and Hamas supporters. Less biased reporters were more likely to use the term "*massacres*." Media such as NBC, the *New York Times* and the *Washington Post,* devoted considerable space in their coverage of the killings, blaming Palestinians for their own slaughter.

Andrew Mills, Lower Gwynedd

The Intelligencer 8/2/2017

Peace May Not Be Sexy, But It Sure Beats War

Peace it seems isn't sexy, but war is. At least that's how the armament industries would like us to feel about it. Our country has a commercial interest in fostering and maintaining selected nations as enemies. Sometimes this leads to war and sometimes it doesn't, but as long as we're made to feel afraid enough, Congress gladly appropriates large sums to the military and the defense industries, as the House did last week (HR 3219).

Large Pentagon budgets don't show support for the troops as much as they do for defense contractors who are campaign donors. Real support for our troops would involve Congress giving serious consideration to where and why we send our men and women into harm's way, and then having the guts to vote for it on the record.

A new Pentagon study, At Our Own Peril: DoD Risk Assessment in a Post-Primacy World by the Strategic Studies Institute of the *US Army War College*, says the U.S. no longer enjoys an unassailable position versus its nation-state competitors. "In brief, the status quo that was hatched and nurtured by U.S. strategists after World War II, and has for decades been the principle beat for the Pentagon is not merely fraying, but may, in fact, be collapsing." In response the Pentagon wants taxpayers to throw more money into their coffers to bring back the good old days.

Colonel Lawrence Wilkerson, former chief of staff to Secretary of State Colin Powell and currently distinguished professor of Government and Public Policy at the College of William & Mary, commented in a Real News Network interview July 30th that the fact the military, the Pentagon study at least, is lamenting the passing of the heyday for the U.S. internationally is notable. The wars during and after the Cold War have all been cash cows for the military, he said. "They're now lamenting the passing of this cash cow." "They want to move out swiftly and reestablish . . . the U.S. hegemony in the world that brings that cash cow into play big time."

I'm afraid we may be on the verge of a larger war, and I'm not alone—in an NBC News poll taken July 10-14th, 76% of responders said they were worried that the U.S. will become engaged in a major war. According to Michael Klare, Professor of Peace and World-Security Studies at Hampshire College, writing in *The Nation* this month, by preparing for war Washington and NATO are setting in motion forces that could achieve precisely that outcome. He cites NATO's plans to deploy four multinational battalions along its eastern flank—one each in Poland, Lithuania, Latvia, and Estonia.

The liberal cable news outlets are fixated on President Trump and the investigations into Russia's meddling in the 2016 elections. It's fine to cover all this as real news, but *not* to the exclusion of other happenings that would affect Americans just as much or more. I'm thinking of war and peace.

The likely candidates we would oppose in a major war are of course North Korea, Russia, Iran and Syria. In the case of the last three, any war would likely be a war of choice on our part, as was the U.S. invasion of Iraq in 2003. Wars of choice are wars waged to gain some advantage in the geopolitical sense, not in response to any attack or threat of imminent attack on our homeland.

Regarding Korea, the North Korean regime in its dealings with the U.S. is likely to have looked to previous models, such as Iraq, where Saddam did not have weapons of mass destruction and he got invaded by the U.S. They can look to Libya, where Gaddafi did have weapons of mass destruction. He gave them up to the U.S. and then he also got bombed, invaded, and executed. This surely goes into the thinking of North Korea right now.

And if Iran looks as if it's getting a nuclear weapon, it would be in the same boat as Kim Jong-un.

Colonel Wilkerson stated in the interview: "The issue of North Korea could probably be solved in 18 months." Real negotiations with North Korea should be started immediately, starting with "trading exercises of U.S. forces on the peninsula . . . for, say, a cessation of ballistic missile testing, which I believe is very feasible. You could get that to happen. You could begin a negotiating process that at the end you would have South Korea fully capable of defending itself, and the U.S. able to augment that defense if it needed to but not visibly present on the peninsula 24/7 and not exercising and training and frightening North Korea."

Peace may not be sexy but it sure beats war. There are many ways to establish better relations with our enemies and avoid war. We simply cannot afford a bloated military budget any longer, and it would be foolhardy to risk getting into a major war. Let's choose peace.

Andrew Mills, Lower Gwynedd, works part time as a consultant in computer programming. Before his retirement, he worked for many years as a consulting water-resources engineer and groundwater hydrologist, including time in India and Egypt.

New York Times 4/17/2017

President Trump rushed to judgment in ordering the attack on the Shayrat airfield in Syria.

There are too many red flags about the chemical weapons attack in Idlib to believe the official version of events that immediately assigned guilt to the Assad government.

I think it's possible that the incident was a false flag operation perpetrated by the rebels with a view to destroying the peace process and prolonging the war. The Assad government would in no way benefit from chemical weapons attacks on innocent people when he is winning the war. The rebels, however, would have something to gain, as they could blame the Syrian government, and hope the United States would attack and thereby weaken the Syrians' position.

At the very least, these questions demand an independent investigation.

Andrew Mills, Lower Gwynedd, PA

The Intelligencer 9/21/2016

Black Lives Don't Matter More; They Matter Equally

I was interested to read two readers' Guest Opinions in the *Intelligencer* on the Black Lives Matter movement. Brian Loutrel and Sean M. Shute on successive days, August 16th and 17th, expressed their anger over the movement and their belief that it is based on lies.

Both authors cite statistics to prove their point but fail to give the sources for them. Of course it's well known that even valid statistics can be used to prove just about anything. But in considering cases such as shootings by police officers, it's essential to compare *rates* of occurrence per capita not the gross numbers. Wikipedia notes that *The Guardian* newspaper runs its own database, *The Counted*, which tracked US killings by police and other law enforcement agencies in 2015, and counted 1140 killed, with rates per million of 2.92 for "White" people, 7.2 for "Black," and 3.5 for "Hispanic/Latino," 1.34 for "Asian/Pacific Islander," and 3.4 for "Native American." According to these statistics, blacks are about 2.5 times more likely to be shot by a police officer than whites.

According to data analysis performed by Washington Post writers, during 2015 and the first half of 2016 U.S. police officers shot and killed the exact same number of *unarmed* white people as they did *unarmed* black people: 50 each. But because the white population is approximately five times larger than the black population, that means unarmed black Americans were five times as likely as unarmed white Americans to be shot and killed by a police officer (*Washington Post*, July 11, 2016).

Thus, it's not black activists' and white liberals' imagination that blacks are more likely to be targeted with deadly force and that the likely major cause of the discrepancy is racism. This is not at all to say that all police officers are racists, and the Black Lives Matter movement isn't saying that either, so Brian Loutrel is wrong on that count. But racism is a major factor in these occurrences as it is in the society as a whole.

The point of the Black Lives Matter movement is not that the lives of black Americans matter more than those of white Americans, but that they matter equally, and that historically they have been treated as though they do not.

If the shoe were on the other foot, I imagine, we whites would be outraged if our white brethren were 2.5 times more likely to be assaulted by police than members of other races in the society. So it is with the black members of the Black Lives Matter (BLM) Movement. As noted by Wikipedia, BLM generally engages in direct action tactics to make people uncomfortable enough that they must address the issue. The BLM movement advocates protests and disruption, in certain cases, but not violence. Those few cases of violence that have occurred at BLM protests are the exception and have not been based on BLM policies. Remember that without the crossing of the bridge in Selma, Alabama led my Martin Luther King in 1965, the advances in civil rights we have achieved in this country may not have occurred. The march from Selma to Montgomery was a major disruption.

The BLM movement reminds us that there is a high level of distrust and suspicion between many black communities and the police, and that it is urgent that we address this as a society. Both sides must reach out to each other—the black communities and the police. In cities where police have received advanced training in community relations, there have been notable decreases in violent confrontations between minority members and the police.

Both Loutrel and Shute seem eager to connect the issue of policing black communities to Presidential politics. Brian Loutrel asserts that since 2014, police have endured relentless attacks from the Obama administration. He provides no basis for this dubious claim.

Sean Shute says that many Americans are looking to Trump as "the law and order candidate" to restore the nation so people can feel safe again in their own neighborhoods. This implies a rising crime rate, while the truth is that the rate of violent crime has been going down since 1991. The July 15, 2016 issue of *The Atlantic* provides data on homicides since 1985. The number of homicides in the U.S. declined from a high of 9.8 per 100,000 people in 1991 to 5.8 in 1999 and to 4.8 in 2014. Also, based on Trump's own words, it is highly unlikely that racial harmony will be enhanced under a Trump presidency.

The issue of police-community relations is a complex one, and it does not help to say in effect to the BLM members: "Just shut up and go away."

Andrew Mills, Lower Gwynedd, works as a programmer for a small firm in Doylestown

The Intelligencer 4/9/2016

Saudi Arabia and the Rise of ISIS

As in many countries, Americans are used to having our mortal enemies in the world defined for us by whichever Party is in power. When they say "make war" on these their pre-defined enemies, we usually don't hesitate. In a similar way our leaders in Washington lay out who our friends and allies are.

Case in point, Saudi Arabia. It's remarkable how consistently all recent Administrations have treated the Saudis as first-rate friends deserving special honors. So much so that at times we have inexplicably given them special treatment ignoring required protocols. Two days after 9/11, before the FAA had lifted its ban on air travel, three Saudi nationals, including at least one member of the Saudi royal family, were allowed to fly on a charter flight from Tampa to Lexington, Kentucky and soon thereafter depart along with other Saudis from the country without being questioned by the FBI.

Then there are the 28 classified pages of the 2002 report on 9/11 by the Joint Congressional Select Committees on Intelligence, which we have been told implicates Saudi Arabia in the attacks. These pages have still not been released by the Administration stating national security concerns. A bipartisan House resolution (HR 428) calls on President Obama to declassify the 28 pages. Former Senator Bob Graham, who chaired the Select Committee in the Senate side, said at a press conference in January, "I believe that the failure to shine a full light on Saudi actions and particularly its involvement in 9/11 has contributed to the Saudi ability to continue to engage in actions that are damaging to the U.S. – and in particular their support for ISIS."

There is evidence that Saudi Arabia and wealthy Saudi donors backed al-Qaeda both before and after 9/11. Zacarias Moussaoui, who is serving a life sentence for his involvement in the planning of the attacks of Sept. 11, 2001, recently testified that he had a role in creating a digital database of al-Qaeda's donors which included several senior Saudi officials and members of the royal family.

A recent Gulf Institute report says that Saudi Arabia's new king, Salman bin Abdulaziz al Saud, and a former Saudi intelligence chief knowingly aided and abetted al-Qaeda in the run-up to 9/11. A December 2009 cable by then Secretary of State Hillary Clinton made public by WikiLeaks states that "Saudi Arabia remains a critical financial support base for al-Qai'ida, the Taliban, LeT [Lashkar-e-Taiba in Pakistan] and other terrorist groups."

The Saudis who are largely fundamentalist Salafi and Wahhabi Sunnis are involved in a life-or-death struggle with their centuries-old enemies the Shia, exemplified especially by the present governments of Syria and Iran. And now the Saudis' proxies, the ISIS fighters, are engaged in a brutal war not only against the Shia but also moderate Sunnis.

So as long as we are supporting Saudi Arabia, we are supporting ISIS. Oh I know, officially the Saudis are making nice by assuring us that they are opposing ISIS. They have even designated ISIS as a terrorist entity, thereby prohibiting Saudi residents from directly supporting the group. But as noted recently by the Washington Institute for Near East Policy, private Saudi individuals still find the means of funneling money to the group. The truth is that Saudi Arabia opposes anything like ISIS's jihad should it threaten their kingdom. But they couldn't be more pleased with what their proxies are doing against the Shia.

It's time for the U.S. to own up to the numerous actions Saudi Arabia has committed against the interests of the American people. Isn't it time to explore the Saudis' possible role in 9/11? Isn't it time to own up to the fact that Saudi Arabia may be more of an enemy than an ally? It may even be the time to consider possible sanctions against the Kingdom until they completely stop all support of jihadis, sanctions that hurt.

Oh, we couldn't do that to big Daddy Oil, you say—or could we?

I'm not optimistic that any Administration would do this because of the cozy relationship this and past Administrations have had with the Saudis, which is rumored to include possible personal business interests. At any rate, here's an important area where sunlight is desperately needed, so we can see more clearly who are our friends and who are our enemies.

Andrew Mills, Lower Gwynedd, works as a programmer for a firm in Doylestown

The Intelligencer 1/7/2015

Deadly Force Not the Only Option for Police

In his Guest Opinion of Dec, 31, Chuck Pizagno sees 'slime' encroaching on all aspects of our society. I think a more nuanced analysis is preferable. Police are important to our society. They routinely put themselves in harm's way and they should be able to protect and defend themselves. On the other hand, there must be a way of their handling of unarmed people who are resisting arrest, besides killing them. For example, two possibilities for Officer Wilson when he confronted Michael Brown in Ferguson could have been: (1) give up on pursuing him that day and go with colleagues to his home and arrest him the next day; (2) if Brown was actually charging toward Wilson, as alleged by two witnesses, aim only at Brown's upper legs, instead of his upper body and head.

Andrew Mills, Lower Gwynedd

Times-Herald 4/29/2013

Torture-based Interrogation Raises Questions

Last week the Constitution Project, a national legal research group, issued a sweeping 577-page report on their non-partisan investigation of the interrogation and detention programs carried out by the Bush Administration in the aftermath of the 9/11 attacks. As reported by the *New York Times* the report details the brutal methods applied to detainees by US personnel at Guantanamo Bay, in Afghanistan and Iraq and at overseas secret prisons. The report found that those methods violated international law with "no firm or persuasive evidence" that they produced valuable information that could not have been obtained by other means.

This story is paralleled by another story that has been largely ignored by the US media. That is the story of a man called Abu Zubaydah, whom the 9/11 Commission called an "al Qaeda lieutenant." After his capture in early 2002, Zubaydah was tortured extensively at the hands of the CIA included at least 83 water-boarding sessions as well as more atrocious torture methods. Khalid Sheik Mohammed (KSM), the supposed mastermind of 9/11, was waterboarded 183 times in March 2003.

In a surprising turn of events, during Zubaydah's habeas corpus petition in September 2009, the government admitted in writing that Abu Zubaydah had never been a member of al-Qaeda, nor involved in any of the al Qaeda attacks. So this nullifies whatever he said while being tortured, which was quoted at length in the 9/11 Commission's report. Khalid Sheik Mohammed, after he was tortured said that he gave the interrogators a lot of false information, telling them what he thought they wanted to hear in an attempt to stop the torture. This forced testimony was also quoted at great length in the Commission's report.

NBC News found that more than a quarter of the 9/11 Commission report's footnotes—441 of some 1,700—referred to detainees who had been tortured. I conclude that not only was the torture all in vain, but a substantial portion of the commission's report on the attacks is now without foundation, a report upon which our war on terrorism is based.

Andrew Mills, Lower Gwynedd

The Intelligencer 6/6/2004

Make Responsible Ones Accountable

The shocking news from the Abu Ghraib prison in Iraq is growing like topsy. The blame keeps rising up the chain of command.

We've learned now that the president has probably known for more than two years that his administration has been pursuing policies that could qualify as war crimes under federal and international law.

In 1996, Congress passed the War Crimes Act, which provides for criminal prosecution of Americans for actions violating the rights granted prisoner and civilians by the Geneva Conventions and for "outrages upon human dignity."

The scandal is shifting from a few "bad apples' among the enlisted soldiers to the administration, which directly or indirectly authorized the torture and humiliation of prisoners.

Those responsible in the administration should be prosecuted to the fullest extent provided for in the Act.

The scandal reveals to us another deeply troubling fact—the training that some of our young people are receiving in the military.

How will these soldiers be able to contribute in a peaceful and tolerant way to our society when they come home?

What are we doing to our young people.

What are we doing in the name of decency and freedom?

Andrew C. Mills, Lower Gwynedd

Bibliography

Adler, Renata. "The Selma March: On the Trail to Montgomery." *New Yorker* (April 10, 1965). https://www.newyorker.com/magazine/1965/04/10/letter-from-selma.

Alvarez, Maximillian. "Nicaragua Presents a Challenge to the International Left." Real News, November 11, 2021. https://therealnews.com/nicaragua-presents-a-challenge-to-the-international-left

Amnesty International. *Instilling Terror: From Lethal Force to Persecution in Nicaragua.* London: Amnesty Interntional, Ltd, October 2018. https://www.amnesty.org/en/wp-content/uploads/2021/05/AMR4392132018ENGLISH.pdf

Blumenthal, Max. "How Nicaragua defated a right-wing US-backed coup," in Nicaragua Notes, "Live from Nicaragua: Uprising or Coup? A Reader." Alliance for Global Justice, 2019. https://secureservercdn.net/198.71.233.230/jwp.e46.myftpupload.com/wp-content/uploads/2019/07/live_from_nicaragua_june_2019.pdf

Blumenthal, Max. "How Washington and Soft Power NGOs Manipulated Nicaragua's Death Toll to Drive Regime Change and Sanctions," in Nicaragua Notes, "Live from Nicaragua: Uprising or Coup? A Reader." Alliance for Global Justice, 2019. https://secureservercdn.net/198.71.233.230/jwp.e46.myftpupload.com/wp-content/uploads/2019/07/live_from_nicaragua_june_2019.pdf

Bokat-Lindell, Spencer. "Did the Supreme Court Just Kill the Voting Rights Act?" *New York Times* (July 6, 2021).

Bow, Juan Carlos, and Maynor Salazar. "Donald Trump Signs the Nica Act to Pressure Ortega." *Havana Times* (December 21, 2018) https://havanatimes.org/news/donald-trump-signs-the-nica-act-to-pressure-ortega.

Britannica. "Nicaragua." https://www.britannica.com/place/Nicaragua.

Bruening, Ben, and David Martin. "To March with Martin", a documentary video of the 1965 bus trip from Davis, California to Montgomery, Alabama, 2013. https://www.imdb.com/video/vi1572253977

Butler, Smedley. *War is a Racket.* New York: Skyhorse, 2013.

Charles, Guy-Uriel E., and Luis E. Fuentes-Rohwer. "The Court's Voting-Rights Decision Was Worse Than People Think." *Atlantic* (July 8, 2021). https://www.theatlantic.com/ideas/archive/2021/07/brnovich-vra-scotus-decision-arizona-voting-right/619330.

Christie, Bob, and Christina A. Cassidy. "AP: Few AZ Voter Fraud Cases, Discrediting Trump Claims." AP News, July 17, 2021. https://apnews.com/article/business-government-and-politics-only-on-ap-election-2020-8260008a320b6c96a15e6884af3fa474

Cohen, Stephen. *War with Russia: From Putin & Ukraine to Trump & Russiagate.* New York: Simon & Schuster, Skyhorse Publishing, 2019.

Dahlin, Dennis. "DCC at 150, Part 4: A Pastor Marches for Civil Rights." Davis, CA: *Davis Enterprise* (September 6, 2019).
Davis Enterprise. "Davisites Board Bus Bound for Rights March in South." Davis, CA: *Davis Enterprise* (March 23, 1965) 1–5.
Davis Enterprise. "Davisites give Impressions of Montgomery March." Davis, CA: *Davis Enterprise* (April 2, 1965).
Davis Enterprise. "Montgomery March Returnees Slate Symposium Tonight." Davis, CA: *Davis Enterprise* (April 1, 1965) 2.
Davis Media Access. "Martin Luther King, Jr–Legacy in Davis," a roundtable discussion on the 1965 march with Lisa Thomas, Terry Turner, John Pamperin, Dick Holdstock and Timothy Malone, Campus Minister, January 11, 2001. https://archive.org/details/dma-Martin_Luther_King_Jr_-_Legacy_in_Davis
Escott, Paul D. *Slavery Remembered: A Record of Twentieth Century Slave Narratives.* Chapel Hill: University of North Carolina Press, 1979.
Fergerson, Cecil. "Interview by Department of Special Collections, University of California, Los Angeles." Online Archive of California, African-American Artists of Los Angeles, July 10, 1991. https://oac.cdlib.org/view?docId=hb7h4nb803&brand=oac4&doc.view=entire_text
Finkelstein, Norman. *Gaza: An Inquest into its Martyrdom.* Oakland, CA: University of California Press, 2018.
Francis, Hilary. "Introduction: Exceptionalism and agency in Nicaragua's revolutionary heritage," in Francis, ed. *A Nicaraguan Exceptionalism? Debating the Legacy of the Sandinista Revolution.* London: Institute of Latin American Studies, School of Advanced Study, University of London, 2020. https://library.oapen.org/bitstream/handle/20.500.12657/39406/9781908857774.pdf?sequence=1&isAllowed=y.
Francis, Hilary, ed. *A Nicaraguan Exceptionalism? Debating the Legacy of the Sandinista Revolution.* London: Institute of Latin American Studies, School of Advanced Study, University of London, 2020. https://library.oapen.org/bitstream/handle/20.500.12657/39406/9781908857774.pdf?sequence=1&isAllowed=y.
Frawley, Joan. "The Left's Latin American Lobby." Heritage Foundation, October 11, 1984. https://www.heritage.org/report/the-lefts-latin-american-lobby.
Griffin-Nolan, Edward. *Witness for Peace: A Story of Resistance.* Louisville, KY: Westminster/John Knox, 1991.
Hendrix, Enrique. "Monopolizing Death: Or how to frame a government by inflating a list of the dead." Tortilla OnDom, 7/15/2018. http://www.tortillaconsal.com/tortilla/node/3546.
Hudson, Jeff. "50 Years after that Long Bus Ride to Alabama." Davis, CA: *Davis Enterprise* (March 22, 2015), A9.
Independent Catholic News. "From: Nicaragua: Pope, World Leaders Concerned at Growing Crisis." Independent Catholic News, August 21, 2022. https://www.indcatholicnews.com/news/45327.
Kaufman, Chuck. "Nicanotes: The MRS is Not 'Left' or Democratic." Alliance for Global Justice, July 11, 2018. https://afgj.org/nicanotes-the-mrs-is-not-left-or-democratic.
Kovalik, Daniel. "Fire from the Mountain: In Search of Omar Cabezas" (Video). Mint Press News, May 3, 2022. https://www.mintpressnews.com/sandinistas-omar-cabezas-interview-daniel-kovalik/280362.

Kovalik, Daniel. "Human Rights in Nicaragua," in Nicaragua Notes, "Live from Nicaragua: Uprising or Coup? A Reader." Alliance for Global Justice, 2019. https://secureservercdn.net/198.71.233.230/jwp.e46.myftpupload.com/wp-content/uploads/2019/07/live_from_nicaragua_june_2019.pdf

Lawyers Committee for Civil Rights under Law. https://lawyerscommittee.org/wp-content/uploads/2015/06/LCCRUL-Sec5-flyer.pdf

Luna, Yorlis Gabriela. "The Other Nicaragua, Empire and Resistance." Council on Hemispheric Affairs–Nicaragua, October 2, 2019. https://www.coha.org/the-other-nicaragua-empire-and-resistance/.

Martin Luther King, Jr. Center for Nonviolent Social Change. "MLK: Beyond Vietnam - A Time to Break Silence." YouTube, April 1967. https://www.youtube.com/watch?v=AJhgXKGldUk.

Martin Luther King, Jr. Research and Education Institute. "Vietnam War." Stanford University. https://kinginstitute.stanford.edu/encyclopedia/vietnam-war.

Mayer, Jane. "The Big Money behind the Big Lie." *New Yorker* (August 9, 2021). https://www.newyorker.com/magazine/2021/08/09/the-big-money-behind-the-big-lie?gclsrc=aw.ds&gclid=EAIaIQobChMI4KjbpN6A-wIVoAOzAB3FTw_7EAAYASAAEgJ6ZfD_BwE&gclsrc=aw.ds.

Moore, Barbara. "CENIDH's False Human Rights Reporting." Tortilla onLun, August 13, 2018. http://www.tortillaconsal.com/tortilla/node/3859.

Moulton, Phillips, ed. *The Journal and Major Essays of John Woolman*. New York: Oxford University Press, 1971.

National Security Archive. "NATO Expansion: What Gorbachev Heard." Washington, DC: George Washington University, 2017. https://nsarchive.gwu.edu/briefing-book/russia-programs/2017-12-12/nato-expansion-what-gorbachev-heard-western-leaders-early.

Nicaragua Notes. "Dismissing the Truth: Why Amnesty International is Wrong about Nicaragua." An evaluation and response to the Amnesty International report 'Instilling Terror: from lethal force to persecution in Nicaragua'. Alliance for Global Justice and Nicaragua Solidarity Campaign Action Group (UK), 2019. https://afgj.org/wp-content/uploads/2019/02/Dismissing-the-Truth-with-links.pdf.

Nicaragua Notes. "Live from Nicaragua: Uprising or Coup? A Reader." Alliance for Global Justice, 2019. https://secureservercdn.net/198.71.233.230/jwp.e46.myftpupload.com/wp-content/uploads/2019/07/live_from_nicaragua_june_2019.pdf.

Nicaragua Notes. "The Revolution Won't be Stopped: Nicaragua Advances Despite U.S. Unconventional Warfare." Alliance for Global Justice, July 15, 2020. https://afgj.org/nicanotes-the-revolution-wont-be-stopped-nicaragua-advances-despite-us-unconventional-warfare.

Norton, Ben. "Debunking Myths about Nicaragua's 2021 Elections, Under Attack by USA/EU/OAS." Monthly Review Online, November 13, 2021. https://mronline.org/2021/11/13/debunking-myths-about-nicaraguas-2021-elections-under-attack-by-usa-eu-oas.

Office of the United Nations High Commissioner for Human Rights (OHCHR). Human Rights Violations and Abuses in the Context of Protests in Nicaragua 18 April – 18 August 2018. Geneva, Switzerland: OHCHR, August 2018. https://www.ohchr.org/sites/default/files/Documents/Countries/NI/HumanRightsViolationsNicaraguaApr_Aug2018_EN.pdf.

Peace, Roger. *A Call to Conscience: The Anti-Contra War Campaign*. Amherst, MA: University of Massachusetts Press, 2012.

Perry, John. "A Year after Nicaragua Coup Attempt, the Media's Regime-Change Deceptions are still Unraveling." Grayzone, July 15, 2019. https://thegrayzone.com/2019/07/15/a-year-after-nicaraguas-coup-the-medias-regime-change-deceptions-are-still-unraveling.

Perry, John. "After 2 Months of Unrest, Nicaragua Is at a Fateful Crossroads." *Nation* (June 22, 2018). https://www.thenation.com/article/archive/two-months-unrest-nicaragua-fateful-crossroad.

Perry, John. "Are Nicaraguan Migrants Escaping 'Repression'—or Economic Sanctions?" Fairness & Accuracy in Reporting (FAIR), November 3, 2021. https://fair.org/home/are-nicaraguan-migrants-escaping-repression-or-economic-sanctions.

Perry, John. "Nicaragua a 'Dictatorship' When It Follows US Lead on NGOs." Fairness & Accuracy in Reporting (FAIR), June 22, 2022. https://fair.org/home/nicaragua-a-dictatorship-when-it-follows-us-lead-on-ngos.

Perry, John. "Sanctions may Impoverish Nicaraguans, but Likely will Not Change Their Vote." North American Congress on Latin America (NACLA), August 6, 2021. https://nacla.org/sanctions-may-impoverish-nicaraguans-will-not-change-their-vote.

Prendergast, Mark. "Contras Seize 29 from U.S." South Florida: *Sun-Sentinel* (August 8, 1985).

Prevost, Gary. "The 'Contra' War in Nicaragua." *Conflict Quarterly* 7 Summer (1987). https://journals.lib.unb.ca/index.php/JCS/article/download/14764/15833/19552

Rawick, G. P., ed. *The American Slave: A Composite Autobiography*. Santa Barbara, CA: Greenwood, 1972.

Ricker, Tom. "Bolton: Symptom of a 'Far Deeper Malady.'" Quixote Center, July 15, 2022. https://www.quixote.org/bolton-symptom-of-a-far-deeper-malady.

Ricker, Tom. "Update on Nicaragua: Interview about Situation in Masaya." Quixote Center, June 6, 2018. https://www.quixote.org/update-on-nicaragua-interview-about-situation-in-masaya.

Ripoll, Santiago. "As Good As It Gets? The new Sandinismo and the co-option of emancipatory rural politics in Nicaragua." Conference paper no. 46 In "ERPI 2018 International Conference on Authoritarian Populism and the Rural World." International Institute of Social Studies (ISS) in The Hague, Netherlands: March 17–18, 2018. https://opendocs.ids.ac.uk/opendocs/bitstream/handle/20.500.12413/13652/erpi_cp_46_ripoll.pdf?sequence=1&isAllowed=y.

Robinson, Nathan, and Noam Chomsky. "What do we owe Afghanistan?" *Current Affairs* (August 3, 2022). https://www.currentaffairs.org/2022/08/what-do-we-owe-afghanistan.

Robinson, William. "Venezuela: The Epicenter of the 'Pink Tide' and now of the Right-Wing Rollback." Real News, February 20, 2019. https://therealnews.com/venezuela-the-epicenter-of-the-pink-tide-and-now-of-the-right-wing-rollback.

Robinson, William. "Nicaragua: Chronicle of an Election Foretold." NACLA, November 9, 2021. https://nacla.org/news/2021/11/08/nicaragua-election-ortega.

Rubenstein, Alexander. "Amnesty International's Troubling Collaboration with UK & US Intelligence." Mint Press, January 17, 2019. https://www.mintpressnews.com/amnesty-international-troubling-collaboration-with-uk-us-intelligence/253939.

Savali, Kirtsen West. "Did You Know? US Gov't Found Guilty in Conspiracy to Assassinate Dr. Martin Luther King, Jr." News One, January 18, 2021. https://newsone.com/2843790/did-you-know-us-govt-found-guilty-in-conspiracy-to-assassinate-dr-martin-luther-king-jr.
Sierakowski, Robert. "'We didn't want to be like Somoza's Guardia': Policing, Crime and Nicaraguan Exceptionalism." in Francis, ed. *A Nicaraguan Exceptionalism? Debating the Legacy of the Sandinista Revolution*. London: Institute of Latin American Studies, School of Advanced Study, University of London, 2020. https://library.oapen.org/bitstream/handle/20.500.12657/39406/9781908857774.pdf?sequence=1&isAllowed=y.
Sikulich, Dick. "Keep Those Cards and Letters Coming." Doylestown, PA: *Intelligencer* (May 12, 2022) 4A.
TheAnalysis.news. "Does Nicaragua Under President Ortega Deserve Progressives' Support?" Debate by UC Santa Barbara Sociology professor William I. Robinson and the Nicaragua-based writer John Perry. Analysis News, March 3, 2022. https://theanalysis.news/does-nicaragua-under-president-ortega-deserve-progressives-support/?cmid=b37087a3-4049-4ca3-9c7a-50ec43acda51.
Thomas, Tansy. "Davis Residents Involved in the Civil Rights Struggle: The 1965 Davis Bus to the 1965 Selma to Montgomery March." Davis, CA: Davisvilletoday, Davis Historical Society. October 28, 2005, 4–5.
United States Institute of Peace. "Truth Commission: El Salvador." Truth Commission: Commission on the Truth for El Salvador (Comisión de la Verdad Para El Salvador, CVES), March 1993. https://www.usip.org/publications/1992/07/truth-commission-el-salvador.
Waddell, Benjamin. "Laying the Groundwork for Insurrection: A Closer Look at the U.S. Role in Nicaragua's Social Unrest." Global Americans, May 1, 2018. https://theglobalamericans.org/2018/05/laying-groundwork-insurrection-closer-look-u-s-role-nicaraguas-social-unrest.
Waddell, Benjamin. "Nicaragua: Better the Devil You Know." *Havana Times* (July 14, 2021). https://havanatimes.org/opinion/nicaragua-better-the-devil-you-know.
Waddell, Benjamin. "One year after Nicaraguan Uprising, Ortega is Back in Control." The Conversation, April 17, 2019. https://theconversation.com/one-year-after-nicaraguan-uprising-ortega-is-back-in-control-113991.
Waddell, Benjamin. "We may be Witnessing the Rise of Fascism in Nicaragua." HuffPost, July 30, 2018. https://www.huffpost.com/entry/opinion-waddell-nicaragua-orteg a_n_5b5e2279e4b0de86f498238b.
Waddell, Benjamin. "Why People Migrate: A Plea for Empathy from Nicaragua." Global Americans, June 27, 2018. https://theglobalamericans.org/2018/06/why-people-migrate-a-plea-for-empathy-from-nicaragua.
Waddell, Benjamin. "Venezuelan Oil Fueled the Rise and Fall of Nicaragua's Ortega Regime." The Conversation, August 21, 2018. https://theconversation.com/venezuelan-oil-fueled-the-rise-and-fall-of-nicaraguas-ortega-regime-100507.
Wikipedia. "2011 Nicaraguan General Election." Wikipedia, last edited October 9, 2022. https://en.wikipedia.org/wiki/2011_Nicaraguan_general_election.
Wikipedia. "2016 Nicaraguan General Election." Wikipedia, last edited May 23, 2022. https://en.wikipedia.org/wiki/2016_Nicaraguan_general_election.
Wikipedia. "2021 Nicaraguan General Election." Wikipedia, last edited October 21, 2022. https://en.wikipedia.org/wiki/2021_Nicaraguan_general_election.

Wikipedia. "Fifteenth Amendment to the United States Constitution." Wikipedia, last edited October 20, 2022. https://en.wikipedia.org/wiki/Fifteenth_Amendment_to_the_United_States_Constitution.

Wikipedia. "History of Nicaragua." Wikipedia, last edited October 22, 2022. https://en.wikipedia.org/wiki/History_of_Nicaragua.

Wikipedia. "Miguel Obando y Bravo." Wikipedia, last edited July 12, 2022. https://en.wikipedia.org/wiki/Miguel_Obando_y_Bravo.

Wikipedia. "Pueblo Nicaraguense." Wikipedia, last edited October 25, 2022. https://es.wikipedia.org/wiki/Pueblo_nicarag%C3%BCense.

Wikipedia. "Selma to Montgomery Marches." Wikipedia, last edited October 24, 2022. https://en.wikipedia.org/wiki/Selma_to_Montgomery_marches.

Wikipedia. "United States Involvement in Regime Change." Wikipedia, last edited October 25, 2022. https://en.wikipedia.org/wiki/United_States_involvement_in_regime_change.

Wikipedia. "Voting Rights Act of 1965." Wikipedia, last edited October 4, 2022. https://en.wikipedia.org/wiki/Voting_Rights_Act_of_1965.

Williams, Virginia S. "Central America Wars, 1980s," in United States Foreign Policy by Historians for Peace and Democracy. http://peacehistory-usfp.org/central-america-wars.

Witness for Peace Documentation Project. *Kidnapped by the Contras*. Washington, DC: Witness for Peace, October 1985.

World Population Review. "Nicaragua Population." https://worldpopulationreview.com/countries/nicaragua-population.

Yellin, Emily. "Memphis Jury Sees Conspiracy in Martin Luther King's Killing." *New York Times* (December 9, 1999). https://www.nytimes.com/1999/12/09/us/memphis-jury-sees-conspiracy-in-martin-luther-king-s-killing.html.

Zeese, Kevin, and Nils McCune. "Correcting the Record: What Is Really Happening in Nicaragua?"in Nicaragua Notes, "Live from Nicaragua: Uprising or Coup? A Reader." Alliance for Global Justice, 2019. https://secureservercdn.net/198.71.233.230/jwp.e46.myftpupload.com/wp-content/uploads/2019/07/live_from_nicaragua_june_2019.pdf.

www.ingramcontent.com/pod-product-compliance
Lightning Source LLC
Chambersburg PA
CBHW051900160426
43198CB00012B/1687